The Belgic Confession

The Belgic Confession

Its History and Sources

Nicolaas H. Gootjes

Baker Academic
Grand Rapids, Michigan

Published by Baker Academic
a division of Baker Publishing Group
P.O. Box 6287, Grand Rapids, MI 49516-6287
www.bakeracademic.com

Printed in the United States of America

Library of Congress Cataloging-in-Publication Data is on file at the Library of Congress, Washington, DC.

ISBN 10: 0-8010-3235-0
ISBN: 978-0-8010-3235-6

Contents

Series Preface

The heritage of the Reformation is of profound importance to our society, our culture, and the church in the present day. Yet there remain many significant gaps in our knowledge of the intellectual development of Protestantism both during and after the Reformation, and there are not a few myths about the theology of the ortho-dox or scholastic Protestant writers of the late sixteenth and seventeenth centuries. These gaps and myths—frequently caused by ignorance of the scope of a particular thinker's work, by negative theological judgments passed by later generations on the theology of the Reformers and their successors, or by an intellectual imperialism of the present that singles out some thinkers and ignores others regardless of their relative significance to their own times—stand in the way of a substantive encounter with this important period in our history. Understanding, assessment, and appropriation of that heritage can only occur through the publication of significant works (mono-graphs, essays, and sound, scholarly translations) that present the breadth and detail of the thought of the Reformers and their successors.

Texts and Studies in Reformation and Post-Reformation Thought makes available (1) translations of important documents like Caspar Olevian's *A Firm Foundation* and John Calvin's *Bondage and Liberation of the Will*, (2) significant monographs on individual thinkers or on aspects of sixteenth- and seventeenth-century Protestant thought, and (3) multiauthored symposia that bring together groups of scholars in an effort to present the state of scholarship on a particular issue, all under the guidance of an editorial board of recognized scholars in the field.

The series, moreover, is intended to address two groups: an academic and a confessional or churchly audience. The series recognizes the need for careful, scholarly treatment of the Reformation and of the era of Protestant orthodoxy, given the continuing presence of misunderstandings, particularly of the latter era, in both the scholarly and the popular literature and also given the rise of a more recent scholarship devoted to reappraising both the Reformation and the era of orthodoxy. The series highlights revised understandings regarding the relationship of the Reformation and orthodoxy to their medieval back-ground and of the thought of both eras to their historical, social, political, and cultural contexts. Such scholarship will not only advance the academic discussion, it will also provide a churchly audience with a clearer and broader access to its own traditions. In sum, the series intends to present the varied and current approaches to the rich heritage of Protestantism and to stimulate interest in the roots of the Protestant tradition.

Richard A. Muller

Author Preface

The Reformation era caused a proliferation of confessional statements. In the struggle to correctly understand and formulate biblical doctrine, many confessional statements were written and published. The differences between the teaching of the Roman Catholic church, the Lutheran views, the Anabaptist statements and the Reformed position needed to be clarified, not only for the clergy but also for the common believers.

Many of these confessions did not survive the sixteenth century, and only a few confessions and catechisms of that period are still used. Among these is the Belgic Confession which had its origin in the southern part of the Netherlands, but is known and used in many countries in the Western world. However, to date no comprehensive study on the background and history of this confession has been published in English. It is my hope that this book will contribute to remedying this situation.

I am indebted to many people for their active support. First of all, I wish to express my gratitude to the Governors of the Theological College for allowing me a study leave during the fall semester of the year 2000, and to Drs. J. M. Batteau for taking over my classes for that period. Our librarian Ms. Margaret Van der Velde was always willing to provide books and other material. In addition, my parents in law, Mr. and Mrs. A. G. J. Stegeman, and my study friend Drs. J. M. De Jong, frequently looked up literature which could only be found in Dutch libraries. We regret that my father in law, who had a great love for history, has not lived to see the result. Rev. Cl. Van der Velde deserves my gratitude for persevering in fine-tuning my English, and my son Albert for all the work done for the final version. Prof. Richard A. Muller is to be thanked for including the book in this series. Finally, I thank my wife Dinie for her constant support, and our children for their encouragement and active participation during research and writing.

Abbreviations

BLGNP	*Biographisch lexicon voor de geschiedenis van het Nederlandse protestantisme.* 5 vols. Kampen: J. H. Kok, 1978-2001.
Winkler Prins	*Winkler Prins Encyclopaedie.* 18 vols. Amsterdam: Elsevier, 1947-55.
Christelijke encyclopedie	*Christelijke encyclopedie.* 6 vols. 2nd ed. Kampen: Kok, 1956-61.
TRE	*Theologische Realenzyklopädie.* 36 vols. Berlin: Walter de Gruyter, 1977-98.

1

The Early History of the Confession

The Belgic Confession first emerged in Doornik, which was then a city in the southern part of the United Netherlands, but now belongs to Belgium. During the early 1560s copies of this confession were found in the houses of some Reformed people in Doornik. This happened during a time of religious persecution, leading up to the Eighty Years' War (1568-1648). The discovery of these books was reported to the national government, which responded by sending inquisitors to Doornik. On arrival, they searched for more copies, and harshly interrogated people found to be in possession of this confession. Later, several hundred copies of this booklet were found in a personal library; these copies were destroyed as they were considered dangerous for the people. In the same library, correspondence with several leaders of the Reformation movement was discovered. These, as well, were destroyed, leading to the loss of probably much valuable background information for the Belgic Confession.

An additional complication is the fact that the confession originated in the southern provinces of the Netherlands. However, already early during the Eighty Years' War the southern provinces became separated from the northern provinces. The northern provinces united as a Protestant nation, while the southern provinces continued to belong to the kingdom of Spain which adhered to Roman Catholicism. As a result of this division, uncertainty concerning the origin of the confession arose at an early date, and the available information was incomplete and often wrong.

The Dutch theologian Thysius stated, about fifty years after the publication of the confession, that it had been written in the French language in 1562, and published in 1563. In the same year, a Dutch language version had been published.[1] The information he provided was later repeated by the influential Remonstrant historian Brandt.[2] Both appear to have been unaware that French as well as Dutch versions had been printed before. Later, by the end of the seventeenth century, the well known theologian Bekker wrote that the confession had been printed in French in 1562, and

---

1. Anthonius Thysius, preface to *Leere ende order, soo Duytsche als Walsche, Ghereformeerde kercken* (Amsterdam: Pieter Pitersz, 1615); quoted in Lambregt A. Van Langeraad, *Guido de Bray, zijn leven en werken: Bijdrage tot de geschiedenis van het Zuid-Nederlandsche protestantisme* (Zierikzee: S. Ochtman, 1884), 103-4 n. 1; for text, see Appendix, Document 7.

2. Geeraert Brandt, *Historie der reformatie*, 4 vols. (Amsterdam: Jan Riemertsz and Hendrik & Dirk Boon, 1671-1704), 1:253.

in Dutch in the next year, 1563.[3] In the eighteenth century, Ens still mentioned 1562 as the year in which the confession was made, but Te Water distinguished the making, which he dates in 1561, from the publication in 1562.[4]

These differences may account for the confusion found in Philip Schaff's comprehensive study of creeds and confessions, published during the later part of the nineteenth century. He first mentions an edition of 1562, but later gives the date of the confession as 1561 or 1562. The underlying reason for this inconsistency becomes apparent in his remark that no copies of the first edition are known.[5]

The situation has changed considerably since Schaff published his books. Several early editions of the confession have been discovered which have been made available for investigation. The time of publication can be determined for these editions as 1561 and 1562.[6] Moreover, the circumstances during which the confession first came into the open have been investigated extensively. Although not all questions can be answered, we are now able to sketch the early history of the confession with much greater clarity.

First Appearance

Printed copies of the confession surfaced in Doornik on four different occasions during the fall and winter of 1561-62. The circumstances were rather unusual.[7] On the occasion of the fair held on September 14, 1561, some Reformed believers from Valenciennes came to Doornik to discuss their common cause with fellow Reformed believers there. Together they decided to stage public demonstrations in their cities. On September 29, about one hundred people began singing the Psalms in French on the streets of Doornik. They soon attracted a following of about six hundred people. The next day, the number of demonstrators grew to three or four thousand.[8] The intention was to stage a peaceful demonstration, to show the strength of the Reformed

---

3. Balthasar Bekker, page 4 of preface to *De leere der gereformeerde kerken van de vrije Nederlanden, begrepen in derselver geloofsbelydenisse* (Amsterdam: Daniel van den Dalen, 1696).

4. Johannes Ens, *Kort historisch bericht van de publieke schriften rakende de leer en dienst der Nederduitsche kerken*, compl. and publ. Regnerus Ens (n.p., 1733; reprint, Kampen: S. Van Velzen, 1864), 65; Willem Te Water, *Tweede eeuwgetyde van de geloofs-belydenisse der gereformeerde kerken van Nederland* (Middelburg: Pieter Gillissen, 1762), 2.

5. Philip Schaff, *The Creeds of Christendom: With a History and Critical Notes* (New York: Harper and Row, 1931; reprint, Grand Rapids: Baker, 1990), 1:505-6.

6. For an early survey, see Van Langeraad, *Guido de Bray*, 94-95. He added the remark that in 1603 Hermannus Moded wrote that the confession was published in 1561. However, the quotation he appeals to merely states that the confession was presented to the king of Spain in 1561.

7. Gérard Moreau, *Histoire du protestantisme à Tournai jusqu' à la veille de la révolution des Pays-Bas* (Paris: Les Belles Lettres, 1962), particularly 168-72; Emile M. Braekman, *Guy de Brès: Sa vie* (Bruxelles: Éditions de la Librairie des éclaireurs unionistes, 1960), 151-55.

8. In a later summary report, dated December 19, 1561, the numbers were reduced to 300 to 400 on the first day, and twice that number on the second day; see Appendix, Document 3.

movement in the city and to receive some kind of public recognition. The first evening, the local government did not respond. However, when another demonstration took place on the next day, the government used its forces to disperse the demonstrators and restore the order. However, they did not notify the governess of the Netherlands, Margaretha of Parma, who was residing in Brussels, governing the Netherlands on behalf of her half brother, King Philip II of Spain. When she heard about it, she was sufficiently disturbed to order the city magistrate to keep her fully informed. She also sent three commissioners to Doornik to investigate this act of rebellion. This committee was given considerable power which was used to arrest people, to interrogate them and, if necessary, to force them to provide answers by torturing them.

Our knowledge concerning the first public appearance of the Belgic Confession is exclusively derived from the reports this committee sent to the governess. It should be remembered that the reports do not present the events in a chronological order. The committee simply summarized what had been done and discovered on a given day. On November 2, 1561, they wrote the following:

> Madame, today at the opening of the gate of this castle, a closed and sealed package has been found, thrown within the first enclosure. This contained a lengthy writing addressed to us or, in our absence, to the [authorities] of this city, in the name of the resident and inhabitant burghers, containing their protests against the persecutions . . .
>
> And in order to make you aware of the purity of their doctrine, we present the booklet here enclosed, containing their confession, which they say more than half of this town present to us with common accord, to which more than one hundred thousand people of these lands agree together. And [they say] that they will not change it even at the risk of losing their goods, tortures, misfortunes, death or the fire, in order not to let themselves deviate from the purity of the doctrine of God. Finally, [they] quote several sentences in Latin, Greek and Hebrew taken from the Scripture.[9]

The explanation the Reformed presented to the government in this unusual way was obviously intended to prevent the impression that throwing the confession inside the outer walls of the castle was meant as an act of defiance. Rather, it was an unusual way to present the Reformed doctrine to the authorities. Since the Reformed were prevented from promoting their doctrine in person, they presented it in writing. They publicly wanted to make known to the authorities what they believed on the basis of God's Word. And they confirmed in the handwritten letter added to the booklet that they were willing to give up their possessions and even their lives for the sake of their faith. The quotations in Latin, Greek and Hebrew cannot be found in the booklet, and

---

9. Van Langeraad, *Guido de Bray*, 32. For text, see Appendix, Document 1.

must have been included in the letter. These were probably added to counteract the impression which could arise from the singing during the fair, that the Reformed movement was merely a popular uprising of unschooled people.

This is the first time the committee of investigation reported on the confession, but it was not the first time they had been confronted with it. Later in the same letter, it is mentioned that the confession had already been found at an earlier occasion: "We send this small book to Your Highness. We had found a similar one in the house of Jean du Mortier."[10] The house of du Mortier had been searched about two weeks earlier, on October 15. The committee reported on that same day that they had found books by Calvin in Latin and French, together with many other books by arch-heretics, but that they had not yet made a complete inventory. Between October 15 and November 2, they must have looked through the confiscated books and discovered this copy of the confession. It is understandable that the confession had not been spotted right away, for it was a small booklet of less than a hundred pages.

The confession is again mentioned in the report of the interrogation of Gilles Espringalles, which took place on November 15, 1561. After the committee had questioned him about Guido de Brès and about the letter included in the package thrown within the walls of the castle, they brought up the confession:

> [He was] interrogated as to who had given him the *confession of the believers which he says to be of Antwerp*, which he mentions in the aforesaid writing to the aforesaid Guy. He says that no one has given it to him, and that he has never seen it; and what he says about it in his writing[11] is because he has heard the aforesaid person talk about it. And in answer to what was said to him, that he in his own writing in several places shows to know it well enough, [he answers] that it comes from the aforesaid confession, as far as he thinks it is good, and he even says that the said Jerome affixed it and made it known at the main doors.[12]

Gilles Espringalles obviously wanted to avoid the impression that he belonged to the congregation of the Reformed in Doornik. It must have struck the committee that he had written some statements which resembled formulations in the Belgic Confession. Espringalles attempted to explain this away by pointing out that the confession had been made public by being nailed to a door, an action that reminds of Luther's nailing his Theses to the door at Wittenberg. In the case of Doornik, the "main doors" may refer to the main entrance of the most important Roman Catholic church in the city. It is doubtful whether this was indeed the source of Espringalles' knowledge of the confession, but the nailing of the confession to the church door must refer to an actual

---

10. See Appendix, Document 1.

11. This "writing" refers probably to the letter Espringalles had written to Guido de Brès, mentioned earlier in the report of the interrogation.

12. See Appendix, Document 2.

event. The name "Jerome" mentioned here refers to Guido de Brès, pastor of the Reformed congregation in Doornik, who used this as his pseudonym.[13] The report appears to indicate that it was he who had brought this confession in the open by nailing it on the door of the church for public perusal. It is not clear when this actually happened; Moreau's opinion that this may have taken place during the *chanteries* at the end of September, or even earlier, cannot be proven.

On the basis of these three reports it can be concluded that the Belgic Confession first came into the open during the fall of 1561. It was thrown within the walls of Doornik's castle in the night of November 1. Prior to that it had been found at the house of Jean du Mortier, on October 15. Since he was a leader in the church, he may have been one of the first to receive a copy. Gilles Espringalles denied that he possessed a copy, but he is the sole source for the report that the printed confession was nailed on the door to make it public. Although we do not know when this happened, the name "Jerome" suggests that Guido de Brès, the minister of the Reformed congregation of Doornik, brought the confession into the open.

The confession is also mentioned in two later reports. The first is found in a summary report presented to the King by the commissioners, dated December 19, 1561:

> Moreover, small booklets have been found, printed in the name of the faithful subjects here, addressing Your Majesty, containing their confession, full of all kind of errors and perverse doctrine of Calvin, and at the end a remonstrance to the magistrates concerning what they are forced to endure. Therefore, it has immediately been made known everywhere that such books are not permitted in these countries, and if someone would find copies of these, that they must be confiscated to know where these come from, who would be the author, and where they had been printed. Nevertheless, we have not been able to know anything further about it with certainty. Except that it is said to be made in France and printed in Rouen, and that these evil spirits from Geneva or France do this to mislead and incite the subjects here.[14]

This report thus provides a table of contents of the booklet the committee had obtained. It contained not only a confession, but also an address to the king of Spain, presumably printed before the confession, and a complaint directed to the local magistrates. It also specified the character of the confession. The teaching is not that of Luther or of the Anabaptists, but of Calvin. In addition, the statement above shows

---

13. Van Langeraad, *Guido de Bray*, 28.

14. Van Langeraad, *Guido de Bray*, xvii; Jan N. Bakhuizen van den Brink, "Quelques notes sur l'histoire de la Confession des Pays-Bas en 1561 et 1566," in *Ecclesia II: Een bundel opstellen door Dr. J. N. Bakhuizen van den Brink* ('s Gravenshage: Martinus Nijhoff, 1966), 297; for text, see Appendix, Document 3.

that the commissioners did not know for sure where the confession had originated, but somehow they knew that it had been printed in Rouen. This statement implies that the name of the publisher was not mentioned on the title page. Instead, their knowledge may have come from interrogation of members of the congregation. Finally, the fact that it was thought to have been printed in France made the confession all the more suspicious to the committee. After all, the riots, together with the Reformed confession, could be taken as part of a movement to gain freedom from Spain. This would then result in the city being again incorporated into France, for the area Doornik belonged to had been part of France till 1513, less than fifty years earlier.[15]

The fifth and final piece of information on the appearance of the Belgic Confession can be found in the report concerning the discovery of Guido de Brès' library. The commissioners reported on January 10, 1562, that they had found out where he lived. From there, the trail had led to Piat Moyeulx and his wife, who were close to him:

> On hearing that the aforesaid Piat had yet another rental property, consisting of a garden and a small summer house in the same parish of St. Brixe,[16] located on the fortifications close to the house of the aforesaid Guido, we went there with several constables and him. On arrival, they found the whole neighbourhood assembled to extinguish the fire which on that same day after lunch someone as yet unknown, having descended into this garden by a stairway, had alighted in a great multitude of books and papers piled up in that house, so that all had begun to extinguish that fire and save those papers and books, as much as they could.
>
> Among those have been saved about two hundred copies of a small booklet entitled *Confession of faith of the faithful in the Netherlands*, of which we have previously sent a similar copy to Your Highness. In order that these people would keep their distance from it, we have made them hand these over by a very strict edict against those who would keep them.[17]

The report goes on to describe other incriminating material discovered in this summer house doubling as a minister's study. Among the "very pernicious books" they had found, were books written by important leaders of the Reformation, such as Calvin, Luther, Melanchthon, Oecolampadius, Zwingli, Bucer, Bullinger and Brent. The library also contained papers with notes in French and Latin. The committee noted that the handwriting was similar to that of the letter thrown into the castle (on

---

15. Jan N. Bakhuizen van den Brink, *De Nederlandse belijdenisgeschriften*, 2nd rev. ed. (Amsterdam: Ton Bolland, 1976), 2.

16. This location was probably intentionally chosen because it did not belong to the diocese of Doornik; for that reason it was not under the supervision of the church authorities; see Moreau, *Histoire du Protestantisme*, 144, 162 n. 2.

17. Appendix, Document 4; see also Braekman, *Guy de Brès*, 179-80, where a misprint occurs that there were 250 copies.

November 1 of the previous year). This provided convincing proof that this letter had been written by Guido de Brès.

The report continues by stating that among these papers they had discovered letters written to de Brès by several prominent people in the Reformed community. They mention a letter by Calvin dating from 1556, a letter by Petrus Dathenus and a letter by Jean Crespin, dating from 1559. All of this led the committee to the conclusion that they had discovered the hideout of de Brès, the supervisor and general minister of the Calvinist sectarians.[18]

It is again the name of Guido de Brès which is closely connected with the confession. He had not only given a copy to Gilles Espringalles, he also kept some 200 other copies in his study. The committee took note of the fact that the confession found in his study was the same confession they had already found in Doornik. Guido de Brès appears to have been rather careful by handing out copies of the confession only to people he sufficiently trusted, to teach them the Reformed faith.

The 1561 Editions

Up to this point, it has simply been assumed that the confession found in Doornik in 1561 was the Belgic Confession. However, this point can be established by relating the accounts of the discovery with original copies of the Belgic Confession. The report of December 19, 1561, provides specific data concerning the copy found in Doornik. It mentioned a booklet printed in the name of the faithful subjects of the Netherlands, addressing the King of Spain. Concerning the content, the committee reported that the booklet contained an address to King Philip of Spain in the name of the believers who live in the Netherlands, several texts from Scripture emphasizing the necessity of confessing, the confession itself and a remonstrance directed to the magistrates. All of these features can be found in copies of the Belgic Confession printed in 1561. The only items not mentioned by the committee are the sonnet and the list of texts dealing with confession, presumably since they were insignificant, consisting of only one or two pages. The confession surfacing at Doornik in 1561 has correctly been identified with the confession now generally known as the Belgic Confession.

However, there are two different printings of the Belgic Confession dated 1561, and this requires us to take a closer look at each. Although they contain the same title, "*Confession of faith, made with common accord by the believers in the Netherlands, who desire to live according to the purity of the gospel of our Lord Jesus Christ,*"[19] they obviously came from different printers. In the one, a printer's mark graces the title page, followed by a quotation of 1 Peter 3:15, and the year is given as 1561. However,

---

18. See Appendix, Document 4.

19. The original French title was: "CONFESSION DE FOY, Faicte d'un commun accord par les fideles qui conversent és pays bas, lesquels desirent vivre selon la pureté de l'Evangile de nostre Seigneur Iesus Christ."

nowhere is the name of the printer mentioned. Since its discovery in the nineteenth century, much attention has been given to the printer's mark, which shows an old man standing among ruins, under a cloudy sky where the name Jahweh is printed in Hebrew letters. The marginal text explains the meaning of the picture. The Latin statement says: "All things grow old but the Lord will always remain." The same mark has been found in two other publications from that same year. The first is a French psalter by Clement Marot and Theodore Beza, printed in 1561, to which the Gallican Confession of 1559 is added.[20] The other publication with the same printer's mark is the fourth edition of Beza's confession.[21] It is noteworthy that the anonymous publisher who printed the Belgic Confession, in the same year printed two more confessions anonymously.

Bakhuizen van den Brink has identified this printer as Abel Clémence of Rouen, in France. He presents three arguments in support of this identification. During an interrogation of a certain Jacques Vrommon, who was involved in covertly selling Protestant books, it was mentioned that Jean Petit and others who imported forbidden Protestant books from France were in contact with a printer named Abel, who lived in Rouen. Secondly, the investigative committee in Doornik reported that a rumor was circulating, that the confession was printed in Rouen. And thirdly, Abel Clémence printed the first edition of *La Racine*, a book written by Guido de Brès and published in 1565.[22] These are obviously interesting and suggestive indications. They do show that Abel Clémence was willing to publish confessions and that a connection existed between the printer of the confession and the minister of Doornik. However, they fall short of proving that the confession had actually been printed by the shop of Abel Clémence.

This circumstantial evidence can be strengthened when this edition of the Belgic Confession is compared with Clémence's edition of Guido de Brès' *Racine*. In this edition of the Belgic Confession three ornamental capitals can be found, an S at the beginning of the letter to the king of Spain, an N at the beginning of article 1 of the confession, and an A at the beginning of the address to the Magistrates. A comparison with the capitals printed at the beginning of the chapters of the *Racine* brings to light that the S used there belongs to a different set. However, the A and the N are identical.[23]

---

20. A reproduction of the title page can be found in Bakhuizen van den Brink, "Quelques notes," opposite page 305.

21. Frédéric Gardy, *Bibliography des oeuvres théologiques, littéraires, historiques et juridiques de Théodore de Bèze* (Geneva: Librairie E. Droz, 1960), 65.

22. Bakhuizen van den Brink, *De Nederlandse belijdenisgeschriften*, 11-12.

23. Guido de Brès, *La racine, source et fondement des Anabaptistes . . .* ([Lyon]: Abel Clémence, 1565). The S printed on page 512 obviously belongs to a different set; the B can be found on pages 804 and 849, and the A on pages 56 and 292.

The fact that of the three capital letters two are identical is hard evidence that the two books were printed at the same printer's shop. This evidence is further confirmed with the data collected by Bakhuizen van den Brink, as listed above. Since it has now been proven that this 1561 edition of the Belgic Confession came from the press of Clémence at Rouen, it can also be concluded that this edition was the one found in Doornik. After all, the committee had stated that the confession, of which it found two hundred copies in de Brès' library, was said to have been printed in Rouen. Since the committee burned the contents of this library,[24] it can be assumed that a majority of the printed copies of the confession were destroyed even before they reached the people.

Another 1561 printing of the Belgic Confession was discovered later in the nineteenth century.[25] Again, the three ornamental capitals allowed identification of the printer. It was Gilmont who identified the printer as Jean II Frellon.[26] A comparison between the two editions may increase our understanding of the early history of the confession. We will call them C and F, after the names of their printers.[27]

Before concentrating on the text of the confession, the general appearance of the two editions should be considered. They contain the same sections: title page, sonnet, epistle to the king, texts on confessing, the actual confession and the remonstrance for the regional magistrates. However, on closer inspection considerable differences can be detected.

To begin with the title page, both editions give the full title of the confession. In C, however, a printer's mark is added, and the statement of 1 Peter 3:15 concerning the importance of confession is printed out. In F, the title page does not show a printer's mark, but provides a more comprehensive description of the content: "With a Remonstrance to the Magistrates of the different regions of Belgium: Flanders, Brabant, Hainault, Artois, Chastelenie de l'Isle and other neighbouring regions." Below this, a small ornamental vignette is printed. The difference between the title pages appears to indicate a difference in emphasis. In C, the emphasis is on the importance of confessing as such, but F concentrates on the content of the book.

Both editions contain the letter to the king, but the layout in C is much nicer, using a larger letter, which results in less text on the page. It also used the exclamation

---

24. Van Langeraad, *Guido de Bray*, 48.

25. Van Langeraad, *Guido de Bray*, 95 n. 5, referring to an article published by A. Van der Linde in 1865. See also Bakhuizen van den Brink, "Quelques notes," 299-300.

26. Jean-Francois Gilmont, "La seconde édition française de la Confessio Belgica [Lyon, Jean Frellon] 1561," *Quaerendo* 4 no. 3 (July 1974): 259-60; Bakhuizen van den Brink, *De Nederlandse belijdenisgeschriften*, 13.

27. Bakhuizen van den Brink refers to the editions by Clémence and by Frellon as A and B, respectively. This may give the impression of a chronological order. To avoid this, the two editions will be identified by the first letter of the printer.

mark to good effect, by using the word "helas!" after having mentioned the tears of wives, children, parents and friends, and following the warning to the king that posterity may not mark his reign as bloody and cruel.[28] The printing in F is much denser, and no exclamation marks are used.

Further, in C the text of the confession is printed in a superior way. For example, here the number of the articles is consistently printed in the blank line between two articles. F, on the other hand, lacks consistency in this respect. With many articles, the number is placed on the line between articles, but in the case of the articles 5, 8 and 9 it is placed on the same line where the previous article ended. However, in the case of articles 23 to 28, a blank line precedes it. There is a lack of consistency in printing. Another difference concerns the way the marginal texts are printed. C always indicates the article to which the texts belong, either by printing these in the margin of the appropriate article, or, if there are too many, by inserting the number of the article before the appropriate texts. In F, however, it is often impossible to know to which article the texts belong. This problem first occurs in the marginal texts belonging to article 7, which begin halfway through article 5, and it continues to article 23.

Overall, C is the better edition, having a printer's mark and showing superior layout. C reflects the use of the Belgic Confession as an apology toward the government. F has a more utilitarian character, listing more of its content on the title page, and cramming the pages with the text of the articles and the proof texts.

The relationship between these two editions has been investigated by Bakhuizen van den Brink.[29] On the basis of a rather detailed investigation of the actual texts, he concluded that F was not meant as a replacement of C, but rather as an improved edition. In his opinion, it is not too hazardous to assume that the Frellon edition was published later, after the commissioners in Doornik had begun their investigation. The fact that copies of C were found during the investigation in Doornik may have brought Bakhuizen van den Brink to this assumption.

The question whether F is indeed an improved edition of C deserves to be investigated, for it may lead to some insight into the history of the Belgic Confession. Reorganizing the data collected by Bakhuizen van den Brink and adding to them, we can distinguish several categories.[30]

First, mistakes which occur in both C and F:

---

28. The examples can be found on pages 10 (twice), 11 and 18 of the letter; there are errors in the pagination.

29. Bakhuizen van den Brink, "Quelques notes," 300-303.

30. The following lists of examples from the confession itself are not exhaustive. The intention is merely to show some clear differences between the printed editions. A survey of the other sections of this publication, such as the Letter to the King and the Remonstrance to the Magistrates, proved that similar problems occur.

In article 14, the apostrophe required in "l' esprit" is missing; it should be added that there is also a slight variation, for C printed "l esprit," and F, "lesprit."

In article 16, a sentence was misunderstood, resulting in a wrong division: "sans aucun esgard de leurs oeuvres iustes: en laissant les autres . . . "; this should have been: "sans aucun esgard de leurs oeuvres; iuste en laissant les autres . . . "[31]

In article 22, the word "requis" needs to be inserted : "tout ce qui est [requis] pour nostre salut."

In the same article, the word "vient" should be "tient" ("la foy est l'instrument qui nous tient avec lui").

In article 32, the word "par" must be inserted ("et par icelles lier les consciences").

In article 37, the statement "toutes l'armes seront essuyees" should read "toutes larmes seront essuyees."

The shared misprints prove that these editions cannot be totally independent. Rather, they must be closely connected. There are several possible ways which may result in these kinds of misprints to occur. One person reading the confession to two copyists may have made the mistakes. Or two copyists may have used the same autograph in which the mistakes occurred. Another possibility is that one copyist made the mistakes, and another simply reproduced this text without thinking.

A second category consists of different spelling:

In article 2, C spells the verb as "conveincre," F as "convaincre."

In articles 3, 4 and 9, C refers to the Bible as "Escritures," F as "Escriptures."

In article 9, C spells the name of one heretic as "Marchion," F spelled his name as "Marcion."

In article 22, C reads "mistere," F "mystere."

In article 34, C has "communiquast," F "communicast."[32]

Concerning the accent, there are several instances where C does not use it and F does, and other instances where the reverse happens. An interesting example is the fact that C wrote "cree" in article 10 and "creé" in article 12, while F, unwittingly reversing this, wrote "creé" in article 10 and "cree" in 12.

These instances of different spelling do not provide an answer to the question which is the earlier edition, for they could be the result of C being read to the copyist of F, or vice versa. However, such differences make it less probable that one edition was copied from the printed version of the other.

In the third place, on a number of occasions, C provides the correct text while F contains a misprint:

---

31. See below, chapter 6.

32. Bakhuizen van den Brink also mentioned a difference in article 26, where A reads "se ranger" and B "se renger," but I could not find this example.

In article 10, C calls the Son "la propre image" of the Father, while F omits a letter ("la prope image").

In article 11, C uses the word "maiesté," while F reads "magesté."

In article 12, C uses the expression "ont persisté et demouré," but F misspells the second word as "domouré."

In article 16, F omits the word "pas" ("de nous-mesmes nous ne sommes [pas] suffisans").

At the very beginning of article 19, C uses "conioincte" to refer to the union of the person of the Son with the human nature, and "incree" to characterize the divine nature. F misspells the first word by writing "conionincte," although two lines down the word is spelled correctly. It also misspells the second word as "increce."

In article 23, C writes "ni de nos merites," but F spells the first word as "n'y."

In article 25, the ceremonies and symbols are referred to in the plural in C: "icelles," but F mistakenly uses the singular "icelle."

In article 36, C writes "afin que Dieu," but F misspells the first word as "affin," although earlier in the same article the word was spelled correctly.

These mistakes are different in character. Some words ("prope," "magesté") are simply misspelled; others ("icelle," "n'y"), however, appear to be the result of a misunderstanding.

Fourthly, on other occasions F provides the correct text:

In both article 4 and 14, C maintains the space between the article and the noun but omits the apostrophe "l apostre" and "s il" (art. 14), where F correctly includes the apostrophe.

In article 14, C states that man has become "semblable au iugement," confusing two results of the fall. F writes "semblable au iuments," using the correct noun, although incorrectly using the plural form.

In article 29, C writes "qu'il n'y ait de grande infirmité," F correctly leaves out the word "de."

In article 35, C misspells the verb "Dieu nous a ordonnez," F writes "ordonne."

In article 37, C confuses two aspects of the day of Christ's return, when it says that all creatures must appear "devant ce grand iour." Remarkably, this word is written correctly earlier in the same article. F correctly uses the word "iuge."

Still in article 37, C says that the evildoers "seront concincus," F correctly reads "conveincus."

How can these errors and differences be explained? If F is a corrected version of C, as Bakhuizen van den Brink thinks, the examples listed in this fourth category can easily be explained, but it would be hard to find an explanation for the mistakes in the third category. The same problem arises if C is seen as a later, corrected version of F. On that premise, the mistakes in C mentioned in the fourth category remain unexplained.

At the same time, it is improbable that the two texts were totally independent, because of the common mistakes mentioned under the first category.

To solve this problem, the possibility must be considered that the two texts are relatively independent. Taking into account the differences in spelling mentioned in the second category, a probable solution is that the original manuscript of the Belgic Confession was dictated to two copyists. This would explain both the common errors as well as the differences between the versions, as two people wrote down the text independently. However, this could have been done either at the same time, or at different times. For that reason, the relative order of the two 1561 editions cannot be determined.

The 1562 Editions

In the year following the original publication of the Belgic Confession, two other editions were printed. Neither shows a printer's mark on the title page, but both use the extended title as found on the F edition. Different from both C and F, not only 1 Pet. 3:15, but also Luke 12:7 and 9 is printed out on the title page. The two 1562 editions have the same sections as the 1561 editions: the sonnet denouncing the persecution, the address to king Philip, the five texts exhorting the believers to profess their faith, the confession itself and the remonstrance for the magistrates.

These editions not only differ from the 1561 editions, they also differ among themselves. The main difference concerns the size of the booklet, for the one edition has a larger page, uses a larger letter and has more pages than the other. For that reason they will be distinguished as Major and Minor.

Several indications suggest that the 1562 editions were printed by two different publishers. One is the fact that different ornamental capitals are used at the beginning of the address to the king, the confession itself and the remonstrance. Those in the Major are embellished with leaves and tendrils, while the capitals in the Minor include a person's head. Another difference concerns the layout. In the Major, the title page and the page containing the five texts proving the importance of confessing are laid out nicely, but in the Minor no effort to produce a pleasing page is noticeable. The Major also has a small vignette at the end of the title, which cannot be found in the Minor. Overall, the presentation of the confession in the Major is much better than that of the Minor.

There is no need to spend much time on the differences between these two printings. A comparison shows a slight variation in the spelling, but the text is basically the same. More interesting is the question how the 1562 editions are related to the 1561 editions. One surprising difference can be found in the sonnet. The 1561 editions made a division between the first six and the following eight lines. Both 1562 editions, however, indicate a division between the first eight and the following six lines. The rhyme pattern proves that the 1562 editions divide the sonnet correctly. This raises the question whether the 1562 editions are independent from the 1561 editions. To find an answer, the same categories used previously to compare the 1561 editions will be used.

The first category listed a number of misprints occurring in both C and F. The same mistakes also occur in the Major and Minor. Several of these make the text unintelligible. The fact that they are repeated in the Major and Minor establishes a connection between the editions of 1561 and the editions of 1562.

The second category comprised examples of different spelling. The two editions of 1562 follow F in the way the words are spelled. The exception is the accent, which is not always inserted in the same place.

The third category consisted of examples of misprints found in F, but not in C. Here, more variations exist between the Major and the Minor, as can be observed in the following examples:

> In article 10, both Major and Minor avoid a misprint by correctly stating that the Son is "la propre image" of the substance of the Father, as C did.
> In article 11, Major follows C by correctly writing "maiesté," but Minor follows F by incorrectly spelling "magesté."
> In article 12, Major and Minor correctly write "demouré," as C did.
> In article 16, both Major and Minor omit the word "pas" at the end of the article, as F had done.
> In article 19, F mistakenly reads "conionincte" and "increce," but Major and Minor use the correct spelling ("conioincte" and "incree").
> In article 23, C has "ni de nos merites," but F misspells the first word ("n'y de nos merites"). Both Major and Minor follow the wrong spelling found in F.
> In article 25, both Major and Minor mistakenly follow F by using the singular form "icelle."
> In article 36, Major as well as Minor follow F in writing "affin."

These examples strengthen the impression that the 1562 editions are based on F rather than C, except in those cases where the mistake was too blatant, such as in articles 10, 12 and 19.

The fourth category listed examples where C was wrong and F was correct. Here, we find the following results:

> In articles 4 and 14, Major and Minor use the apostrophe, different from C but in agreement with F.
> In article 14, Major and Minor use the expression "semblable aux iuments," exactly as F had done. This means they use the correct word, avoiding the mistake "iugement" in C. In addition, they print the same incorrect plural form as F. This is another strong indication that Major and Minor follow F, rather than C.
> In article 29, Major and Minor follow F: "il n'y ait grande infirmité" without inserting the word "de" which occurred in C.

In article 35, Major and Minor again do not follow C: "Dieu nous a ordonnez," but rather F, even to the point of omitting the accent: "Dieu nous a ordonne."

In article 37, Major and Minor correctly write: "devant ce grand juge," following F.

These examples allow us to conclude with confidence that both Major and Minor are closer to the Frellon edition of 1561 than to the Clémence edition. The title page as well as the examples from the text of the confession point in that direction. This becomes a certainty when the mistake made in the location of the proof texts belonging to article 11 in the Major and Minor is considered. There was already a problem with the proof texts of article 11 in the editions of 1561,[33] but the problem in the 1562 editions is different.

The marginal proof texts as given in the margin are: Rev. 1, 2, 3, 4, 5, 6; John 8:58; John 7:5; 1 Cor. 0 [read: 1 Cor. 10] :9; Gal. 4:4; Mi. 5:2; Col. 1:5; Ps. 2; Heb. 13:8. These texts do not make sense. Article 11 deals with the Holy Spirit, but this list of texts concentrates on the Son of God, particularly if John 7:5 is taken as John 17:5.

This mistake cannot be explained if it is assumed that C was the model for the 1562 editions, for here it is clearly indicated in the margin to which article the proof texts belong. However, in the margin of F, no indication is given as to which texts belong to which article. In the case of article 11, dealing with the Holy Spirit, the corresponding texts were actually placed in the margin of article 12. As a result, the printer of the 1562 edition, confused by the way the texts were printed, had the impression that the texts printed in the margin of article 11 actually belonged to that article. The mistake in the 1562 editions can only be explained on the premise that they were based on the F edition. The use of F as basis for the 1562 editions is also understandable for the reason that, as noted above, the majority of the C edition had been destroyed.

Concerning the two 1562 editions, the fact that both contain the same mistake in the proof texts of article 11 implies that they are related. This can be confirmed by comparing the proof texts of other articles. Notwithstanding slight differences, overall the same list of texts is used, and the texts are frequently found to be in the wrong place. However, at this moment it cannot be determined which of the two 1562 editions is the earlier.

The fact that within two years four editions were printed shows that already during that time of persecution the Belgic Confession was used by the Reformed believers. There must have been considerable demand for the confession for printers to publish four editions within two years, and this is further confirmed by the Dutch language editions published in 1562, 1563, 1564 and 1566.[34] The fact that several printings

---

33. This will be discussed later in this chapter.
34. The Dutch editions will be further discussed in chapter 8.

were made proves that the confession established itself very quickly as an important document within the Reformed churches of the Netherlands.

The Earlier History

The records of the persecution in Doornik during the fall of 1561 prove beyond doubt that printed copies of the Belgic Confession were in the hands of Reformed leaders early in October. The question must now be considered whether information is available concerning the earlier stages of the confession, prior to the *chanteries*. Several leads need to be investigated.

Braekman has pointed to a statement made by Guido de Brès in his *Baston de la Foy*, concluding that he was considering writing a confession as early as 1555.[35] At this point the questions do not focus on the authorship of the Belgic Confession, but rather on the time when this confession was made. It is true that de Brès' statement referred to a "confession of faith," but it is questionable whether he was indicating that he was planning to write one. His remark can be found in the preface of his *Baston*, the book in which he argues on the basis of quotations from the church fathers that the Reformed are not heretics:

> . . . that if I intend to present this book (in which there is nothing of mine, but all things are from the ancients) as a confession of my faith to these enemies of the fathers, I do not doubt that at the same time I am not like an evil heretic, condemned to be burned alive to ashes.[36]

When this statement is carefully considered, it can be acknowledged that Guido de Brès did refer to a confession of his faith, but he did not say he was intending to write one. Rather, he presented his book consisting of quotes from the church fathers, as an expression of his own faith. De Brès wanted to emphasize that he was in agreement with the church fathers for he believed the same doctrines already stated by them.

Moreau drew attention to a remark in the Acts of the consistory of the francophone Dutch refugee church in London, which had not previously been

---

35. Braekman, *Guy de Brès*, 156-57.

36. Guido de Brès, *Le Baston de la Foy Chrestienne . . . Reveue et augmentee de nouveau par luy, avec un abregé d'icelle* (n.p.: Nicolas Barbier et Thomas Courteau, 1558), 7: " . . . que si ie veux presenter le present livre (ou il n'y a rien du mien ains tout des anciens) pour confession de ma foy a ces ennemis des Peres: ie ne doute pas que quant et quant je ne soye comme un meschant heretique condamné a estre brusle toutvif en cendre."

connected with the Belgic Confession.[37] The entry can be found in the Acts under April 9, 1561:

> It was also brought to our attention . . . that the brothers of Antwerp have made a supplication to the magistrates of Antwerp which they sent here together with their confession, desiring to have it printed. Concerning this, they are told that everyone will give his considered opinion on this at another time.[38]

At the time, there was another refugee congregation in London, consisting of Dutch-speaking refugees. Their records contain a statement on the same issue:

> Concerning the petition of the Antwerp church to the Antwerp magistrate, they respond that it is dangerous to resolve that it should be printed. Galasius wants to consult the bishop of London concerning this issue.[39]

Moreau connects the report with the fact that during the persecution in Doornik, in 1561, the Belgic Confession was called the confession of the believers at Antwerp. Macquet had called it the "confession of the believers at Antwerp," and Gilles Espringalles had stated that the confession was that of Antwerp.[40] Moreau, combining these data, concluded that the Belgic Confession represented not only the views of Guido de Brès, but that of the church at Antwerp, as well.

This reconstruction would make it easier to understand why these two inhabitants of Doornik referred to the Belgic Confession as the "confession of Antwerp." On the other hand, the testimony of these members of the congregation does not have much weight, for the records of the interrogations show that those who had attended meetings did not know much beyond that. The actual proof must be found in the consistory records. These records themselves need to be considered carefully.

A closer look at the request Antwerp presented to the French-speaking Dutch refugees in London shows that it did not deal with the publication of the Belgic

---

37. Moreau, *Histoire du protestantisme*, 156. His view was accepted by Bakhuizen van den Brink, *De Nederlandse belijdenisgeschiften*, 15, and by Guido Marnef, *Antwerp in the Time of the Reformation: Underground Protestantism in a Commercial Metropolis, 1550-1577*, trans. J. C. Grayson (Baltimore and London: John Hopkins University Press, 1996), 106, 124.

38. Moreau, *Histoire du Protestantisme*, 156 n. 1: " . . . fut aussi proposé . . . que les frères d'Anvers ont faict une supplication aux magistratz d'Anvers laquelle il [sic] ont ycy envoiet avec leur Confession désirant la faire imprimer; surquoy l'on leur dit que sur cela chaschun en prendre avis jusques a ung aultrefois."

39. Moreau, *Histoire du Protestantisme*, 156 n. 1: "De supplicatione ecclesiae antwerpianae ad magistratum antwerpianum. Respondent periculosum esse consulere ut imprimatur, vult ea in re Galasius consulere episcopum londinensem."

40. The report on Espringalles can be found Appendix, Document 2; see also note 12 above. For Macquet, see Moreau, *Histoire du Protestantism à Tournai*, 156 n. 1.

Confession, after all. First of all, the actual text of the request shows that it concerned a supplication to the magistrates, which they would like to be printed in London. Further, although it is true that a confession was sent along, there is no indication that this refers to the Belgic Confession. The statement refers probably to Beza's confession. There is an indication from around the same time that his confession was known and used in Antwerp. In a letter dated April 10, 1561, Olevianus wrote to Beza:

> Dr. Johannes Junius Senator of Antwerp sent to you your confession translated into Dutch, so that by confessing your faith, you also in the future may enlighten many people in Flanders.[41]

This means for the Belgic Confession that the request to the congregation in London cannot be used to prove that this confession existed in manuscript as early as April 1561.

Another indication concerning the printing of the Belgic Confession was passed on by Braekman. He gives an exact date and place: it was published in Rouen on May 25, 1561.[42] This was based on a published speech by Panchaud, originally given on the occasion of the tercentenary of the Belgic Confession.[43] In view of the fact that the confession was first discovered in Doornik in October, this date is altogether probable. However, this date remains uncertain, as Panchaud did not provide the source for this information.

Therefore, although regrettable, the conclusion must be drawn that, due to a lack of sources, we have no information concerning the actual making of the confession outside of the confession itself. However, a closer look at a mistake in article 11 of the confession may provide us with some details to shed some light on the preparatory stage of the confession.

In both 1561 editions, it is clearly indicated which proof texts belong to this article. This is especially the case in C, where "artic. xi" is printed in the margin, followed by a list of fourteen texts. Below this, one finds "article xii," followed by another list of texts. F does not provide these headings in the margin, but it gives the same list of proof texts, inserting a blank line in order to separate these texts from the

---

41. His letter to Beza was published in Theodore Beza, *Correspondence de Théodore de Bèze*, coll. H. Aubert, ed. A. Dufour, F. Aubert, and H. Meylan (Geneva: Libraire E. Droz, 1963), 3:96-97. The preface to the translation of Beza's confession is dated March 20, 1561; see 97 n. 3.

42. Braekman, *Guy de Brès*, 161.

43. Eduard Panchaud, *Souvenir du jubilé tricentenaire de la publication de la confession de foi* (Brussels: Librairie chrétienne évangélique, 1861), 12. I am grateful to Dr. Braekman for presenting me with a copy of this brochure.

texts belonging to the previous article and those belonging to the following article. The list of texts in both editions is identical, but something has gone wrong.[44]

Article 11 deals with the Holy Spirit, but most of the marginal texts do not refer to him.[45] Actually, the first eight texts do not speak of the Spirit at all. They are followed by one text specifically dealing with the Holy Spirit, John 15:26. The next two texts again have nothing to do with the subject of article 11, but the final references mentioned in this section, John 14:16 and 26, do speak of the Holy Spirit. As a result, only three of the original marginal texts of article 11 actually belong to this article. The texts that do not match article 11 all refer to God's creation work, which is the subject of the following article, 12.

A similar problem can be noted concerning the proof texts in the margin of article 12. The first two deal with creation, but the following six (Matt. 28:19; 1 John 5; Acts 5:3; 1 Cor. 3:16 and 6:11; Rom. 8:9) mention the Holy Spirit, who was the subject of the previous article. In other words, the texts belonging to the articles on the Spirit and on creation have been mixed up.

This raises the question how it may have come about that so many texts ended up in the margin of the wrong article. At this point, it must be taken into consideration that articles 10, 11 and 12 all have many marginal texts. Even the printed versions, where a smaller letter could be used for the margin, show that there are too many texts to be fitted in the margin of the appropriate article. The problems will have been even greater in the original manuscript. The mix-up of the texts can be explained if it is assumed that in the written version, the texts belonging to article 10 spilled over into the margin of article 11, so that the texts belonging to article 11 began more than halfway down the article, continuing in the margin of article 12. The many proof texts for article 12 were written in a second column beginning at the level where article 11 began. When the texts were merged into one column, it was no longer visible that they belonged to different articles.

At what point in the process from writing to publication were they combined? It would be easy to suppose that the printer misunderstood the handwritten copy he had received. He could have merged two columns of texts belonging to different articles into one, causing the confusion. However, there is one fact that makes this reconstruction improbable. The two 1561 editions were published by different printers but both contain the same garbled list of proof texts. This suggests that the mistake was not made by the printers who misunderstood the copies they had received. Rather, it points to the existence of two similar handwritten copies, each of which had the

---

44. See also Nicolaas H. Gootjes, "Problems with Proof Texts: The Proof Texts of Article 11 of the Belgic Confession and Their Implication for the Confession," *Calvin Theological Journal* 36 no. 2 (2001): 372-78

45. The texts are: Gen. 1:1; Heb. 1:3 and 11:3; John 1:3; Ps. 33:6 and Ps. 110:3; Jer. 32:17; Mal. 2:10; John 1:3; John 15:26; Ps. 104; Amos 4:13; John 14:16, 26. It is noteworthy that John 1:3 is mentioned twice.

same mistake. The confused list of texts must have come about when a copyist misunderstood the two columns of texts in the original manuscript, something the printers did not catch.

In addition to the copyist and the printer, the author, too, made mistakes. In the original editions, the last two articles were introduced as the final one. Article 37 correctly begins with the formula: "Nous croyons finalement," but already article 36 opened with a similar statement: "Finalement nous croyons." It is improbable that this was intended as a double conclusion.[46] Rather, this mistake must have been made by the author, who failed to change the beginning of article 36 after he had added article 37. Such a mistake can easily occur, but is also easily noticed. At any rate, this suggests that the Belgic Confession was printed with some haste, without being carefully checked over by either the printer or the author.

---

46. Cornelis Vonk explained this double "finalement" as a parallel intended by the author, for article 36 is an appeal to the earthly government, and article 37 to the heavenly government; see his *De voorzeide leer, III: De Nederlandse Geloofsbelijdenis*, 2 vols. (Barendrecht: Drukkerij Barendrecht, 1955-56), 2:549. This interpretation is improbable for neither article is presented in the form of an appeal. The possible background for the double use of the word "finally" will be given in chapter 4.

2

The Author of the Confession

The title page of the sixteenth century editions of the Belgic Confession states that the confession was made "with common accord by the believers who dwell in the Netherlands, who desire to live according to the purity of the gospel of our Lord Jesus Christ." This title was obviously an adaptation of the Gallican Confession of 1559, for one of the two versions of this confession was entitled: "Confession of faith, made by common accord by the French who desire to live according to the purity of the gospel of our Lord Jesus Christ."[1] Neither the title page of the Gallican Confession nor that of the Belgic Confession provides an indication of who had authored these confessions. The issue of the author of the Gallican Confession will be discussed briefly in the next chapter. In this chapter, the much more complicated question of the author of the Belgic Confession will be dealt with.

During the century in which the confession was published, no one claimed authorship. Nor was it generally known who was the author. This can be demonstrated from Crespin's *Book of Martyrs*, which was published during that period. In this book, an abbreviated version of the Belgic Confession was included as early as 1570, and from 1582 onward the first edition of the confession was inserted in its entirety. Neither of these editions provides an indication concerning the author of this confession.[2] Traditionally, Guido de Brès is considered to be its author. However, his contemporary Crespin, who dealt extensively with the life and work of Guido de Brès as martyr,[3] does not give any indication that he may have been involved in the Belgic Confession.

The question of the authorship of the confession began to receive attention in the seventeenth century, when it became part of the debate on the authority of the confession between the Reformed and the Remonstrants. This debate has clouded the issue considerably. The Remonstrant leader Johannes Uytenbogaert stated in his posthumously published *Ecclesiastical History* (1646) that he is unable to say with certainty who had drawn up the Belgic Confession and published it in the name of

---

1. On this title, see Hannelore Jahr, *Studien zur Überlieferungsgeschichte der Confession de foi von 1559* (Neukirchen-Vluyn: Neukirchener Verlag, 1964), 20, 94.

2. Jean Crespin, *Histoire des martyrs*, 3 vols. (Toulouse: Société des livres religieux, 1889), 3:102-3

3. Crespin, *Histoire des martyrs*, 3:533-75.

the Dutch churches.[4] He had not found any evidence that a synod of the Dutch churches had dealt with it beforehand, nor that a general instruction had been given for making it, let alone that it had been scrutinized and adopted as being in full agreement with God's Word. In that context, he discusses two sources for the origin of the Belgic Confession, listing only a few names of people who had been involved. Obviously, Uytenbogaert used the information on the authorship in order to present this confession as someone's personal project without any authorization from the Reformed churches.

The Reformed historian Jacobus Trigland responded to Uytenbogaert. He started off by emphasizing that the confession cannot be credited to one particular author. The pious martyr Guido de Brès who was knowledgeable in theology, together with his helpers in the congregations of Rijssel, Casselrye, Doornik, Valenciennes and other places, and the scholarly and God-fearing Godfried Van Wingen with his helpers in Flanders, Brabant, Holland and so forth, were the first authors. Next, he points out that it is no wonder that no record exists of a synod dealing with the confession, for it was made during a time of persecution. After the confession had been made, it was published only upon consultation with as many people as possible. Trigland then enumerates the names of thirteen people who had been consulted. Following this impressive list, he concludes by pointing out that the Belgic Confession had been officially revised during an ecclesiastical meeting held in Antwerp, in 1565. In listing so many names, Trigland is obviously countering Uytenbogaert so as to establish the confession's authority for those years where he is unable to produce ecclesiastical records confirming such authority.

The Remonstrant historian Geeraert Brandt mentions that Guido de Brès was the author, adding that Saravia, Moded, Van Wingen and two others were his helpers. This is followed by quotations from Saravia and Junius concerning the making of the confession.[5] An extensive note added at the end of the book serves to provide the proof that the Belgic Confession had never received public authority.[6] By organizing his material in this way, Brandt, like Uytenbogaert, intends to present the Belgic Confession as a personal confession, which inadvertently had received official status at a later date.

This Reformed-Remonstrant discussion is apparently about authorship, but in reality it is concerned with the confession's authority. Although this debate and its sources have traditionally been used to settle the issue of the authorship, we must distance ourselves from this approach. In the context of the seventeenth century it

---

4. The views of both Uytenbogaert and Trigland can be found in Johannes Trigland, *Kerckelijcke geschiedenissen* (Leiden: A. Wijngaerden, 1650), 145. For text, see Appendix, Document 6.

5. Brandt, *Historie der Reformatie*, 1:253-54.

6. The text of the note can be found in Brandt, *Historie der Reformatie*, vol. 1, endnote section 31-32.

was understandable that the issue of authorship was tied up with authority. However, it has not been helpful for the historical question of authorship, and has only clouded the issue.

When the issue of the author is discussed, we are particularly interested in the background and origin of the confession. Five statements, all dating from the seventeenth century, constitute the center of the discussion concerning the authorship of the Belgic Confession. A remarkable feature of these statements is that the later their origin, the more specific their content. We need to take a close look at each in turn.

Saravia

Foundational information concerning the author of the Belgic Confession can be found in a long letter written by Adrianus Saravia to Uytenbogaert. Almost all of the following discussion goes back in one way or another to this letter. It is therefore important to place this letter in its historical context.[7] Saravia was probably born in January 1532 in Hesdin, Belgium. After having become an adherent to the Reformation in 1557 or 1558, he had a checkered career in the Netherlands and England. In 1562, he became a minister in Antwerp. The following year, he was in England, where he served as headmaster at two different schools (1563-1578). Back in the Netherlands, he became minister at the Reformed church at Ghent, and later at Leiden (1578-1584). He became professor at the University of Leiden (1584) until his dismissal (1587). Then he returned to England, serving in several functions in the church till he eventually rose to become Canon of Westminster Abbey (since 1601). He died in Canterbury on January 15, 1613. His letter to Uytenbogaert was written in the year before his death, on April 23, 1612.[8]

Saravia's letter was a response to a letter Uytenbogaert had sent him, together with a book he had written. Uytenbogaert's book was published during the doctrinal struggles between the Reformed and the Remonstrants leading up to the Synod of Dort. In it, he dealt with the task of the government in ecclesiastical affairs, defending the position that the government has decisive authority in the church. Saravia was in agreement with this view, for as early as 1593 he had published a book advocating the same position. We may assume that Uytenbogaert had included a letter with the book, in which he asked Saravia some questions concerning the Belgic Confession, for Saravia had already been active as a minister when the confession first appeared and he had many contacts in the area. At any rate, in his

---

7. On Saravia, see Willem Nijenhuis' biography *Adrianus Saravia: Dutch Calvinist* (Leiden: Brill, 1980); see also "Saravia, Adrianus," in *BLGNP*, 2:382-87.

8. Nijenhuis, *Adrianus Saravia*, 355. The date of the letter is adjusted to the way the years are counted today; the original date, following the old style still used in England at the time, was April 13, 1612.

response, Saravia dealt not only with the role of the government in the church but also with the Belgic Confession.

Saravia begins by elaborating on the role of several Dutch noblemen in the early history of the confession.[9] This is followed by a passage on the origin of the Belgic Confession:

> I acknowledge having been one of the first authors of this confession, just as Herman Moded; I do not know whether others are still alive. It was first written in the French language by the servant of Christ and martyr Guido de Brès. But before it was published he showed it to those ministers of the Word he could reach and offered to change whatever displeased them, to add and to delete, so that it would not be seen as the work of one person. But none of those who were involved ever intended to publish a rule of faith, but to prove his faith from the Canonical books. Yet in my opinion there is nothing in it which I disapprove of or would want to change.[10]

At the end of this section, Saravia makes a statement on the authority of the confession. But before that, he provides more general information about its background.

Since the time Saravia's statement became known, it has been used to prove that the Belgic Confession was made by several authors. Some he mentions by name, in addition to himself, referring to Moded and Guido de Brès; others he indicates without identifying them. The fact that he did not provide the names of these other ministers who were involved has provided opportunity for considerable speculation. When later authors dealt with the authorship of the confession, they made up longs lists of possible candidates. It can be questioned whether this is a correct interpretation of Saravia's statement. In fact, there are several indications that make this view untenable.

In the first place, the text of the letter itself does not favor this interpretation. If this is what happened, one would expect Saravia to begin with Guido de Brès as the first author, before mentioning himself and Moded as co-authors. However, the names occur in a different order, beginning with his own role and that of Moded, before stating that Guido de Brès had written the confession. Further, on this interpretation the statement would be almost contradictory. Why would Saravia first say that there were more authors, and later that de Brès had written it? Why did Saravia not reverse the order of his sentence, stating that the confession was first written by de Brès, and that the others had made additions later? It should also be noted that Saravia's statement that de Brès was willing to change things is an

---

9. See chapter 5 for a discussion of this section.
10. For the text, see Appendix, Document 5.

indication that he was the author. It is unknown whether any of these ministers used the opportunity to contribute to the confession; we are only told that they had the opportunity to propose changes. This would make them consultants, rather than co-authors.

In the second place, the historical circumstances make it impossible that Saravia was one of the authors of the confession. In 1561, when the confession was published, he had not even been ordained as a minister. Actually, he was living in England at the time, although he made regular trips to Belgium.[11] It is unlikely that at this stage in his life he would have been involved in making a confession.[12] Another problem concerns the fact that Saravia mentions Moded as the other "first author." In view of his life, it is improbable that he was involved in the making of the original Belgic Confession. Moded was born in Zwolle, in the northern, Dutch-speaking part of the Netherlands. He was a minister of the Reformed church in Antwerp from 1560-1567, serving the Dutch speaking part of the congregation. From there, he moved around and preached in Breda, 's Hertogenbosch and Gorkum, cities in the northern provinces of the Netherlands.[13] He was involved in the early history of the Belgic Confession, as noted in the previous chapter. However, he himself did not say that he had made it but that he had promoted it.

We need to reconsider the original quotation in its context. Prior to stating that he was one of the first authors of the Belgic Confession, Saravia referred to an event that took place in 1566, several years after the publication of the confession. In that year, the confession was presented to the Prince of Orange and Count Egmond. The brother of Saravia's wife was gentleman-in-waiting to Count Lodewijk, a brother of the Prince of Orange. Saravia recounts that through this courtier he had been able to approach the Count and to present him with a copy of the recently printed confession. It is at this point that he also says he was one of the first authors of the Belgic Confession. If by this he intended to say that he was involved in the actual writing of the confession, this would hardly be a fitting place for such a statement.

On closer inspection this does not appear to have been Saravia's intention either. The word "author" has more than one meaning and can be used in different ways. In this case, he calls himself "author" in the context of approaching the Prince of

---

11. Nijenhuis, *Adrianus Saravia*, 12-14.

12. Nijenhuis recognized the problem that at this time, Saravia had not yet been ordained as a minister. His solution is that the minister of the London refugee church, Des Gallars, "and his close friend Saravia, future minister of Antwerp, would undoubtedly have deliberated together about the Belgic Confession. Perhaps the opinion which [Saravia] expressed on this occasion became the source of the report that spread here and there that he was one of the Confession's authors" (*Adrianus Saravia*, 17). This ingenious solution is untenable. That Saravia was involved was not a rumor; this was stated by Saravia himself. The context of this statement shows clearly that Saravia is not referring to the making of the confession, but to making the confession known.

13. For a survey of Moded's life, see Gerrit P. Van Itterzon, "Moded," *BLGNP*, 3:267-71.

Orange through his brother, and this word must therefore be understood as "instigator" or "promoter."[14] Saravia wants to state that at one time he had been involved with the confession, but this cannot be a statement on authorship. Rather, he means that as early as 1566, he had actively been involved in promoting the Belgic Confession, particularly by making it known to important noblemen.

This interpretation of Saravia's statement is confirmed by the mention of Hermanus Moded's name in the same context. As Moded came from the northern, Dutch-speaking provinces, it is improbable that he would have been involved in the composition of the Belgic Confession because it was originally written in French. On the other hand, there is evidence that he was a supporter of the confession, for he was present at the synod of 1566 where the confession was revised and adopted. The question may arise why Saravia would mention only two names of all the people who had promoted the Belgic Confession at that synod. The reason for singling out these names is spelled out in the letter itself: Saravia mentions only those who were still alive at the time he wrote this, over fifty years later. If the word "author" is taken in the sense of supporter, the elements of the letter fall into place. Saravia clearly states that Guido de Brès had written the Belgic Confession, and adds that of the early supporters of this confession only he and Moded are still alive.

Another issue that needs to be considered is whether Saravia's statement is reliable. There was an early attempt to cast doubt on the authenticity of Saravia's letter.[15] This letter is dated April 13, 1612,[16] but Saravia had died on January 15, 1612, according to the inscription on his gravestone. This would mean that Saravia wrote this letter not only more than thirty years after he had left the Netherlands, but even after his death. Since the autograph is lost, the date on the original letter can no longer be checked, but there is an easy solution for this problem. At the time, the new year in England did not begin on the first day of January but on March 25. In today's reckoning, Saravia died on January 15, 1613.[17] The authenticity of the letter is therefore not in doubt.

Since Saravia was eighty years old at the time of writing, the question may be raised whether he would still remember events which by that time had occurred about fifty years earlier. However, his letter does not show any signs of a weakened memory. In fact, later that same year Saravia wrote a second letter to Uytenbogaert, in connection with the debates concerning Vorstius' book on God and his attributes, published in 1610. This second letter confirms the impression of the first letter that even at his advanced age he was fully aware of the issues.[18]

---

14. For this sense of the word "auctor," see Charlton T. Lewis and Charles Short, *A Latin Dictionary*, s.v. "auctor," sub II.C; and *Oxford Latin Dictionary*, s.v. "auctor," sub 12.

15. Willem Te Water, *Tweede eeuw-getyde*, 43.

16. Nijenhuis, *Adrianus Saravia*, 357.

17. Nijenhuis, *Adrianus Saravia*, 158.

18. For the text of this letter, see Nijenhuis, *Adrianus Saravia*, 359-66.

Another question is whether Saravia would have been in a position to be familiar with the early history of the Belgic Confession. His letter does not provide concrete information concerning the source of his knowledge, but his biography indicates that he had been close enough to know of its origin. Saravia had been in a monastery near Saint-Omer, in the southern part of the Netherlands. After having become acquainted with the Reformed faith, he had escaped from the monastery with the help of Jacques Taffin. Saravia had been invited to the castle of the Taffin family, and had even preached there. He later stated that he was deeply indebted to the Taffins for important and well founded reasons.[19] As this family played an important role in the Reformed church at Doornik served by Guido de Brès, Saravia could easily have heard about the author of the Belgic Confession from a member of the Taffin family. Moreover, even after Saravia joined the Dutch church in London in 1561, the contact was not broken off, for he continued to visit Belgium regularly.[20] He was still involved in promoting the Belgic Confession among the nobility in 1566, as we saw before.

We can therefore conclude that Saravia was sufficiently close to the Belgic Confession in its early years to be sure of the information he gave. His remark on the author of the Belgic Confession may be taken as trustworthy.

Thysius

The next theologian to discuss the authorship of the Belgic Confession is Anthony Thysius. He made his remarks only three years after Saravia, but his contribution is markedly different, both in character and in value. He presented his view in a book devoted to the defense of the doctrine and church order of the Dutch churches. This was published in 1615, during the debates between the Reformed and the Remonstrants leading up to the Synod of Dort. Thysius was a strong proponent of the Reformed doctrine, and this shows in the way he presented the material available to him.[21] His views concerning the author of the Belgic Confession can be summarized in four statements. He begins by downplaying the importance of the question of authorship:

> And although it is not sufficiently clear who were the author or authors of this (which is of little importance), nevertheless it was written by scholarly and pious men, who did not have an uncertain, intellectual knowledge of God and the divine things concerning our salvation, but a sure and active knowledge, and who were

---

19. Nijenhuis, *Adrianus Saravia*, 89.
20. Nijenhuis, *Adrianus Saravia*, 12-13.
21. Thysius' introduction to the Belgic Confession can be found in his *Leere ende Order*. The original text, as published by Van Langeraad, is provided in Appendix, Document 7.

willing to give their blood for the confirmation of the truth summarized in the confession.

This is followed by a statement emphasizing that many people were involved in making the confession:

> We are informed by the older people [that it was drafted] by the faithful minister and martyr Guido de Brès, who was well grounded in the Word of God and in all godliness, and by his helpers in the congregations of Rijssel, Casselrije, Doornik, Valenciennes, among others, and by Godfried Van Wingen, whose exceptional scholarship in theology and ability in Greek and other languages is well known . . . and his coworkers in Flanders, Brabant, the Netherlands and elsewhere.

Concerning its publication, Thysius mentions that the confession:

> was not made nor published without previous communication with, and approval . . . by the faithful ministers who at the time were everywhere in the Dutch churches.

Thysius goes on to list the names of fourteen ministers who had worked in congregations in and outside of the Netherlands, ending with the well-known Calvin:

> It has even been shown and shared by the very knowledgeable, Godfearing and active Jean Crespin with the ministers, and particularly with that exceptional and precious man of God John Calvin at Geneva, where it was also first printed.

This long list of impressive names ending with the reference to Calvin clearly shows Thysius' intention in writing this section. He is not so much interested in the name of the author, as can be noticed at the beginning of the first and third statements. Rather, his concern is the authority of the Belgic Confession, which at the time was greatly debated between the Reformed and the Remonstrants. That also explains why he drew attention to the fact that the confession had been submitted to leading ministers for their approval, and even to Calvin.[22]

Thysius' knowledge of the early history of the Belgic Confession is not the result of direct involvement, for he was born in 1565 in Antwerp, four years after its

---

22. Van Langeraad subjected this list of names to an extensive and critical investigation, concluding that many of the persons mentioned cannot have been involved in the making of the confession. In his opinion, the list contains much improbable and untrue information, cf. *Guido de Bray*, 104-16. Later research has qualified this criticism to some extent. All the same, the common understanding that the list of names refers to co-authors is a misunderstanding of Thysius' statement.

publication. For study purposes, he had traveled widely in many European countries. After having served as a curate in churches in the Netherlands and France, he became a professor of theology at the university in Harderwijk, and later in Leiden.[23] He says that his information is based on reports, but it is unclear which reports on the authorship of Guido de Brès he knew. Thysius may have become acquainted with Saravia's remarks, written a few years earlier.

Concerning the making of the confession, Thysius' most striking remark is that Guido's helpers in the congregations of Rijssel, Casselrije, Doornik and Valenciennes contributed to the confession. This formulation is presumably the result of his combining the title page of the Belgic Confession, which notes that this confession was made with common accord by the believers in the Netherlands, with the section on de Brès in the *Book of Martyrs*, where three of these congregations are mentioned.[24] Only the name Casselrije is missing, but Van Langeraad explains that its inclusion in Thysius is based on a misunderstanding, since Casselrije is simply another name for Doornik and surrounding areas.[25] That he did include this fourth name is presumably the result of the fact that it is mentioned in the Remonstrance to the Magistrates, included in the original editions of the confession.[26] This then proves to be another indication that Thysius did not have clear, first-hand knowledge of the circumstances.

In short, Thysius is not an independent witness to the authorship of the Belgic Confession. With the original edition of the confession, Saravia's statement and the *Book of Martyrs*, the information he had available was the same we have today. His statement is merely his own interpretation of these data.

Uytenbogaert

We can now return to the debate between Johannes Uytenbogaert and Jacobus Trigland mentioned at the beginning of this chapter. Uytenbogaert was born four years before the publication of the Belgic Confession, in Utrecht, a city located in the northern part of the Netherlands. Both time and place therefore show that he had no personal, direct knowledge of the origin of the Belgic Confession. He himself indicates that his opinion is based on two sources, Saravia and Junius.[27]

Saravia, Uytenbogaert writes, had mentioned three or four authors of the confession, and the Remonstrant leader interpreted the word "authors" as referring

---

23. Hendrik Kaajan, "Thysius," in *Christelijke Encyclopedie*, 6:373; Anthonie J. Lamping, "Thysius, Anthonius," in *BLGNP*, 5:505-8.

24. Crespin, *Histoire des martyrs*, 3:581.

25. Van Langeraad, *Guido de Bray*, 104.

26. The name can be found on page d. iii in the Clémence edition of the Belgic Confession.

27. This section is quoted in its entirety by Trigland, *Kerckelijcke geschiedenissen*, 145; for text, see Appendix, Document 9.

to theologians who had actually written the confession. As we have argued above, this is a misunderstanding of Saravia, but Uytenbogaert is the source for the widespread opinion that this remark did refer to the actual composers of the Belgic Confession. The original letter was not published until later in the seventeenth century, and by that time, Uytenbogaert's interpretation determined the way Saravia's letter was read and understood.[28]

Uytenbogaert combines this misunderstanding of Saravia, however, with a statement from Franciscus Junius that Guido de Brès made the confession, together with Herman Moded, Saravia, and Junius himself. One or two other persons were mentioned, but Uytenbogaert writes that he has forgotten their names. However, the information he attributes to Junius cannot be correct. Junius was of French origin and born in 1545 in Bourges. He began his study in law in 1558, but after his conversion he turned to theology, pursuing studies in Geneva in 1562. He became a minister in the French-speaking Reformed congregation of Antwerp in 1565 at the young age of twenty. In 1561, the year the Belgic Confession was published, Junius was even younger, and he had not even started the study of theology. Clearly, he could not have been among the authors of the confession.

Uytenbogaert is aware of the problem posed by Junius' age and attempts to resolve it by stating that he was merely secretary to a committee of ministers who made the confession. However, this is again a misunderstanding. In Junius' autobiography, published in 1595, a somewhat similar statement can be found:

> At that time, I sent the confession of the Dutch churches, revised according to the decision of the synod held at the beginning of May, to the brothers in Geneva, so that they, after having approved it, would permit it to be printed if that seemed useful, and commend our doctrinal teaching to the Lord.[29]

According to Junius' own statement that he was responsible for sending the confession to the churches, his role was clearly that of a secretary. However, the events he is describing took place in 1566.[30] Uytenbogaert, therefore, mistakenly applied Junius' statement concerning the revision of 1566 to its composition in 1561.[31]

A careful reading of Uytenbogaert's argument shows that he interpreted the information from Junius in light of his (mis)understanding of Saravia's letter.

---

28. The reason why Saravia's letter was suppressed will be discussed in chapter 5.

29. Franciscus Junius, *Opuscula theologica selecta Francisci Junii*, ed. A. Kuyper (Amsterdam: Fredericus Muller, 1882), 26: "Quo tempore Confessionem Belgicarum Ecclesiarum de Synodi, quae ineunte Maio habita fuerat, sententia recognitam ad fratres Geneuenses misi, ut a se probatam excudi sinerent, si videtur utile, & institutum illud nostrum Deo precibus commendarent."

30. Bakhuizen van den Brink, *De Nederlandse belijdenisgeschriften*, 17.

31. This problem was already noted by Brandt, *Historie der Reformatie*, 1:254.

Therefore, Uytenbogaert's statement is based on the same sources we still have, but it contains several misrepresentations. In short, he does not provide independent, additional information concerning the author of the Belgic Confession.

Trigland

In connection with Jacobus Trigland's statement concerning the authorship of the confession,[32] the same questions must be considered: What were his sources and did he have access to additional information? He begins by stating that the confession was made by Guido de Brès, with approval of his helpers in the congregations of Rijssel, Casselrije, Doornik, Valenciennes and others, and by the very scholarly and God-fearing Godfried Van Wingen. This is similar to what Thysius wrote.

He also provides a list of names of the ministers who had been involved in the confession before it was printed and published. He mentions two ministers who worked in the Netherlands, and ten ministers who worked in Dutch congregations outside of the country. The list is identical to that of Thysius, and the names are presented in the same order.

Trigland, who was born in 1609, did not have personal knowledge of the events leading to the publication of the Belgic Confession. Although he does not mention his source, it is obvious that he relies heavily on Thysius. It has already been shown that Thysius had no direct knowledge of the background either, but interpreted information taken from the life of Guido de Brès. We must conclude that Trigland, as well, based his opinion concerning the author of the Belgic Confession on earlier information, without providing new data.

Trigland goes on to discuss Junius' statement, which he does not connect with the origin of the Belgic Confession, as Uytenbogaert had done, but correctly with the authority of the Belgic Confession. However, as far as the authorship of the Belgic Confession is concerned, we must conclude that Trigland had nothing new to contribute to the discussion.

Schoock

The last of the seventeenth century authors to be discussed is Martinus Schoock.[33] He presents several new pieces of information on the issue of the authorship of the Belgic Confession. He states that as early as 1559, Guido de Brès

---

32. Trigland, *Kerckelijcke geschiedenissen*, 145.

33. Schoock published his remarks in *Liber de bonis vulgo ecclesiasticis dictis* (1650); they can also be found in Nijenhuis, *Adrianus Saravia*, 17; Van Langeraad, *Guido de Bray*, 97-98; Henrikus E. Vinke, *Libri symbolici ecclesiae reformatae nederlandicae*, xiii-xv. The text has been printed in Appendix, Document 10.

wrote a number of articles on which the Reformed agreed. By means of Saravia, these articles were first shown to Calvin and other theologians in Geneva, around the end of the year. However, Calvin urged the author and other ministers in Belgium rather to agree with the ministers of France on the confession that had been adopted at the Synod of Paris in that same year. On his return, Saravia reported the advice of Calvin and his colleagues to the author, who kept the articles to himself till 1561. On the advice of Godfried Van Wingen, de Brès sent them to the church of Emden, where Cornelius Cooltuyn and some colleagues reviewed and approved them. Later, these articles were sent to several ministers in Belgium, and to the ministers in Metz, Frankenthal, Frankfurt and London, as well as to the leaders of the French church. After the confession had been seen, and tacitly approved, by most ministers in Belgium, it was published by the author in the original French language in 1562, and in Dutch in 1563.

The information presented by Schoock has long been considered the authoritative statement concerning the early history of the confession.[34] However, the question arises how he acquired all this new information about the early history of the Belgic Confession.[35] He had no personal knowledge of that time, for he was born in 1614, over fifty years after the publication of the confession. Nor was he particularly knowledgeable in the area of the Reformed confessions. He had studied broadly in areas such as law, philosophy, literature and theology, obtaining an M.A. degree in 1636. His statement on the Belgic Confession dates from the time he was teaching logic and physics at Groningen University. Actually, it was published in 1650 in a section on Dutch church history, which Schoock included in a book dealing with ecclesiastical property.

The reason Schoock's statement on the background of the Belgic Confession has long been considered authoritative is that he appealed to certain documents to be published at a later time. However, Van Langeraad subjected this statement to a lengthy critical investigation.[36] For our purpose it is not necessary to evaluate his argument in its entirety, but it is obvious that Schoock made several questionable assertions. For example, the information that Calvin saw the Belgic Confession but did not like the fact that the Reformed churches in the Netherlands would have their own confession sounds suspiciously similar to Calvin's advice concerning the Gallican Confession. When asked to provide a draft for a confession for the French churches,

---

34. Vinke called it the "locus classicus" on the Belgic Confession (*Libri symbolici*, xiii); Te Water considered this statement to be more certain than the other accounts on the confession (*Tweede eeuw-getyde*, 7).

35. Cornelis Bezemer, "Schoock, Martinus," in *BLGNP*, 2:394-95. Evaluating Schoock's literary production, Bezemer states that he published on a great variety of subjects, even though he often was not knowledgeable.

36. Van Langeraad, *Guido de Bray*, 98-116. He raises many questions, particularly in connection with the list of theologians who saw and approved the confession before it was published.

Calvin was initially reluctant, stating he preferred that they would use an existing confession.[37] Schoock must have confused the Gallican and the Belgic Confession. If that is the case, then his statement that the drafting of the Belgic Confession began in 1559 can be attributed to the same misunderstanding. In fact, it was the Gallican Confession that was made in that year.

Another problematic aspect of Schoock's statement is his opinion that Saravia had traveled to Geneva in 1559 to show the confession to Calvin. Van Langeraad has questioned the reliability of this remark, for during that period Saravia was mostly in England. Moreover, the fact that Galasius, the minister of the congregation of Dutch refugees to which Saravia belonged, wrote a letter of introduction for Saravia to Calvin at the end of 1561 must be considered. This indicates that up to this point in time Saravia was unknown to Calvin.[38] In defence of Schoock, Nijenhuis has pointed out that Saravia may have been in Geneva without Calvin's knowledge.[39] This remark is correct in itself but not to the point, for Schoock stated explicitly that Saravia had shown the confession to Calvin. And Nijenhuis himself increases our doubt concerning Saravia's stay in Geneva by pointing out that Saravia, although quite knowledgeable of church life in Geneva, never even hinted at having personally encountered the Genevan theologians.[40] In addition, Saravia's letter to Uytenbogaert concerning his involvement with the Belgic Confession must be considered. If he had brought Guido de Brès' articles to Calvin in Geneva, he would surely have mentioned that in his letter. The fact that Saravia himself never mentioned this makes Schoock's statement about Saravia submitting the Belgic Confession to Calvin in 1559 all the more unreliable.

What were Schoock's sources? He states that he derived his knowledge from certain documents which he hoped to publish later.[41] He never published these documents, but one of his sources is obviously Thysius' book published about forty years earlier,[42] although Schoock did not use the information carefully. But there is another document on the history of the Belgic Confession which had not yet been made public at the time Schoock published his book: Saravia's letter! Uytenbogaert had used part of this letter without revealing that he had been the recipient. Others had followed Uytenbogaert without actually having seen the letter. It is probable that at one point Schoock had seen Saravia's letter, and that his mistakes were caused by the fact that he quoted it from memory. However, Saravia's letter was first made

---

37. Jacques Pannier, *Les origines de la Confession de Foi et la Discipline des Églises Réformées de France* (Paris: Librairie Félix Alcan, 1936), 89-90.
38. Van Langeraad, *Guido de Bray*, 99-103.
39. Nijenhuis, *Adrianus Saravia*, 18.
40. Nijenhuis, *Adrianus Saravia*, 19.
41. Vinke, *Libri symbolici*, xiii.
42. Van Langeraad, *Guido de Bray*, 103.

public in a collection of letters by Remonstrant leaders, published in 1660,[43] ten years later than Schoock's book.

We must conclude that Martinus Schoock did not work with newly discovered information. Rather, he was careless in the use of the available sources. Not only did he quote Thysius incorrectly and confuse the Gallican Confession with the Belgic Confession, he also misunderstood Saravia's remarks. Schoock's statement on the Belgic Confession, therefore, cannot be used as a reliable source.

An Earlier Source: Thomas Van Tielt

The seventeenth century theologians dealing with the authorship of the Belgic Confession all go back, in one way or another, to Saravia's statement that Guido de Brès is the author of the Belgic Confession. However, there is another, older source of information of which they were not aware. Van Langeraad, the nineteenth-century biographer of de Brès, found a handwritten note in a copy of te Water's study on the Belgic Confession published in 1762:

> Thomas Van Tielt wrote to Arent Cornelisz, minister at Delft, from Antwerp, July 17, 1582: I have spoken with Taffin about the confession, which he says was written by Guy de Brès.[44]

This statement on the authorship of the confession is very concise, and it needs to be considered carefully. It shows first of all that when Van Tielt wrote his letter in 1582, it was not generally known that Guido de Brès had written the Belgic Confession. Thomas Van Tielt had not known before he was told, and in telling Arent Cornelisz, he obviously expected that he would not know this either.

Considering his life, it is not surprising that Arent Cornelisz was not aware of this information. Born in Delft, he hailed from the Dutch-speaking part of the Netherlands. He studied theology at Heidelberg and Geneva, and after having worked among Reformed refugees in Frankenthal, he became a minister in Delft.[45] He therefore had no direct connections with the churches in the southern provinces of the Netherlands. In the case of Thomas Van Tielt, however, it is remarkable that

---

43. It is letter 181 in the collection published by C. Hartsoecker and Ph. A. Limborch, *Praestantium ac eruditorum virorum epistolae ecclesiasticae et theologicae varii argumenti.* The first edition of this book was published in 1660 in Amsterdam; see Vinke, *Libri Symbolici,* xii. The second edition was published in 1684, and the third in 1704. A Dutch translation of this letter was published in 1662 in [Geerardt Brandt], *Brieven van verscheyde vermaerde en geleerde mannen deser eeuwe* (Amsterdam: Jan Riewertsz, 1662), 52-57.

44. Van Langeraad, *Guy de Bray,* 117: "Thomas van Thielt schreef aan den Delftschen predikant Arnoldus Cornelii uit Antwerpen 17 Julij 1582: Ic hebbe Taffinum gesproken van de Confessie, de welcke hy seyt van Guy de Bres gestelt te sijne."

45. Doede Nauta, "Arent Cornelisz," in *Christelijke encyclopedie,* 2:304.

he had never heard the name of the author. He was born in the southern part of the Netherlands (Mechelen) in 1534, and spent much of his life in that area until, in 1572, he became minister to the Dutch refugees in Geneva. That neither Cornelisz nor Van Tielt had heard that Guido de Brès was the author of the confession indicates that as late as 1582, even among the Reformed leaders, this was not generally known.

The source cited for de Brès' authorship is Taffinus. This Latinized name refers to Jean Taffin, born at Doornik in 1528, who had become a minister in the Reformed church at Antwerp in 1557. After having served several refugee congregations, he eventually became minister at the court of William of Orange in 1574. As he was a member of the Taffin family, which had proven to be strong supporters of Guido de Brès during his ministry,[46] Jean Taffin's statement can be used as reliable information.

The problem with this quotation has been that for a long time its provenance was unknown. However, I was able to find the original source.[47] The statement is part of a letter of over two pages, written by Thomas Van Tielt to Arent Cornelisz of Delft, and dated July 17, 1582. The section dealing with the Belgic Confession is actually longer than presented by Van Langeraad:

> I have spoken with Taffin about the confession, which he says was made by Guy de Brès and presented in French to his Majesty. [He] has given me this copy of the same confession which I send to you.[48]

The final remark refers to a French language copy of the second, revised edition of the Belgic Confession of 1566. The Dutch-speaking churches in the northern provinces of the Netherlands needed to consult this particular text, for as late as 1582, no Dutch translation of the second, revised edition was available. Now that an official copy of the revised French edition had been found, an updated Dutch translation could be made for use in the churches.[49] While Thomas Van Tielt was looking for a copy of the second edition of the Belgic Confession, he also received information he had not originally been looking for. He was told that the author of the confession was no other than Guido de Brès, well known through Crespin's *Book of Martyrs* as a defender of the faith and as a martyr. This information, coming from a member of the influential Taffin family in Doornik, which supported the Reformation, is reliable.

---

46. Moreau, *Histoire du protestantisme*, 345-47.

47. Gootjes, "The Earliest Report on the Author of the Belgic Confession (1561)," *Nederlands archief voor kerkgeschiedenis* 82 no. 1 (2002): 93-94.

48. The original statement is: "Ic hebbe Taffinum gesproken van de co[n]fessie, de welcke hij seijt van Guij de Bres gestelt te sijne en[de] in Walsch aan sijne M[ajesteit] gepresenteert te sijne: heeft mij dit exemplaar gegeven vande zelviger co[n]fessie, twelck ic u l[ieden] seijnde."

49. See chapter 6 for further information concerning this revised edition.

Interestingly, there is not only a connection between Van Tielt and a member of the Taffin family, but also between Saravia and this family. Jacques Taffin, a brother of Jean Taffin, is said to have been instrumental in Saravia's leaving the monastery. He also provided him with money. Moreover, Saravia is reported to have stayed at the Taffin castle, and to have preached Reformed sermons there.[50] And in a letter of recommendation for a nephew of the Taffin brothers, Saravia singled out Jean Taffin as a minister of the gospel who was noted both for his piety and for his erudition.[51] The Taffin brothers, belonging to the congregation where Guido de Brès had worked, were in a position to know who had written the Belgic Confession.

In the final analysis, there are two sources for Guido de Brès' authorship of the Belgic Confession: the letter of Arent Cornelisz, written in 1582; and the letter of Saravia, written in 1612. Both authors are reliable, the sources for their information can be traced back to Doornik, and the content of these statements is in agreement with what is known about the early history of the confession. Saravia added that Guido de Brès consulted several ministers who were within reach. This is likely, but it is not known whether they contributed anything to the actual text of the confession. At any rate, this historical evidence points to Guido de Brès as the actual author of the Belgic Confession.[52]

Guido de Brès

In view of the fact that the sources identify Guido de Brès as the author of the Belgic Confession, it needs to be considered what we know about him. Is it possible and probable that he wrote the Belgic Confession? Who was he and what did he do?[53]

De Brès was born in Bergen, in the province of Henegouwen, one of the southern provinces of the Netherlands. His date of birth is unknown, but he was probably born in 1522. He had been trained as a painter of stained glass, but there are no indications whether he ever established himself in that profession. Around 1547, he embraced the Reformed doctrine. When, during the persecution of the Protestants

---

50. Nijenhuis, *Adrianus Saravia*, 8.

51. This letter can be found in Nijenhuis, *Adrianus Saravia*, 288.

52. See also Braekman, *Guy de Brès*, 159; Bakhuizen van den Brink, *De Nederlandse belijdenisgeschriften*, 9.

53. The earliest source of information is Crespin's *Book of Martyrs*, where de Brès' life is described under 1567, the year in which he died; see the *Histoire des martyrs*, 3:533-75. Among the older studies on Guido de Brès, the doctoral dissertation by Van Langeraad, *Guido de Bray*, published in 1884, is still the basic source for information concerning his life and work. He provided additional information and made corrections in "De liturgie bij de hervormden in Nederland I," *Theologisch Tijdschrift* 35 (1901): 130-31, 143-50. The more recent biography by Braekman, *Guy de Brès: Sa vie*, describes Guido de Brès' life in the context of his time and country. Van Itterzon gives a brief survey of his life and work in "Guido de Brès," in *BLGNP*, 2:97-100.

in Belgium, de Brès was sought, he went to England and stayed there from 1548 until 1552. It may be assumed that he studied theology during this period, but no specifics are known.

In 1552, he returned to the Netherlands to take care of several congregations from his home base of Rijssel. Here he published his *Le Baston de la Foy Chrestienne* (1555) in response to a book written by Nicolas Grenier, *Le Bouclier de la Foy*. In this book, de Brès refuted many Roman Catholic positions, beginning with their view on the Lord's Supper. Usually, he is very concise in presenting his own opinion, allowing the issues to be decided on the basis of quotations taken from Scripture and the church fathers. The book shows that he was familiar with their teaching.[54]

During the fall of 1555, when the persecution of the Protestants became fiercer, Guido de Brès fled the country and went to Frankfurt. He continued to upgrade his theological training by going to Lausanne and Geneva for further study. At the end of 1558 he was back in the Netherlands, settling in Doornik, and from there visiting other Reformed congregations such as those in Rijssel and Valenciennes. He married Catharine Ramon sometime in 1559, and they had five children. When the authorities discovered his hiding place in Doornik, they found that he had been living in rooms at the back of a house in St. Brixe, not far from his study near the walls of the city.

The persecution in Doornik resulting from the *chanteries* caused him to abandon his possessions, flee the city and establish his residence in the French city of Sedan. While living there, he contributed to the *Book of Martyrs*. He published his second major work, *La Racine des Anabaptistes*, in 1565. In this book, he discussed several groups under the common name of Anabaptists. However, he distinguished clearly between the teachings of the different groups, dealing separately with each.

In 1566, de Brès returned to his native country, where the situation for the Reformed population appeared to have improved. Under the protection of the nobility, the Protestants began publicly to organize their worship services. De Brès became a minister in Valenciennes. When the majority of the population had been won for the Reformation, the people demanded church buildings for their worship services. The city's refusal to make these available led to the Reformed taking possession of several buildings and destroying the images in these churches. Although Guido de Brès had been opposed to taking these church buildings by force, he did preach in these churches. However, the city was besieged as a result of the iconoclasm, and consequently conquered. Guido de Brès and his fellow minister Pérégrin de la Grange were captured and publicly executed by hanging, on May 31, 1567.

---

54. For information on this book see the biographies of Guido de Brès, and particularly the article by Detmer Deddens, "Rondom het eerste geschrift van G. de Brès, 'Le baston de la Foy,'" *Lucerna* 3 no. 6 (1962), 817-31.

This brief biography shows that Guido de Brès fulfills all requirements for being the author of the Belgic Confession. The confession was written in French, which was his native language. Moreover, in his *Baston de la Foy* he had already proven that he was able to discuss theological issues. This is confirmed by his later, more comprehensive book about the views of the different Anabaptist groups.

Considering his two books more specifically, it can be noted that the first focused on Roman Catholic teachings and the second on Anabaptist teachings. The same focal points can be noticed in the Belgic Confession. To mention only the clearest examples, articles 5, 6, 7, 23, 24, 26 and 35 oppose Roman Catholic positions, and articles 10, 18, 25, 34 and 36 oppose Anabaptist positions. Further, the references to the patristic church and its struggles in articles 9, 10, 11, 12, and 15 are in character for one who had collected numerous patristic quotations as in the *Baston de la Foy*. Moreover, like the Belgic Confession, the *Baston* opens with an address to the princes, judges and magistrates, appealing to them to bring justice.[55]

These arguments do not all have the same weight. The opposition to both Roman Catholic and Anabaptist teaching is commonplace in Reformed literature of the sixteenth century. To give a well known example, Calvin does the same in his *Institutes*. However, taken together, they provide strong support for the trustworthy reports that the Belgic Confession was made by Guido de Brès.

Several considerations can be added to strengthen the case for de Brès' authorship. The Belgic Confession was first discovered in Doornik, the city where he was ministering to the Reformed congregation. It was accompanied by a handwritten letter with an appeal to the government. When his hiding place was discovered, a comparison of his handwriting with this letter showed clearly that he had written the letter.[56] A further indication is the fact that two hundred copies of the confession were discovered in his library. Traveling book peddlers would have taken along a limited number of copies at a time, but only the author could be expected to have the bulk of the printed copies.

All these indications confirm that Guido de Brès was the author of the Belgic Confession. The testimonies of Van Tielt and Saravia, which were shown to be trustworthy, are in complete agreement with the data in the confession itself and with the circumstances of its discovery.

The Importance of Guido de Brès

De Brès' authorship of the Belgic Confession is further supported in view of his important position among the Reformed ministers. There are several indications that

---

55. De Brès, *Le Baston de la Foy Chrestienne*, 8-10.

56. For the text of the report concerning the committee's discovery of Guido de Brès' library, see Appendix, Document 4.

already in his own time this importance was recognized. One is his description. When the authorities were looking for ways to arrest Guido de Brès, they published the following notice:

> Description of a heretical preacher, formerly named Guy, presently named Jerome, of whom the surname is still unknown. This person is a man of between 36 and 40 years, tall, long face, thin and pale; with a beard more reddish than black, which he sometimes wears long, sometimes shorter. He also has a rather stooped back and high shoulders. He sometimes wears a coat with hat, at other times he wears a long gown with a cap.[57]

It can be assumed that his characteristic features were mentioned in this description. He might change his hairstyle and wear different clothes, but age and the physical features of head and body would be harder to hide. As such, this description has been used to provide us with a fairly accurate impression of how he must have looked. However, it should not be overlooked that the purpose of this particular description was not to make the people acquainted with an important author and minister, but to capture someone who was seen as a leader in the Reformation movement, and as such constituted a danger for the population.

The same applies to another description, which is part of the testimony of a certain Guillemette, when she was interrogated concerning Guido de Brès. According to her, he was about forty years of age. She described his face as rather pale and long, the color of his beard tending towards red, his shoulders high and his back rounded. Concerning his clothes, a black coat with turned down collar is mentioned.[58] Also in this case, the description was actually given in the course of an interrogation, proving how important it was for the committee to lay hands on this preacher.

In a different way, the importance of Guido de Brès can be gauged from the reports about him after his death. In Crespin's *Book of Martyrs* the section dealing with him is not limited to a summary overview of his life and death.[59] In this case, the description is much lengthier than average. It includes reports on discussions

---

57. Braekman, *Guy de Brès*, 136, referring to an article by W. Brulez, "Nadere bijzonderheden over Guy de Bray," published in 1953: "Description de certain hérétique prédicant, par ci-devant appelé Guy, et présentement nommé Jérôme, duquel ne se peut encore entendre le sûr nom. . . . Ledit personnage est homme de 36 à 40 ans, haut de stature, la face longue, maigre et pâle; ayant barbe plus tirante sur le roux que noire, qui'il porte quelquefois longue, quelquefois plus courte; si a aussi assez gros dos, et hautes épaules, se vêt quelquefois de manteau avec chapeau, autrefois de longue robe avec une toque."
58. Van Langeraad, *Guido de Bray*, 38: "Ledit homme est de quarante ans ou environ, haut de stature, pâle de face et assez maigre et long visage, et la barbe tirant sur le roussart, avec les épaules hautes, un gros dos. Et étant mal en ordre avec un manteau noir à collet rabattu."
59. Crespin, *Histoire des martyrs*, 3:533-75.

with visitors who had come to argue with him. This is followed by a letter he wrote to his congregation at Valenciennes in which he reports on the debates he had with visitors. They show that de Brès did not only quote from Scripture, but that he also was able to refer to statements of the church fathers. In addition, a lengthy report is included of a discussion initiated by a bishop, François Richardot from Arras, who wanted to engage him in a debate on the Mass. These are clear indications that de Brès was seen as an important leader on the side of the Reformed.

His importance is also confirmed by a sixteenth-century painting, made not long after his death, in which Guido de Brès is depicted. This painting is not well known, and the significance of the fact that he is included has not been noted. It will prove useful to consider the implications of this Haarlem panel for his position at this time.[60]

The painting depicts the Roman Catholic church and the heretics. In the center of a large rock, the church is pictured as a woman wearing a triple crown. She is surrounded by the seven sacraments, represented by seven huge vats from which many people receive the grace from Jesus Christ who is seated in heaven. However, outside of the church which is founded on the rock, several people are shown in the water. Some are portrayed behind a pulpit, others are drowning, and some have already gone under. Each is identified by a caption, and one of them is called Bretius, a Latinized form of the name of Guido de Brès. The meaning of the picture as a whole is obvious, and the different elements of this picture are further explained in many framed statements included in the picture.[61]

The date of this panel can be determined to within a relatively narrow period of time. The painting goes back to an Italian copper engraving published by Luca Bertelli in 1574.[62] However, the engraving and the panel are not identical, and several differences should be noted. A rather striking difference can be found in the lower part, where the heads of Jesus Christ and of Peter are portrayed upside down in the original engraving, but right side up in the painting. However, the overall message is the same, for both the engraving and the picture represent the church as the bride of Christ who is dispensing the blood of the crucified Christ to its members through the seven sacraments. As the engraving obviously served as model, the painting must have been made after 1574. The latest date for its origin can be set at 1585, since it portrays Pope Gregory XIII, who died in that year.[63] The picture can therefore confidently be dated between 1574 and 1585.

---

60. This painting has been reproduced below, 54-55.

61. D. P. R. A. Bouvy, *Kerkelijke kunst* (Bussum, 1965), 1:61-63; Paulus P. W. M. Dirkse, "De katholieke kerk en haar genadeleer," in *Geloof en satire anno 1600* (n.p.: RMCC, 1981), 20-24. The panel itself can be seen in the Catharijne Convent in Utrecht, the Netherlands.

62. Dirkse, "De katholieke kerk en haar genadeleer," 21.

63. Dirkse, "De katholieke kerk en haar genadeleer," 22.

It may be possible to narrow the time span even further. The same image was painted on the wall of the now demolished Galilean Church in Leeuwarden, a city in the northern part of the Netherlands. This church building, completed at the end of the fifteenth century, went through a tumultuous time during the 1560s. In 1566, when the Protestants had the upper hand in the city, the church buildings were renovated to make them suitable for their worship services. When in the next year the army of the Roman Catholic general Aremberg conquered the city, the church was again designated for Roman Catholic worship. The restoration may have begun as early as 1567, or, if this was delayed till the new bishop arrived in Leeuwarden, in December 1569, and it was probably completed by 1577.[64] This building had to be demolished in 1940, but sections of the murals were preserved, among others the part portraying Zwingli and Calvin drowning in the water. As Zwingli was not shown on the original engraving, but only on the Haarlem panel that also depicted de Brès, we can assume that the Leeuwarden mural resembled the latter. It is therefore possible that in the 1570s Guido de Brès' picture was shown not only on the Haarlem panel, but also on the wall of the Galilean Church in Leeuwarden.

The picture on this panel, and presumably also on the mural, provokes the question why Guido de Brès was included. In all, eleven opponents of the Roman Catholic church were represented on the panel. On the left hand side, five names are shown, from left to right: Martin Luther, Flacius Illyricus, Andreas Fricius, Stancarus and Theodore Beza. On the right hand side, another six are portrayed: Bretius (de Brès), Servet, Bernhard Ochino, Viret, Calvin and Zwingli. These heretics are portrayed in different ways. Luther, Calvin and Zwingli are shown standing behind a lectern, so that their upper bodies are visible. Three others, Illyricus, Bretius and Ochino, are so deep in the water that only their heads are visible. And Andrea, Stancarus, Beza, Servet and Viret appear to have already drowned for they are not pictured but only represented by a book floating in the water.

We must now consider whether these pictures are accurate representations of the persons they are said to portray. To begin with the best known theologians, Luther is portrayed with both hands extended; in his left hand he holds up a book, and he appears to be speaking. He has a dark covering on his head, and wears a gown with a wide collar. His face is not clear enough in its details to identify him; however the overall impression is somewhat similar to pictures which show him with gown and doctor's beret.[65]

---

64. Gerhard Jansen, "De muurschilderingen in de Galileërkerk te Leeuwarden," *Gildeboek* (May 1942): 3-7; Bouvy, *Kerkelijke kunst*, 1:61-63. Sections of the wall paintings are preserved in the Fries Museum in Leeuwarden; here, the date is given as between 1567 and 1577.

65. Several pictures of Luther can be found in Hanns Lilje, *Portret van Luther in de lijst van zijn tijd*, ed. Willem J. Kooiman (Amsterdam: W. Ten Hoor, 1967). Of these, the woodcut of the young Luther on page 116, the 1521 engraving by Cranach Sr. on page 147 and his 1526 painting on page 186 show some similarity.

On the opposite side, Calvin, too, is pictured as standing behind a pulpit. His representation mirrors that of Luther, for his face is turned towards the left, and he holds a book in his right hand. He does not wear a hat, and he appears to be bald, with a rather long beard. It is hard to find specific similarities between this picture and the portraits made of Calvin.[66] In all portraits, Calvin is shown wearing a cap which covers his ears partly or completely, but in this picture he is bareheaded. The only characteristic traits the panel shows are the long face and the long beard.

The hardest to recognize is Zwingli. His right hand is gripping the edge of the pulpit, and with his left hand he holds up a sword. He appears to be wearing a kind of cape from which his arms protrude. He has a darkish beard, and he is wearing a rather tall dark hat. I have not been able to find a picture of Zwingli that shows some similarity to the depiction on the panel. However, the inclusion of the sword could be an allusion to the fact that Zwingli marched out with the army of Zürich to defend freedom of religion by force of arms. This leads to the tentative conclusion that the representations shown on the Haarlem panel and on the wall of the Galilean Church are not to be taken as lifelike portraits, although they do imply some knowledge of the persons portrayed.

Before concentrating on Guido de Brès, another fact must be considered in connection with Zwingli. As it occurs in the painting, his picture upsets the balance. Five people are portrayed on the left hand side, but six on the right. Luther on the left and Calvin on the right are nicely mirrored, each keeping one hand on the pulpit and holding up a book with the other hand. But Zwingli disturbs this nice balance, because his portrait crowds that of Calvin. It is also awkward because Zwingli faces the wrong way. Moreover, a comparison with the original engraving shows that the latter did not portray anyone in that corner. Here only ten heretics are shown, five on each side. The reason for this difference must be that in Italy there was no need to include Zwingli, but in the Netherlands his picture could not be lacking from a collection of heretics, even at the expense of its artistic quality. For the panel, the original engraving was adapted to the local situation.

This observation is important when considering Guido de Brès' portrait on the panel. He is not shown on the Italian engraving; in his place, a round head is portrayed, with receding hairline, curly hair on top and a curly beard, facing right. Remarkably, no name is added to the figure, although the other heretics are all identified. In the Dutch painting, however, the head still faces right, but it is represented quite differently. There is no indication of baldness, and the shape of the head is not round but long. The hair is not curly but straight and rather long, and the shape of the brownish beard is different. And where the engraving only showed the head, the painting also shows the neck. Obviously, the painter attempted to portray

---

66. All existing paintings are reproduced and explained in Jan Weerda, *Holbein und Calvin: Ein Bildfund* (Neukirchen: Verlag der Buchhandlung des Erziehungvereins, [1955]).

a different person from that in the engraving. However, since he did not include the characteristic features of de Brès, his reddish brown hair and his stooped shoulder, it is unlikely that he actually saw him.

That raises the question why his picture was included in this collection of eleven international heretics. By portraying Luther, Calvin and Zwingli as standing behind a pulpit, the painter singled them out as the instigators and leaders of the Reformation movement that had been growing in the Netherlands. However, he also included others from a wide variety of nations and with different views.[67] A remarkable aspect is that several are only represented by a book. This requires us to pay particular attention to the books they wrote.

To begin from the left, the name "Flatius Illyricus" refers to Mathias Flacius Illyricus (1520-1575), a Lutheran theologian who was involved in many debates with both fellow Lutherans as well as others. During the 1560s, he wrote three anti-Roman Catholic treatises, one against the Council of Trent, one against the recommended catechism by Canisius and one to prove that unity did not exist in the Roman Catholic church because of the many groups and disagreements. "Andreas Fricius" (1503-1569) does not hail from the Dutch province of Friesland. His name is the Latinized form of the Polish family name Frycz. Although he never actually joined the Reformation movement, he argued that the Roman Catholic church had deteriorated so much that leaving it and reestablishing the church was the only possibility. Later in life he joined the Unitarians. Next to him, the name "Stancarus" (around 1500-1574) is written above a hand holding up a book. He was an Italian Protestant who had to leave his fatherland. He was involved in many theological disputes, also with theologians belonging to the Reformation movement. His place among the heretics may be the result of the fact that as a professor in Krakau in 1549 he attacked the veneration of the saints which led to him being accused of heresy. The final heretic presented on the left hand side is "Theodore Beza" (1519-1605). He was born in France, but spent most of his life in Switzerland. He became the close friend and colleague of Calvin in Geneva. The reason why he, too, was portrayed among the drowning heretics may have been the publication of his stage play "Abraham's sacrifice" of 1551, but it is also possible that the many polemical sections in his confession earned him this distinction.

On the right hand side of the painting, the theologian next to Guido de Brès is indicated as "Servetus." This refers to Michael Servet (around 1509-1553) who is here represented by a book. Although among his books there is one which is directed against Calvin's theology, he is particularly known for his rejection of the doctrine

---

67. Gebhard Voorvelt has deciphered the explanatory texts included in the painting and reported on this in "De fresco-fragmenten van Leeuwarden en het Haarlemse paneel," *De Vrije Fries* 38 (1946): 69-85. He also provides some information about the heretics portrayed in the water, which will be used in the following explanation.

of the Trinity. His views were rejected by both Roman Catholic and Protestant theologians. "Bernardinus Ochino" (1487-1565) was an Italian who began as a preacher in the Roman Catholic church. He joined the Reformation movement late in life, in 1542, and traveled widely in Switzerland and Germany. His inclusion in this painting is probably due to his writings against the Roman Catholic church, in particular a tragedy published in 1549, containing a harsh attack on the origin and development of the papal system. The next is "Viretus," again represented by a book. This refers to Peter Viret (1511-1571), born in the French-speaking part of Switzerland, who was ordained as a Reformed minister by Farel in 1531. He wrote several polemical books against Roman Catholic doctrine: tracts about the clergy and the sacraments, and satyrical dialogues against the papal system, the mass and purgatory.

The fact that Guido de Brès is included in this company proves that he was seen as one of the main opponents of the Roman Catholic church. When this picture, originally made in Italy, was adapted for the Netherlands, the painter (or his patron) felt that Zwingli had to be added, for he was one of the original instigators of the Reformation in that part of Europe. However, Guido de Brès' portrait was also added. He may not have been as prominent a leader as Luther, Zwingli or Calvin, but in this Dutch survey he had to be included. Since his authorship of the confession was not known at the time, this distinction must be the result of his anti-Roman Catholic book, *Le Baston de la Foy*, which he did publish under his own name. At any rate, this painting highlights that Guido de Brès' importance was recognized already in his own time.

3

Calvin and the Confession

The Belgic Confession has often been characterized as a Calvinistic confession.[1] As mentioned in the previous chapter, specific Roman Catholic and Anabaptist doctrines are identified and rejected. In addition, it must be pointed out that the confession also distances itself from certain Lutheran views. This is particularly noticeable in the article on the two natures of Christ (art. 19) and the article on the Lord's Supper (art. 35). And it presents the typical Reformed teaching on several doctrines, such as revelation (art. 2) and the church (arts. 27-29). Moreover, Calvin's influence on the Belgic Confession was recognized as soon as it was published. When the commissioners in Doornik found a copy, they reported that it was "full of all kind of errors and perverse doctrine of Calvin."[2]

The question arises whether a direct relationship between John Calvin and the Belgic Confession can be established. Publications dealing with Calvin as well as studies dealing with the Belgic Confession have argued that such a relationship did exist. In an extensively annotated study on the influence of Calvin on the Reformation in the Netherlands, the well known Dutch historian F. L. Rutgers included Guido de Brès among the students of Calvin.[3] De Brès' biographers Van Langeraad and Braekman both elaborated on the connections between Calvin and de Brès, and Strauss published an article on this issue, as well.[4] This opens the way for explaining the Belgic Confession against the background of Calvin's theology, as is done by Polman and Vonk.[5]

As the issue of the relationship between Calvin and the Belgic Confession is rather complicated, it will be approached from three different angles. First we will consider whether there is evidence for personal contact between Calvin and de Brès.

---

1. See, for example, Schaff, *Creeds of Christendom*, 1:506.

2. See their report of December 19, 1561, in Appendix, Document 3.

3. Frederik L. Rutgers, *Calvijns invloed op de Reformatie in de Nederlanden* (Leiden: Donner, 1899), 16, 139-40; see also William R. Godfrey, "Calvin and Calvinism in the Netherlands," in J. Stanford Reid, ed., *John Calvin: His Influence in the Western World* (Grand Rapids: Zondervan, 1982), 97.

4. Van Langeraad, *Guido de Bray*, 21-23; Braekman, *Guy de Brès*, 104-18; Siebrand A. Strauss, "John Calvin and the Belgic Confession," *In die Skriflig* 27 no. 4 (1993): 505-15.

5. Andries D. R. Polman, *Onze Nederlandsche geloofsbelijdenis*, 4 vols. (Franeker: T. Wever, 1948-53), especially 1:105, 108; Vonk, *De Nederlandse geloofsbelijdenis*, especially 1:96-104.

A second section will deal with the possibility of a relationship between Calvin and the Belgic Confession through the Gallican Confession. A third issue to be considered is whether a direct connection between Calvin and the Belgic Confession can be established.

Calvin and de Brès

As Calvin was one the most influential theologians of his time, it would not be surprising if he had been in personal contact with the author of the Belgic Confession. It has been stated repeatedly that de Brès met Calvin on at least two occasions, first in Frankfurt and later in Geneva. Rutgers argued that Guido de Brès must have met him in September 1556 in Frankfurt, and that he came to know him even better when he studied for two years in Lausanne and Geneva.[6]

The only source for Guido de Brès' stay in Frankfurt is his own account in *La Racine*. Here he describes a meeting he had with some Anabaptist leaders in the presence of John à Lasco.[7] De Brès does not indicate at what time this meeting took place, nor does he mention having met Calvin. The fact that à Lasco was present allows dating de Brès' visit to some time in 1555 or 1556, for à Lasco went to Frankfurt to help the congregation in April 1555, was absent from the middle of April to the end of May 1556, and left to go to Poland in October 1556.[8]

Calvin had traveled to Frankfurt in order to help the local congregation, staying there for a period of about three weeks in September 1556. Therefore the possibility cannot be altogether excluded that Guido de Brès met with Calvin sometime during those three weeks, but this is not probable. One reason is that no positive indication has been found that they met in Frankfurt during this brief period. Further, what is known concerning their work there does not point to a meeting. Calvin was in Frankfurt in order to resolve some difficulties within the congregation, while de Brès was involved in a debate with Anabaptists. It is also noteworthy that Calvin nowhere mentioned de Brès in any of his letters written from Frankfurt in which he reported about the work he had done. Nor does de Brès anywhere refer to a meeting with Calvin in Frankfurt. There is not a shred of evidence that such a meeting took place.[9]

---

6. Rutgers, *Calvijns invloed op de Reformatie in de Nederlanden*, 139-40; Strauss expresses himself more carefully when he states that Guido de Brès "could have met Calvin personally then" (see his "John Calvin and the Belgic Confession," 504).

7. De Brès, *La racine*, 91-92; see on this, Van Langeraad, *Guido de Bray*, 20-21; Braekman, *Guy de Brès*, 112-13.

8. See Doede Nauta, "Lasco," in *BLGNP*, 4:295-96.

9. The letters from and to Calvin can be found in *Ioannis Calvini opera quae supersunt omnia*, 59 vols., ed. G. Baum, E. Cunitz, and E. Reuss (Brunswick: Schwetschke, 1863-1900), vol. 16, nos. 2531, 2532 and 2535. More material in connection with the visit to Frankfurt can be found in *Johannes Calvins Lebenswerk in seinen Briefen*, 3 vols., trans. Rudolph Schwarz (Neukirchen: Neukirchener

The report concerning the discovery of Guido de Brès' library provides more solid information.[10] The committee wrote to the governess that they had found some letters addressed to de Brès. Among these was "a letter of John Calvin from the year 1556 in which he responds to certain questions which the aforesaid Guido had submitted to him, of which we send a summary to your Highness." This letter did not only establish the identity of the owner of the library, it also made clear that he was in contact with the center of the Reformed movement in Geneva. The committee concluded that de Brès had learned his errors from Lausanne and Geneva. Regrettably, the details of this epistolary contact cannot be recovered because Calvin's letter has not been preserved. The governess ordered that everything found in the study be carefully investigated and then burned.[11]

Calvin's letter was written in the same year Guido de Brès visited Frankfurt. It is possible that de Brès wrote to Calvin after having met him, but it is equally possible that Calvin wrote in response to a letter from de Brès without a previous meeting. At any rate, de Brès obviously considered Calvin, who was twelve years his senior, a trustworthy adviser.

Another opportunity for contact came when de Brès journeyed to Geneva. Again, there is only one source for this event, a remark found in his biography in Crespin's *Book of Martyrs*:

> Afterwards, since he was eager to increase his knowledge needed in the ministry, he traveled to Lausanne and Geneva, for that purpose and in order to learn Latin. After having stayed there for some time, on his return to the Netherlands, he reorganized the churches in Lille, Doornik and Valenciennes.[12]

Van Langeraad has demonstrated that de Brès left for Lausanne at the end of 1556 or the beginning of 1557,[13] although he could not determine when de Brès departed from there for Geneva. It can also be determined that de Brès had returned to Belgium by late 1559.[14] Between the end of 1556 and the fall of 1559 de Brès could therefore have attended some of Calvin's sermons and lectures. However, it must be

---

Verlag, 1962-63), vol. 3; letters 508, 509, and 510 were written while he stayed in Frankfurt, and letters 511, 513 and 514 deal with the situation in Frankfurt.

10. For the text of this report, see Appendix, Document 4.

11. Van Langeraad, *Guido de Bray*, 48.

12. Crespin, *Histoire des martyrs*, 3:581: "Depuis, comme il estoit studieux de savoir plus amplement ce qui est requis au ministere, il s'achemina vers Lausanne et Geneve, à ces fins, et pour apprendre la langue Latine. Apres y avoir demeuré quelque temps, revenu qu'il fut au Pays-bas, redressa les Eglises à Lisle, Tournay et Valenciennes . . ."

13. Van Langeraad, *Guido de Bray*, 22.

14. Van Langeraad, *Guido de Bray*, 24-25.

taken into account that part of this time was spent in Lausanne, and further, that there are no positive indications that he actually went to listen to Calvin.

Although the above evidence fails to prove conclusively that there was direct contact between them, it is certain that Calvin influenced Guido de Brès through his publications. The report concerning the discovery of his library stated that the committee had found several very pernicious books of Calvin, Luther, Melanchthon, Oecolampadius, Zwingli, Bucer, Bullinger, Brent and other arch-heretics.[15] It was not recorded which book—or books—by Calvin was found in his library, but Guido owned and must have read publications of Calvin. However, de Brès was not exclusively dependent on Calvin, for he is only one of the sixteenth-century theologians whose books were included in his library. Other Protestant leaders such as Luther and Zwingli were represented as well.

The fact that Guido de Brès did not limit himself to Calvin is also apparent in the foreword of his 1565 publication against the Anabaptists. Here he mentions Calvin as one of his sources, together with à Lasco, Bullinger and Micron.[16] This probably refers to different books than those he owned when he lived in Doornik, for when in 1561 his books were destroyed at the order of the committee, any books by Calvin, too, would have been destroyed.

In conclusion, Guido de Brès read at least one book written by Calvin, owned at least one book by him, and exchanged at least one letter with him. He may have met him in Strasbourg, and more likely in Geneva. But classifying de Brès exclusively as a student of Calvin does not reflect the actual situation. He was in contact with more Reformed theologians, and he owned books written by a variety of theologians, including some outside of the strictly Calvinistic tradition.

Calvin and the Gallican Confession

The history of the Gallican Confession is rather complicated, but for our purpose it is not necessary to discuss it in detail.[17] François de Morel mentioned in a letter to Calvin that the upcoming synod of the French churches intended to draw up a confession for the Reformed churches. Calvin responded by providing a draft for a confession consisting of 35 articles,[18] which was based on the Confession of Paris of

---

15. See Appendix, Document 4.

16. De Brès, *La racine*, a.iii r.

17. See Pannier, *Les origines de la confession de foi*, 85-94, 119-31; Hannelore Jahr, *Studien zur Überlieferungsgeschichte*, 19-29; Detmer Deddens, "De eerste synode der Franse Gereformeerde kerken te Parijs 1559," *Lucerna* 1 no. 3 (1959): 107-9; Wulfert De Greef, *The Writings of John Calvin: An Introductory Guide*, trans. Lyle D. Bierma (Grand Rapids: Baker, 1993), 142-43.

18. It has been suggested that Calvin was reluctant to see another confession be added to the already existing Reformed confessions. This could be the origin of Schoock's statement that Calvin first gave a negative advice concerning the making of the Belgic Confession (see chapter 2). In fact, however, in this letter Calvin was not dealing with the Belgic Confession. Further, he did not object

1557. In this form, it became the confession of the Waldenses in Piemont, and of the Italian refugees' congregation in Geneva.

An expanded version of Calvin's draft became what is now known as the Gallican Confession. In a letter to Calvin, Morel summarized the relationship between Calvin's proposal and the Gallican Confession: "It was decided to add several things to your confession but to change only very few things."[19] This implies that the additions are much more substantial than the changes. That is confirmed when the two versions are compared.

To begin with the additions, the greatest change took place right at the beginning of the confession.[20] Calvin had opened his confession with an article on the foundation of faith, revelation as recorded in Scripture. The second article dealt with the doctrine of God, mentioning several attributes, and summarizing the doctrine of the Trinity. In the Gallican Confession, the content was not only expanded but also reorganized. It begins with the attributes of God, of which many are listed. In addition, Calvin's article on revelation became four articles, each of which expanded on the earlier content (arts. 2-5). Finally, the doctrine of the Trinity was dealt with separately (art. 6). Overall, the number of articles increased from 35 to 40.

In the context of a discussion of the Belgic Confession, it is not necessary to provide a comprehensive list of all the changes made to Calvin's original contribution in arriving at the Gallican Confession. The character of the revision can be determined from the following general survey. First of all, words and phrases have been added to many articles of Calvin's version. The more important of these occur in articles 7, 8, 13, 26, 27 and 28 of the Gallican Confession. There are also instances where words have been deleted from Calvin's version. For example, important deletions occur in articles 12, 16, 26, and particularly in articles 22 and 30. Further, the original article 35 was divided into two articles (39, 40). The most common type of change is rephrasing; examples can be found in almost every article.

However, in spite of these alterations, the similarity is much greater than the difference, and nowhere do the changes represent a doctrinal change. This provides an interesting perspective on the place Calvin had in the Reformed world of his time. He was obviously seen as an important leader. When the Reformed in France wanted to have their own confession, they turned to him for advice. But they did not follow

---

to the making of the confession, but to its publication, for he wrote: "Si confessionis *edendae* [emphasis added] tam pertinax quosdam zelus sollicitat . . . " See Calvin's letter to Morel, dated May 17, 1559, in *Calvini opera*, 17:526. It is likely that this is connected with the fact that Calvin had been notified at a late stage, and had made his concept in haste. On this, see Deddens, "De eerste Synode," 107, 118 n. 51.

19. *Calvini opera*, 17:540: "Confessioni vestrae nonnulla visum est addere, perpauca vero commutare."

20. The changes have been indicated in *Calvini opera*, 9:739-52; they can also be reconstructed from Bakhuizen van den Brink, *De Nederlandse belijdenisgeschriften*, 70-146.

him to the letter. They carefully looked over his proposal and felt free to add, remove and change as it appeared profitable in their situation.

The Gallican Confession, in turn, became the pattern for the Belgic Confession, something that can easily be proven. This is evident already from the title pages, for even a quick glance will show that they are virtually identical:

Gallican Confession:	*Belgic Confession:*
Confession de foy,	Confession de foy,
faicte d'un commun accord par les	Faicte d'un commun accord par les
François,	fideles qui conversent és pays bas,
qui desirent vivre selon la pureté	lesquels desirent vivre selon la pureté
de l'Euangile de nostre Seigneur	de l'Evangile de nostre Seigneur
Iesuchrist.	Iesus Christ.
I. Pier. 3	I. Pier. III.
Soyez tousiours appareillez à	Soyez tousiours appareillez à
respondre à chacun, qui vous	respondre à chacun qui vous
demande raison de l'esperance	demande raison de l'esperance
qui est en vous.[21]	qui est en vous.[22]

The similarity is so obvious that there is no room for doubt that the author of the Belgic Confession not only looked at the title page of the Gallican Confession, but that he consciously followed it as well.

Striking similarities also exist between a number of corresponding articles. This can be illustrated by a comparison of two versions of a brief article.[23]

Gallican Confession (art. 23):	*Belgic Confession* (art. 25):
Nous croyons que toutes les	Nous croyons, que les ceremonies et
figures de la Loy	figures de la Loy
ont prins fin	ont cessé
a la venue de Iesus Christ.	à la venue de Christ,
	tous les ombrages ont fait fin,
Mais combien que les ceremonies	de sorte que l'usage en doit estre osté

---

21. On this title page, see Jahr, *Studien zur Überlieferungsgeschichte*, 20; see also the many editions listed on 94-97.

22. Bakhuizen van den Brink has reproduced the title page opposite page 1 in *De Nederlandse belijdenisgeschriften*.

23. For the text of the Gallican Confession, see Bakhuizen van den Brink, *De Nederlandse belijdenisgeschriften*, 116. The text of the Belgic Confession has been taken from the Clémence edition, 18-19.

ne soyent plus en usage,	entre les Chrestiens:
neantmoins la substance et verité	cependant la verité et substance
nous en est demeuree	d'icelles nous en demeure
en la personne de celuy,	en Iesus Christ,
auquel gist tout	en qui elles ont leur
l'accomplissement.	accomplissement:
Au surplus il nous faut aider	toutesfois nous usons encore
	des tesmoignages prins
de la Loy et des Prophetes	de la Loy et des Prophetes
tant pour reigler nostre vie	pour nous confermer en l'Evangile,
que pour estre confermez	et aussi pour reigler nostre vie en
aux promesses de l'Evangile.	tout honneur à la gloire de Dieu.

Ro. 10:4	Rom. 10
Gal. 3 et 4	Gal. 3 et 4
Colos. 2:17	Colos. 2:17
Jean 1	
2 Pier. 1:19	2 Pier. 1:19 et 2:19
1 Tim. 3	
2 Pier. 3:2	
Jaq. 5	

This example shows beyond doubt that Guido de Brès followed the Gallican Confession. The two articles deal with the same issues in the same order, and have several texts in common. At the same time, he did not follow the article of the Gallican Confession slavishly, for he introduced several changes:

clarification: the word "figures" is further explained by the addition of "ceremonies";
different expression: the words "ont prins fin" are replaced by "ont cessé";
change in the sentence structure: the beginning of a new sentence, "Mais combien que les ceremonies ne soyent plus en usage", has become a conclusion, "de sorte que l'usage en doit estre osté";
change in the word order: "la substance et verité" has become: "la verité et substance";
another clarification: "en la personne de celuy" has become: "en Iesus Christ";
change of character: the final sentence was an addition, but it has become a qualification;
addition: the word "tesmoignages" has been inserted;
change of words: the two functions of the Old Testament have been reversed.

It is obvious that this article, although retaining the same overall teaching, was extensively rephrased. The same happened to many other articles, particularly in the first part of the confession. A comparison of articles 2, 4, 7, 8 and 13 in the Belgic

Confession with the corresponding articles of the Gallican Confession shows that many statements were changed.[24]

Another notable change concerns the content. Although the Belgic Confession in general follows the Gallican Confession in its organization, it does express the teachings more fully. This can already be seen in the earlier articles. The Gallican Confession begins with the doctrine of God, followed by revelation and Scripture in the articles 2 through 5, and then returns to the doctrine of God in its discussion of the Trinity in article 6. The Belgic Confession deals with the same doctrines, but explains them at greater length. The articles 2, 5 and 8 are expansions of previous articles, while articles 3 and 6 are new. In addition, several articles were inserted to provide scriptural proof for the Trinity, and to summarize the doctrine of the Son and of the Holy Spirit (arts. 9, 10 and 11). This resulted in a much more comprehensive explanation.

Interestingly, while early on the Belgic Confession has more articles than the Gallican Confession, later the reverse is true. This does not mean, however, that from this point onward the Gallican Confession is richer in content. It deals with original sin in two articles (10, 11), but the one article in the Belgic Confession (15) states about the same. This can also be said in connection with justification and faith. The Gallican Confession devotes five articles to this (18-22), while in the Belgic Confession only two articles are included (23, 24), which in actual fact say more. The Gallican Confession discusses the church in nine articles (25-33), but in the six articles devoted to this in the Belgic Confession (27-32) the issues are more comprehensively explained. The same can be noticed in the discussion of the sacraments. In the Gallican Confession this section contains more articles (35-38), but the Belgic Confession gives a more comprehensive explanation in two articles (34, 35). The two articles in the Gallican Confession devoted to the civil government (39, 40) are brought together in one article in the Belgic Confession (36). Overall, the Gallican Confession consists of more articles, but the Belgic Confession explains the doctrines more comprehensively.

A third difference is that in the Belgic Confession the rejection of the doctrines promoted by Anabaptist groups is more pronounced.[25] In article 18, dealing with the incarnation of God's Son, the "heresy of the Anabaptists, who deny that Christ assumed human flesh from his mother" is rejected, maintaining that Christ shared in the flesh and blood of infants. The Gallican Confession did not mention the Anabaptists at this point, but rather referred to heresies troubling the patristic church, and the contemporary teaching of M. Servet. Another example can be found in the statements on baptism. The Gallican Confession, in article 35, deals rather

---

24. More examples of dependence on the Gallican Confession will be given in the next chapter.

25. This was noted by Herman H. Kuyper in a 26-article series entitled "Guido de Brès," *De Heraut* no. 3426-51 (1943-44). His observation can be found in article 17.

briefly with baptism, stating that we baptize only once. This is said to reject an early Anabaptist custom of repeated baptisms, although this is not mentioned explicitly. The article also defends infant baptism on the basis that Christ receives the infants in his church. The Belgic Confession, on the other hand, explicitly mentions and rejects two Anabaptist positions, repeated baptism and rejection of infant baptism, and presents an argued defense of the Reformed positions.

The only occasion where the Gallican Confession does turn directly against a position of the radical Anabaptists can be found in article 40, dealing with the government: "Therefore we detest those who would like to reject the authorities, to establish community and confusion of property, and to overturn the order of justice." Even in this case the name "Anabaptists" is not mentioned. Article 36 in the first edition of the Belgic Confession stayed remarkably close to this formulation, which may explain why the name is not mentioned in this article, either. To sum up, the Belgic Confession is more comprehensive and more pointed in its rejection of the Anabaptist positions. This will have been occasioned by the fact that their doctrines were much more influential in the Netherlands than in France. For the same reason, Guido de Brès would later publish *La Racine,* an extensive work dealing with the teachings of the several Anabaptist groups.

A fourth difference is the addition of new articles in the Belgic Confession. We already mentioned articles 3 and 6, both of which added new elements to the doctrine of Scripture as found in the Gallican Confession. Article 37, dealing with the final judgment, was also new and is in no way related to the Gallican Confession.

Having traced the development from Calvin's draft through the Gallican Confession to the Belgic Confession, we can conclude that his influence, though indirect, is unmistakable. Whether Guido de Brès was aware that Calvin had been involved in the making of the Gallican Confession is not known, although it cannot be totally excluded since he had connections in France. At any rate, under his hands the Belgic Confession grew far beyond Calvin's original draft and even beyond the Gallican Confession, with the result that it became a confession in its own right.[26]

Calvin on the Belgic Confession

The Dutch church historian H. H. Kuyper argued in an article that Calvin had seen and approved the Belgic Confession. He published this in one of the installments of a lengthy series on Guido de Brès, which appeared in 1943-44, close to the end of the Second World War. At the time, all attention was drawn to the progress of the allied forces as well as the doctrinal struggles within the Reformed churches in the Netherlands. It is therefore understandable that at the time Kuyper's

---

26. Van Langeraad came to the same conclusion; see "De liturgie bij de Hervormden in Nederland," 139-42.

study went unnoticed, till years later Deddens drew attention to it. Kuyper based his view on a response written by Calvin, which had been published among his advices.[27] Calvin wrote this letter in the name of the brothers of Geneva and throughout used the "we" form.[28] This letter may therefore be taken as the official response by the ministers of Geneva concerning this confession.

The name of the confession is not mentioned in the letter containing the advice, but it can be identified from the following passage:

> In your confessional statement[29] we have not noticed anything which does not agree with the holy oracles of God and the orthodox faith. Therefore, we willingly approve the summary of the doctrine contained in it. However, we would wish the letter to the Hebrews was not attributed to Paul, for we are convinced by strong arguments that the author is someone else.

Kuyper pointed out that article 4 of the original edition of the Belgic Confession, when listing the canonical books, referred to the fourteen epistles of Paul and the seven other epistles. This meant that the epistle to the Hebrews was attributed to Paul. Kuyper had found only one other example of a confession attributing Hebrews to Paul. This was the Confession of Erlauthal (1562), which for a brief period of time was the accepted confession of the church in Hungary.[30] Calvin's advice, however, could not refer to this Hungarian confession, for it had not been sent to Geneva, nor was it ever approved by him. Kuyper noted further that the Confession of Erlauthal mentioned the canonical books in a haphazard fashion, beginning with the book of Revelation, going back to the gospels and ending with the epistles of Paul.

This reasoning is suggestive, but it does not definitively prove that Calvin's advice concerned the Belgic Confession, and not the Confession of Erlauthal. After all, it would not have been impossible for someone from Hungary to contact Calvin. Moreover, although Calvin would not have condoned an intrinsically indefensible

---

27. H. H. Kuyper, "Guido de Brès," article 15; see also Detmer Deddens, "De Nederlandse geloofsbelijdenis: Een en ander over haar geschiedenis," *De Reformatie* 37 no. 6 (1961): 46.

28. This letter was published under the somewhat misleading title: "Ad quaestiones circa disciplinam ecclesiae responsa," *Calvini opera*, 10/1:224-26. The text of this letter can be found in Appendix, Document 5.

29. Calvin used the Latin expression "forma vestrae confessionis." It would be tempting to translate the word "forma" as "sketch" in the sense of "draft," implying that Calvin received only a draft for the confession. However, the word can also be used for a brief account, see *Oxford Latin Dictionary*, s.v. "forma," sub 15. We may compare this use of "forma" with the expression "the three forms of unity," which within the Reformed churches is still used as a general term for the confessions.

30. The main body of this confession has been published in E. F. Karl Müller, *Die Bekenntnisschriften der reformierten Kirche* (Leipzig: A. Deichert, 1903; reprint, Zurich: Theologische Buchhandlung, 1987), 265-376; the statement concerning the epistle to the Hebrews can be found in the section on the Councils (327).

position, he might have accepted a lack of organization, which this confession certainly shows. Kuyper's conclusion, that Calvin's advice could not have referred to the Erlauthal Confession, is rather proven by this confession itself. Calvin speaks about a confession for members of the congregation,[31] but the confession of Erlauthal is much too large and scholarly to be useful for that purpose.[32]

When the whole of Calvin's advice is taken into consideration, however, the likelihood that this letter refers to the Belgic Confession increases. The first issue Calvin discusses concerns the question whether those who request to be admitted to the church must publicly testify of their faith. The underlying issue appears to be that the confession contains a rejection of errors, for Calvin wrote:

> We do not see, however, how it would be hard for anyone who wants to be counted among the household of the church to sincerely be enlisted under Christ its head. This is impossible unless he clearly assents with upright piety, and honestly condemns errors by which the sincerity of the religion is corrupted.

Calvin states here that the two requirements for sincere church membership are agreement with the faith and rejection of wrong teaching. It appears that particularly the latter, the rejection of errors, had caused the problem, for Calvin continues:

> Now the rejection of errors often depends on the circumstances. For, as Satan thinks up new ways to cause disturbances, it is necessary to counteract wisely. We know how much Paul commends to us the unity of the spirit in the bond of peace (Eph. 4:3). Further, this solemn profession of faith is even more necessary in order to foster and retain agreement between the believers. Finally, all who want the church of God to stand firm, bear with it without being annoyed that it is supported by this means. We do not think there are people who would quarrel with this general confession, but it would be ineffective unless everyone would clearly denounce both heretical and corrupt teachings.

This is followed by Calvin's remark that he fully agrees with the confession, with the exception of the one statement in which Hebrews is called an epistle of Paul.

Calvin's defense of including passages rejecting errors strengthens the identification of this confession as the Belgic Confession, for in many of its articles errant views are distinguished and refuted. This confession not only expresses agreement with the condemnation of certain teachings by the patristic church, it also rejects contemporary errors by referring to Roman Catholic and Anabaptist

---

31. "Porro ad fovendum et retinendum inter pios consensum, plusquam necessaria est illa solennis fidei professio." For the text of the whole letter, see Appendix, Document 5.

32. Müller, *Die Bekenntnisschriften der reformierten Kirche*, xxxvi-xxxvii; Lourens Doekes, *Credo: Handboek voor de gereformeerde symboliek* (Amsterdam: Ton Bolland, 1975), 93-95.

doctrines. We can therefore agree with Kuyper when he concluded on the basis of this letter that Calvin did receive the Belgic Confession and expressed agreement with it. As Calvin wrote his advice on behalf of the ministers of Geneva, his letter means an official stamp of approval from the entire ministers' council of Geneva on the Belgic Confession.

At what time did the Genevans state their agreement with the Belgic Confession? In the printed version of the *Calvini Opera*, the year of Calvin's advice is not mentioned, but Kuyper says that it must have been written in 1560.[33] This is improbable. The Belgic Confession was printed and published in 1561, and, as was mentioned in our first chapter, Guido de Brès was careful in handing it out. The situation described in Calvin's letter must refer to a later time when copies of the Confession were being distributed among members of the congregations, something de Brès had not yet done in Doornik in the fall of 1561.

In short, although Calvin's role was indirect, he clearly was involved in the early history of the Belgic Confession. Three connections have been noted. He influenced its author in several ways, and his draft was used for the making of the Gallican Confession on which the Belgic Confession is based. Finally, in a letter he expressed his hearty approval of the confession itself.

---

33. H. H. Kuyper, "Guido de Brès," article 15.

4

Beza and the Confession

The previous chapter has shown that the Belgic Confession was constructed after the model of the Gallican Confession. The similarity is not limited to the general pattern, but extends to the content as well. Bakhuizen van den Brink has therefore argued the Belgic Confession should first of all be compared to the Gallican Confession. However, he added that this would not be sufficient for a complete historical evaluation.[1] This can be confirmed by comparing the two confessions as they are printed side by side in his text edition.

Several scholars have pointed to Beza's confession as another background for the Belgic Confession. H. H. Kuyper stated that Guido de Brès must have consulted this confession in making article 37. In fact, the first part of this article was actually taken from it.[2] Another indication in the same direction can be found in Braekman's biography of de Brès. Following Veltenaar, Braekman drew attention to the fact that parts of articles 27 and 29 resemble sections from Beza's fifth chapter.[3] These are merely incidental remarks by Kuyper and Braekman, but they invite further investigation into the connections between these two confessions.

In the following the relationship between Beza's confession and the Belgic Confession will be traced in some detail. However, when in the process derivations from the Gallican Confession are encountered, these, too, will be identified. Such a survey should also further our understanding of the way de Brès actually composed the Belgic Confession.

Beza's Confession

Before beginning our survey, it will be useful to introduce Beza's confession briefly. Beza originally made this not as a confession for the church but as a personal confession for his father. Born in 1519 into a Roman Catholic family, he was sent to Orléans in 1528 to study in the home of Melchior Wolmar. Here, he became

---

1. Bakhuizen van den Brink, *De Nederlandse belijdenisgeschriften*, 53.

2. H. H. Kuyper, "Guido de Brès," article 17.

3. Braekman, "Les sources de la Confessio Belgica," *Bulletin de la commission de l'histoire des Églises Wallonnes* 7 (1961): 19-22, referring to the study of C. Veltenaar, *Théodore de Bèze et ses relations avec les théologiens des Pays-Bas* (Kampen: J. H. Kok, 1904).

acquainted with the Reformation movement. In an autobiographical letter originally written to Wolmar and later added to his confession, Beza explains that he wrote this confession first of all to clear his name from the slander of people who had given his father the impression that his son was an impious man and an heretic. His second reason for making it was to win his father for Christ.[4]

In 1558, Beza accepted an invitation to become professor of Greek at the newly-founded Academy in Geneva. In the same year, he received permission to publish his confession, which became available in 1559 from the press of Conrad Badius.[5] In the preface, Beza acknowledged that many had written about the same issues, among them Calvin, whom he calls his second father. He defended the publication of his own confession by pointing out that it is possible to repeat the same festive meal with only a slight change in the arrangement, to the enjoyment of the partakers.[6]

We are unable to determine whether Beza revised this personal confession before publishing it. At any rate, his confession became very popular, and between 1559 and 1563 no less than ten printings of the French text were made.[7] One of these came from the same printer who also published the Belgic Confession, as can be concluded from the identical printer's mark.[8] Beza himself later produced an expanded Latin translation, which was first published in 1560.[9]

---

4. Beza did not state this explicitly in the French edition; this information can be found in the preface of the Latin edition. See the footnote in "La confession du foi du chrétien," ed. and trans. Michel Réveillaud, *La Revue Réformée* 6 no. 23-24 (1955): 11 n. 1.

5. Jill Raitt mentions two original French editions, one published in 1558 and the other the next year (*The Eucharistic Theology of Theodore Beza: Development of the Reformed Doctrine* [Chamsburg, PA: American Academy of Religion, 1972], 11). This is probably based on a misunderstanding. Badius' request for printing Beza's confession was discussed on September 15, 1558, and granted on September 20, before Beza arrived in Geneva; see *Calvini Opera*, 21:703, 706. However, Badius actually published the confession in 1559. See also Walter Hollweg, *Neue Untersuchungen zur Geschichte und Lehre des Heidelberger Katechismus* (Neukirchen: Neukirchener Verlag, 1961), 1:90 n. 10. Unless otherwise noted, references to Beza's confession are keyed to this Badius edition.

6. The letter to Wolmar was printed in the second edition of Beza's *Tractationes Theologicae*, published in Geneva in 1582. A translation can be found in Henry M. Baird, *Theodore Beza: The Counsellor of the French Reformation*, 2nd ed., (New York: B. Franklin, 1970), 355-67; see on the confession, 366-67.

7. See Gardy, *Bibliographie*, 60-69, correcting Hollweg, who stated that the sixth edition was published in Geneva in 1563, *Neue Untersuchungen*, 90. Beza's confession was also translated into Italian (1560) and English (1563). After some changes had been made, it was adopted as the confession of the Protestant Church in Hungary. See Hollweg, *Neue Untersuchungen*, 91, and for the text, Müller, *Bekenntnisschriften*, 376-449.

8. For the printer's mark of Beza's confession, see Gardy, *Bibliographie*, 65; for that of the Belgic Confession, see Bakhuizen van den Brink, *De Nederlandse belijdenisgeschriften*, opposite page 1. See also our discussion in chapter 1.

9. Raitt, "Beza," in *TRE*, 5:766.

General Features of Beza's Confession

For a comparison between Beza's confession and the Belgic Confession we can begin by looking at some general features. As mentioned before, Beza himself stated that his confession shows a slight change in arrangement compared to other confessions. Careful investigation brings to light that this is an understatement, for the differences in structure are far from minor. His confession has a number of characteristics which set it apart from other confessions, including the Belgic Confession.

In the first place, Beza's confession is divided into seven chapters, the first six dealing with the Trinity, God the Father, Jesus Christ the Son of God, the Holy Spirit, the church, and the last judgment. The order of the topics shows that he presented his material after the structure of the Apostles' Creed. The final chapter is different in character, for it consists of a comparison between the doctrine of the papal church and the catholic church.[10] The confession concludes with a warning addressed to kings and princes, judges and magistrates not to persecute the church, to which is added a call for all to remain faithful. The chapters differ considerably in length. The first and second are rather short, three and four sections respectively, but from then on the chapters increase in length. The third chapter has twenty-six sections, chapter four as many as fifty-two, and chapter five comes close with forty-five. Even a quick glance at the Belgic Confession will reveal that it did not derive its structure from Beza's confession.

A second difference concerns the order in which the doctrines themselves are discussed. This will become obvious even when only Beza's first two chapters are compared with the beginning of the Belgic Confession. Beza's confession starts off by dealing with the Trinity in the first chapter, followed by a discussion on God the Father in the second chapter. The chapter on the Trinity is subdivided into three sections, explaining successively the oneness of God, the three Persons who are distinct within the unity of the essence, and God's eternal providence. In the chapter on God the Father four issues are discussed: the Person of the Father, the Father as the creator and preserver of all things, the creation of the angels and finally, how the works of the Trinity are inseparable.

The order followed by the Belgic Confession is much different. Article 1 does not deal with the Trinity but rather with God. This is followed by a discussion of revelation and Scripture, in articles 2 through 7. Articles 8 and 9 deal with the Trinity, while the next two focus on the divinity of the Son and of the Holy Spirit. Only then are creation and providence discussed, in articles 12 and 13.

---

10. This chapter has been left out in the edition of Réveillaud; see "La confession de foi du chrétien," 6. The same happened in the translation by James Clark. However, the original conclusion is now called chapter seven, causing confusion; *The Christian Faith*, trans. J. Clark (East Sussex: Focus Christian Ministries Trust, 1991), 121-27.

Even this limited comparison shows clearly that the Belgic Confession did not follow the order of Beza's confession. This negative result confirms the conclusion of the previous chapter, that the Belgic Confession dealt with the same material as the Gallican Confession, and organized it in a similar way as well.

Thirdly, the character of Beza's confession changes in the course of the discussion. In the early chapters, the doctrines are discussed rather briefly, but later, more extensive explanations are given. The sections become longer in the course of the third chapter dealing with the Holy Spirit and faith, and even lengthier halfway through the fourth chapter.

This can be demonstrated when the confession turns to temptations.[11] Four temptations are described at length and refuted at length, with the discussions varying from three to fifteen pages in length. To give some other examples, the meaning of the sacrament in general is discussed in over twenty pages, followed by another five pages devoted to baptism and six to the Lord's Supper.[12] It is probably unintentional, but at the same time undeniable, that the explanations in the later sections of Beza's confession go beyond a believer's confession and assume the character of a theological exposition. In comparison, the Belgic Confession is much more even in its explanation of the doctrine. It does not even deal with the temptations and is much more succinct when discussing the sacraments.

Fourthly, a remarkable difference can be noticed in the use of the church fathers. During the time of the Reformation, the question as to which point of view was supported by the theologians of the early church was an important part of the discussion. Calvin, for example, frequently quoted their writings in his *Institutes* and also in his other works.[13] Guido de Brès was familiar with this practice, for he worked extensively with patristic evidence in his first major publication, the *Baston de la Foy*. The Belgic Confession, however, is very restrained in this respect. It refers to council

---

11. In chapter IV, dealing with the Holy Spirit, the temptations are discussed in sections 10-20, stretching from pages 34 to 68 in the first edition printed by Conrad Badius (Théodore Beza, *Confession de la foy chrestienne . . . Reveue et augmentee de nouveau par luy, avec un abregé d'icelle* [N. p.: Conrad Badius, 1559]). This is longer than the first three chapters together, which take up pages 11-27 in the same edition. The same can be observed in the modern French edition published by Réveillaud (33-55 compared to 15-28) and in the English translation by Clark (19-40 compared to 1-14).

12. In the Badius edition, the sacraments in general are discussed on 89-104; baptism on 104-8 and the Lord's Supper on 109-14.

13. For a comprehensive study on the quotes Calvin included in his works, see Remko J. Mooi, *Het kerk- en dogmahistorisch element in de werken van Johannes Calvijn* (Wageningen: H. Veenman & Zonen, 1965). From the side of the Roman Catholic church, the same emphasis on the support of the patristic church can be observed in the marginal references added to the decisions of the Council of Trent. See for example the decision on original sin in Henricus Denzinger and A. Schönmetzer, *Enchiridion Symbolorum definitionum et declarationum de rebus fidei et morum* (Barcinone: Herder, 1965), 368, 371-79.

decisions in article 9 and to ancient heresies in articles 9, 12 and 15, but names of church fathers are never mentioned in the text, and their works are not referenced in the margin.

Beza's confession, on the other hand, appeals extensively to patristic literature. On many occasions, references to the fathers are given in the margin of his confession. To give only one example out of many, the statement concerning original sin in chapter III, 11, is supported by four references to Augustine, specified in the margin.[14] Beza even frequently inserted quotations from the fathers in the text of his confession. For example, in chapter III, 13, three statements of Augustine are quoted to prove that the doctrine of the corruption of the will was really taught by him. And in chapter III, 16, another quotation from Augustine is given to show how God uses sin to manifest his power and wrath.

Augustine is probably the most frequently quoted patristic author, but references to many others are included as well. There is no need to provide a comprehensive list of all the quotes inserted in this confession; the following examples will be sufficient to give an impression of their range. In chapter IV, 15, Bernard of Clairvaux is quoted as teaching assurance of the forgiveness of sins. In the lengthy section chapter IV, 16, three quotations from Chrysostom have been inserted in the text. They are followed by two statements taken from Ambrose.[15] To chapter IV, 46, a relatively brief section on the communication of the sacraments, eight marginal references from Irenaeus are included, two from Augustine, and one each from Prosper, Innocent, Cyprian, Origen, and Hilary. To give only one more example, in chapter V, 35 of his confession, Beza deals with the controversial issue that in an established church those who are in office must be freely and lawfully elected. The marginal notes refer to the Acts of a council held in Rome at the time of Hilary,[16] statements made by Augustine and Athanasius, a letter by Leo, a canon of the Council of Laodicea, and a statement by Cyprian. These are followed by references to a canon from an early bishop of Rome, statements by Leo I and by Gregory, and finally a reference to the rules for the election of the Pope, given by Nicholas II.[17]

The range of the quotations and references is impressive, and they attest to Beza's scholarship. However, for our purpose it is more important to note that it underlines the different intention of his confession compared to that of Guido de Brès. As Beza's confession progresses, it becomes more and more a theological exposition of the Reformed faith. This is different from the Belgic Confession which is not scholarly

---

14. These references have been written out in the edition published by Réveillaud, "La confession de foi du chrétien," 21.

15. These were taken from the Commentary on Romans, incorrectly attributed to Ambrose; see Réveillaud, "La confession de foi du chrétien," 44.

16. This refers presumably to Canon 13 of the Council of Laodicea; Réveillaud, "La confession de foi du chrétien," 133.

17. Réveillaud, "La confession de foi du chrétien," 133.

in its presentation. The comparison with Beza's confession clearly shows the Belgic Confession to be a different kind of confession, made for the general believers who believe with the heart and confess with the mouth.

In the fifth place, the conclusion of the previous section is further confirmed when the presentation of the doctrines is considered. Beza's confession repeatedly develops into a scholarly treatise. A case in point is the discussion of the similarities and differences between preaching and the sacraments. In IV, 34, four similarities are mentioned, the third of which is introduced with the words, "As we have said above," a reminder suitable for a treatise. This is followed by a discussion concerning the specific character of the sacraments. Again, four characteristics are discussed, the first explaining that sacraments are appendages to the Word. The following quotation is part of a comprehensive explanation concerning the character of sacraments in general:

> Since the sacraments are like subordinate additions to the Word, and since they are appointed to seal what is already in us, namely, the union and communion which we already have in Jesus Christ, it is sufficiently clear that the plain preaching of the Word must have precedence, and even that there should be a clear profession of faith before the sacraments may be duly administered. I mean that of those who are of the age of discretion, for as far as the baptism of the infants of the believers is concerned, there is a specific consideration of which we shall speak below. (IV, 35)

The style of this passage resembles a scholarly exposition rather than a confession for members of a Reformed congregation.

Another example can be found in the discussion of ecclesiastical orders. Beza goes through an explanation of the four minor orders that come up in patristic literature, and concludes:

> All these small tasks which properly belong to church work, also serve to, little by little, try out and test those who could be used for important charges. And when a good organisation would be established in the church for such a good purpose, we would not be averse to it, provided consideration is given to what is necessary for edification. (V, 31)

In this context, Beza is considering several options for introducing people to church work. The statement is useful in itself, but it does not function well in a summary of the Reformed doctrine. Also in this respect, the Belgic Confession is different in character. It is consistent in maintaining the style of a confession of believers, as is stated on its title page.

All of this leads to the conclusion that these confessions are altogether different. This shows, first of all, in the way the confessions are structured. Beza's confession has a double division, its seven chapters being subdivided in sections. In addition, there is a considerable difference in the manner of discussion. As the confession progresses, it evolves into a treatise. It can easily be ascertained that this confession did not influence the Belgic Confession in its structure and general approach. In these respects, Guido de Brès followed the pattern of the Gallican Confession.

Content of Beza's Confession

Another question concerns the extent to which Beza's confession may have influenced the content of the Belgic Confession. This influence has already been noted in two instances: the explanation concerning the church in articles 27 and 28, and the explanation of the final judgment in article 37. A careful comparison of the two confessions proves that there are more instances that show dependence on Beza's confession. In fact, many articles of the Belgic Confession include material derived from it, although the extent of the borrowing differs considerably. While surveying the derivations from Beza's confession, it will be useful to note what Guido de Brès did with them.

The first instance of borrowing is, unfortunately, no longer noticeable in the later editions of Beza's confession. As can be seen in the Badius edition, Beza's confession ends with a number of texts. These are introduced with the remark: "Several passages from the New Testament, by which the believers are exhorted to give confession of their faith before the people." This is followed by five passages, identified by book and chapter: Matt. 10 [:32, 33]; Mark 8 [:38]; Luke 9 [:26]; Rom. 10 [:10]; 2 Tim. 2 [:12b]; 1 Pet. 3 [:15]. In the first edition of the Belgic Confession, exactly the same texts are used, introduced by exactly the same formula. However, two differences must be noted. In the first place, they are not included at the end of the confession, but are found at the beginning, between the letter to King Philip and the confession itself. Moreover, the texts are organized in a slightly different order. Since 1 Peter 3 here precedes Romans 10, the texts are no longer presented in order of the books of the Bible. As a result, in the edition of the Belgic Confession the actual confession is preceded by two sets of texts on confessing. The first moves from denial to confessing, the second reverses the order, ending with the warning that Christ will deny those who deny him.

In the following, an extensive survey of corresponding sections will be provided, presented in the order of the Belgic Confession.[18]

---

18. In the following examples, the translations are mine, based on the text edition by Bakhuizen van den Brink for the Gallican Confession, the Badius edition for Beza's confession and the Clémence edition for the Belgic Confession.

Article 1

This article deals with God's existence. It has often been compared with the corresponding article of the Gallican Confession, but it is interesting to include a comparison of the opening sentence of this article with Beza's confession.

Gallican Confession: We believe and confess that there is a single God. (art. 1)

Beza's confession: We believe that there is a single divine essence, which we call God. (I, 1)

Belgic Confession: We all believe with the heart and confess with the mouth that there is a single and simple divine essence, spiritual, which we call eternal God. (art. 1)

This shows that for the opening phrase, the Belgic Confession takes its starting point in the Gallican Confession by using the same two verbs "believe" and "confess." The statement is expanded by the insertion of an expression taken from Romans 10:8, 9, in order to give full weight to the importance of confessing. The rest of the article, however, appears to be drawn from Beza's confession, which de Brès elaborated upon.

It appears that Guido de Brès intended to continue in the tradition, choosing the best formulation, and making the confession his own by expanding on it. Obviously, he did not feel restricted to a simple repetition of the tradition.

There are no further derivations from Beza's confession in the section on revelation and Scripture (arts. 2-7), for Beza approaches this doctrine from the distinction between law and gospel. (IV, 22-27)

Articles 8 and 9

The way the Trinity is confessed provides further insight into the making of the Belgic Confession. A good example can be found in the beginning of this section.

Gallican Confession: This Holy Scripture teaches that in this single and simple divine essence, which we have confessed, there are three persons, the Father, the Son and the Holy Spirit. (art. 6)

Beza's confession: The Word of God teaches us clearly that this divine essence is really, truly and eternally distinct in three persons, namely the Father, the Son and the Holy Spirit, who are one God. (I, 2)

Belgic Confession: Following this truth and the Word of God, we believe in one God, who is one in essence and substance, but three in persons, Father, Son and Holy Spirit. (art. 8)

The Belgic Confession opens the doctrine of the Trinity by reminding the believers that there is one God. This expression itself can also be found in article 1 of the Gallican Confession as well as in Beza's confession, but in de Brès' formulation it becomes the starting point for the discussion of the Trinity, leading to an improved statement.

The concluding statement on the Trinity provides another point of comparison:

> *Gallican Confession:* And on this we approve what has been determined by the councils, and detest all sects and heresies which have been rejected by the holy teachers, such as St. Hilary, St. Athanasius, St. Ambrose, St. Cyril. (art. 6)
>
> *Beza's confession:* As the church has decided by means of Holy Scripture, against Sabellius, Samosatenus, Arius, Nestorius, Marcion, Eutyches and all other heretics. (I, 2)
>
> *Belgic Confession:* This doctrine of holy Trinity has always been maintained in the true church since the time of the Apostles to the present, against the Jews, Muslims, and against certain false Christians and heretics such as Marcion, Mani, Praxeas, Sabellius, Samosatenus and such like, who have been rightfully condemned by the holy fathers. We willingly receive on this issue the three symbols, that of the Apostles, of Nicea and of Athanasius, and likewise that which has been determined by the holy councils. (art. 9)

The Gallican Confession thus ends positively by accepting the decisions of the councils and emphasizing the holy teachers in their rejection of heresy. The Belgic Confession does refer to the holy teachers, but also follows Beza by mentioning specific heretics. However, Beza was not followed slavishly, for Guido de Brès included Mani among those who did not follow the orthodox doctrine of the Trinity. Nestorius and of Eutyches, on the other hand, were left out, for their deviation from the orthodox teaching did not so much concern the Trinity, but rather the natures of Christ. It appears that de Brès left these names out intentionally as not directly relevant for the doctrine of the Trinity.

Article 10

The Gallican Confession does not devote a separate article to the Son, but Beza's confession and the Belgic Confession do. The following comparison shows the relationship:

> *Beza's confession:* We believe that Jesus Christ, as to his divine nature, is the unique Son, eternally begotten and certainly not made, one with the Father in essence, coeternal, consubstantial, equal to God his Father in all and over all. (III, 1)
>
> *Belgic Confession:* We believe that Jesus Christ, as to his divine nature, is the unique Son of God, eternally begotten, certainly not made nor created (for he would be a creature): he is one in essence with the Father, he is coeternal, he is the proper image of the Father and the reflection of his glory, being in all and through all alike to him. (art. 10)

Beza's statement was obviously used as the basis for the confession of the Son in the Belgic Confession, but de Brès did make changes. He added to several statements: the unique Son "of God"; certainly not made "for then he would be a creature." He also replaced the technical expression "consubstantial" by the descriptive statement "he is the proper image of the substance of the Father." He added another expression to emphasize his divinity: "and the splendor of his glory." Finally, he turned Beza's "equal to God his Father" into a more emphatic statement: "being like him in all and through all." De Brès was obviously concerned with clarity in the presentation of the doctrine.

Another difference concerns the proof texts. Beza's confession followed the normal procedure of simply listing texts in the margin. For the Belgic Confession, however, de Brès included a selection of texts in the article itself, and added many more in the margin.

This comparison proves that de Brès used Beza's confession concerning the Son, while at the same time expanding it, particularly by adding an explicit biblical basis for the eternal divinity of the Son of God.

Article 11

Remarkably, the situation is rather different in the case of the article dealing with the divinity of the Holy Spirit. Beza's confession stated: "We believe in the Holy Spirit, who is the coeternal and consubstantial power of the Father and the Son, with whom He resides and from whom He proceeds, being one God with them, yet distinct in person" (IV, 1).

De Brès did not follow this statement at all when formulating article 11 of the Belgic Confession. Rather, he borrowed the first sentence of his article from article 6 of the Gallican Confession and elaborated on it.

Article 12

Most of this article dealing with creation in general, and more specifically with the angels and the devils, can be traced back to the sources. Following the order of the article, we can begin by noting that in Beza's confession creation is rather emphatically attributed to the Father: "We believe in one God the Father, a person distinct from his Son and from the Holy Spirit. It is he who has created . . ." (II, 1 and 2). In the original edition of the Belgic Confession, a shorter formulation of this statement is used: "We believe that this one God has created . . ." (art. 12). Remarkably, from the second edition of 1566 onward, the creator is identified as the Father. The reason for this change is presumably the formulation of the Apostles' Creed.

The section dealing with the task of the creatures is not derived from either the Gallican Confession or Beza's confession. Part of this teaching can be found in

Calvin's *Institutes*,[19] but the formulation is likely de Brès' own. However, the following statement on God's work in the world follows Beza's formulation ("He also sustains and governs everything according to his eternal providence by his infinite and essential providence" [II, 2]) almost to the letter. To this the Belgic Confession adds: "to serve man, in order that man serves his God." This last phrase appears to be from de Brès' own hand, since it cannot be found in either the Gallican Confession or in Beza's confession.

At this point, the article makes a transition to the angels. The same combination of creation and angels can already be found in both article 7 of the Gallican Confession and in the next section of Beza's confession (II, 3). However, the explanation of the Belgic Confession goes beyond its predecessors. This was even more pronounced in the original edition, which included an additional explanation of the wicked devices of Satan in the following statement: "to the point of letting himself be adored by everyone by promising great things to people; and that is small wonder in view of the fact that he even dared to present himself to Christ to be adored by him."

Finally, the rejection of the errors of the Sadducees and Manicheans is based on Beza's confession, although slightly rephrased.

The conclusion is that Guido de Brès chose the more elaborate confession of Beza as the model for this article. At the same time, he felt free to remove or to add sections according to his own insight.

Article 13

The article on God's providence is based on article 8 of the Gallican Confession, but it has been greatly expanded. One of the additions is taken from Beza's article on providence, where he states: "For his power and goodness is so great and so incomprehensible that He even ordains and works rightly and justly what the devil and the people do wrong and injustly" (I, 3).

Article 14

A similar change was made in the article dealing with the creation and fall of man. The article itself is an elaboration on article 9 of the Gallican Confession, but one phrase from Beza's confession more or less found its way into the Belgic Confession. Beza wrote that man "voluntarily and without being forced has allied himself with the devil, and so has made himself culpable of the first and second death" (III, 10). The Belgic Confession used part of this expression, when it states that "man has made himself culpable of the first and second death."

---

19. Calvin, *Institutes*, 1.14.20; see also Polman, *Onze Nederlandsche geloofsbelijdenis*, 2:47-49.

Article 15

Articles 10 and 11 of the Gallican Confession have obviously been used in the making of article 15 of the Belgic Confession, which deals with original sin. However, its beginning is an adaptation of the summary statement in Beza's confession: "Original sin is therefore a total corruption of the whole nature of man, which corruption has proceeded from Adam unto his whole race" (III, 15). The Belgic Confession has taken over this expression, adding some words: "original sin has been spread out over the whole human race, which is a corruption of the whole nature and a hereditary evil."

Article 16

This article speaks of God's mercy and justice for sinful people. The Belgic Confession follows a tradition when referring to these attributes of God in connection with election, for both article 12 of the Gallican Confession and sections III, 3 and 16 of Beza's confession mentioned the same attributes. However, a difference in approach between these earlier confessions is apparent. The Gallican Confession took its point of departure in the situation of the fall. Beza, on the other hand, mentioned God's justice and mercy (III, 3) even before dealing with creation and fall (III, 16).

The Belgic Confession follows Beza's example by placing God's mercy and justice side by side. This results in an article that is more clear than that of the Gallican Confession. However, theologically speaking, it follows the Gallican Confession in two respects. Different from Beza's confession, which began with God's justice, the Gallican Confession begins with God's mercy. Further, where Beza emphasized God's punishment, the Gallican Confession referred to God leaving people in their sins. In both these instances, the Belgic Confession followed the Gallican Confession.[20]

Article 18

This article is an ingenious combination of Beza's confession and the Gallican Confession, together with de Brès' own additions. The opening section, all the way to the mention of the virgin birth, is almost literally taken from Beza's confession (III, 21). The only substantial difference is that in the latter the Son of God is the main subject, when it speaks of "the true and unique eternal Son of God [who] has taken the form of a servant." In the Belgic Confession, on the other hand, God is the subject: "God . . . by sending his own unique and eternal Son."

The second section deals with the completeness of Christ's human nature, emphasizing that he had both a human body as well as a human soul. This was also mentioned in article 14 of the Gallican Confession, but the formulation of the Belgic

---

20. The original article of the Belgic Confession was twice the length it is today. The reduction of this article and the reason for it will be discussed in chapter 6.

Confession is closer to Beza's confession: " . . . having a true human soul and a true human body formed from the substance of the virgin Mary" (III, 23). The Belgic Confession continued with the explanatory statement that "Jesus Christ needed to have both a human body and a human soul." As a comparable phrase cannot be found in either the Gallican Confession or Beza's confession, this must have been contributed by Guido de Brès.

At first glance, the Gallican Confession and the Belgic Confession are similar in the fact that both contain a rejection of errors. However, the difference is greater, for the earlier confession identified these as "the heresies which have troubled the church in ancient times, and particularly also the diabolical imaginations of Servet." The Belgic Confession, on the other hand, formulates its explanation of the incarnation of Christ in opposition to "the heresy of the Anabaptists," thereby adapting the statement to its specific situation.

Finally, the Gallican Confession proves Jesus' true human nature by stating that he was "the true seed of Abraham and David." The Belgic Confession uses this statement, but goes far beyond it by supporting this doctrine with no less than thirteen expressions from Scripture, including several references to his descent from Abraham and David. Notwithstanding similarities, the difference in focus results in different articles.

Article 19

In this article, still belonging to the section on Jesus Christ, the implications of the incarnation are discussed. The first, shorter paragraph contains several statements intended to emphasize the unity of his person, while the second section explains that the differences between the two natures were not obliterated. This second part is an expanded rewriting of article 15 of the Gallican Confession. However, the beginning of this article is a rephrasing of Beza's confession: "We confess that from the moment of this conception, the person of the Son has been inseparably united with the human nature, so that there are not two Sons of God, nor two Jesus Christs, but one single Son of God, Jesus Christ" (III, 22). Bringing these two sources together and successfully unifying them allowed Guido de Brès to present a balanced summary of the doctrine, dealing with both the unity of the person as well as the two natures of Jesus Christ.

Article 22

This article deals with justification by faith. It opens with a sentence partly derived from article 20 of the Gallican Confession: "We believe that we are made participants of this justice by faith alone."[21] However, the main part of the first section of article 22 is taken from Beza's description of the object of true faith. He noted that two issues need to be kept in mind. The one states that where no Word of God exists but only the word of man, there is no faith. The other is: "Faith embraces and appropriates Jesus Christ and all that is in him" (IV, 6). This second statement was used for the beginning of article 22 of the Belgic Confession.

In the following section, Beza described justification by faith as follows: "This does not mean that faith would be a virtue which makes us righteous in ourselves before God . . . but we understand that by faith we are justified in that it embraces him who justifies us, namely Jesus Christ" (IV, 7). This sentence appears to be the basis of the original text of the Belgic Confession, since it, too, begins with a negative statement, followed by a positive expression: "We do not understand [this to mean] that properly speaking it is by faith that we are made righteous, for it is only an instrument by which we embrace Jesus Christ our righteousness."

However, the expression at the end that "faith is the instrument which keeps us with Him in the communion of all his benefits" appears to be Guido de Brès' own formulation.

Again we notice de Brès freely borrowing from existing confessions, although the resulting statement is clearly his own.

Article 27

In the Belgic Confession, the doctrine of the church is extensively discussed in six articles, from 27 to 32. The Gallican Confession provided much of the material for the later articles of this section, but, remarkably, the opening article 27 does not resemble the opening article on the church in the Gallican Confession (art. 25).

Beza dealt with the church in a long chapter, consisting of no less than 43 sections. De Brès did not follow this pattern, but he did borrow from this chapter. Beza began by giving two reasons for the existence of the church, the first being that the work of the three Persons would be in vain if there were no people to enjoy its fruit. This was followed by the statement: "Since Jesus Christ has an eternal reign, it is necessary that he is never without subjects" (V, 1). De Brès obviously used this reason in his confession, when he wrote: "It is known that Christ is an eternal king; it follows from this that he cannot be without subjects."

In the same article, Beza had stated:

It is therefore necessary that from the beginning of the world there has been a church, that is to say, a multitude and assembly of such people as it has pleased God

---

21. This is not noted by Bakhuizen van den Brink in his text edition, but it can be confirmed by a comparison of article 22 of the Belgic Confession with article 20 of the Gallican Confession. See his *De Nederlandse belijdenisgeschriften*, 106 and 110, respectively.

to choose by his grace, who have acknowledged and served the true God according to his will, by means of the one Jesus Christ appropriated by faith.

The author of the Belgic Confession used this, but with considerable changes. He omitted the reference to election, retained the statement on salvation in Jesus Christ, and added a phrase concerning sanctification by the Holy Spirit. He also placed this section at the beginning of the article on the church. This allowed him to connect the statement that the church has been from the beginning of the world with the remark that it will remain to the end, which had been kept apart in Beza's confession.

At the end of article 27, the Belgic Confession states that the church is not limited to a certain place or attached to certain people. This is a rephrasing of Beza's remark that the church is not limited to a certain place, time, or nation (V, 3).

Article 28

This article is an expanded version of article 26 of the Gallican Confession. The similarity can be seen, for example, in the striking expression "the yoke of Christ," which occurs in both confessions. At the beginning of the article, however, an expression is used that did not occur in the Gallican Confession but was probably occasioned by Beza's confession. Here, the introductory article on the church ended with the following statement:

> Finally, we must necessarily confess, since outside of Jesus Christ there is no salvation at all, that anyone who dies without being a member of this assembly is excluded from Jesus Christ and from salvation, for the power to save which is in Jesus Christ belongs only to those who recognize him as their God and only Saviour. (V, 1)

Since Beza used the expression that there is no salvation "outside of Christ" in a statement on the church, he had to include a rather involved reasoning to make the connection with the church again. The Belgic Confession avoided this problem by using the traditional expression "outside the church no salvation," which can already be found in the writings of Cyprian and Augustine. It is probably de Brès' familiarity with the church fathers that allowed him to use the original expression for his confession.

However, another phrase in article 28 is actually derived from Beza's confession. Originally, it was part of a convoluted statement that had an argumentative character. It sounds as if he is debating with his father:

> The duty of the children of God is not only to serve God wherever they are and whatever decay exists in the church, but also, when it pleases God to rebuild these ruins here or there since he is not limited to any people or nation—that means, when it pleases him to raise his standard again, which is the ministry of the holy

Word—then the duty of the children of God, I say, is to join themselves to the flock and to separate themselves from those who do not belong to it. (V, 9)

A comparison with the Belgic Confession shows that Guido de Brès left out Beza's argumentation but retained his conclusion. This is confirmed by the fact that he included three of Beza's four proof texts (Isa. 49:22; 52:11, 12; Matt. 24:28).

Article 29

Three related issues are discussed in this article: the marks of the true church, the marks of the Christians, and the marks of the false church. The introductory sentence is taken from article 27 of the Gallican Confession, which characterized the church as the company of believers who agree to follow God's Word and the pure religion which is based on it.

Beza's confession stated the following:

The mark of the true church is the preaching of the Word of the Son of God as it has been revealed to her in the prophets and apostles and by them made known to the world, containing therefore the sacraments and the administration of the ecclesiastical discipline, as God has ordered it. (V, 7)

This is followed by references taken from both Scripture and the church fathers to support the statement that there is no other Word or other preaching. Beza concludes:

Wherever the Word of God is purely preached, the sacraments purely administered, with the church discipline conducted in conformity with the holy and pure doctrine, there we recognize the church of God, however small the number or the appearance is according to people.

Both of these statements were used for the Belgic Confession. Guido de Brès did not quote them exactly, but he did list the same three marks and used elements from the final phrase to formulate his summary.

A remarkable aspect of the Gallican Confession is that the marks of the true church are not formulated, although several characteristic elements of the false church are. It states in article 28:

Therefore, we condemn the congregations of the Papacy since the pure truth of God is banished there, the sacraments are corrupted, degenerated, falsified or altogether destroyed, and all kind of superstitions and idolatries are popular.

De Brès used this section in formulating the marks of the false church in article 29 of the Belgic Confession.

However, for the statement concerning those who are true members of the church, he turned to a long section in Beza's confession. This statement begins as follows:

> Those belong to the church, who have the mark of the Christians, that is the faith. One knows those who have the faith in that they receive only one Savior Jesus Christ, as has been said, flee from sin, pursue righteousness, that is, they love the true and only God and their neighbor according to the Word of God, without turning to the right or to the left. Not that there are no great weaknesses in the most perfect people, but because there is a great difference between those in whom sin reigns and those in whom there are still remnants of sin. (V, 8)

When preparing the articles on the church, Guido de Brès obviously looked at the Gallican Confession and Beza's confession. Bringing together statements from both, he was able to forge them into a well-balanced and well-organized article.

Article 33

This article on the sacraments in general shows considerable influence from the Gallican Confession. For example, the words "insensitivity and weakness" were borrowed straight from this confession, although they were placed in a different position.

However, a section was also taken from Beza's confession. Here it was stated that:

> the sacraments are sure signs, marks or visible witnesses commanded by God for continual use by his whole church, added by himself to the Word of his gospel, by which he wants to save us graciously in Jesus Christ his Son; added, I say, to better represent to our external senses all that he gives us to understand by his Word and that he does internally in our hearts, as well as to seal and ratify in us the salvation which we only possess in faith and hope. (IV, 31)

Guido de Brès took two phrases out of the latter part of this long sentence to insert them in his confession.

This is followed by a lengthy article devoted to each of the sacraments. These are, in fact, considerable expansions of the articles in the Gallican Confession. Although Beza, too, provided an extensive explanation of each sacrament, there is no clear indication that de Brès made use of his confession on this point.

Article 37

In the case of this article it has already been noted that the Belgic Confession was influenced by Beza's confession. Now we must consider to what extent article 37 is dependent on Beza's explanation of the last judgment, in his chapter VI. A comparison of the original texts will provide a clear answer.

Beza's Confession	*Belgic Confession*
Finalement nous croyons,	Finalement, nous croyons
selon la parole de Dieu,	selon la parole de Dieu,
qu'au temps ordonné de Dieu,	que quand le temps ordonné du Seigneur sera venu,
et lequel les Anges mesmes	lequel est incongnu à toutes
ne scavent pas, Iesus Christ	creatures,
voyant le nombre des eleus	et que le nombre des esleus sera
accompli,	accompli,
viendra du ciel	nostre Seigneur Iesus Christ viendra du ciel
corporellement	corporellement et visiblement, comme il y est monté
avec sa Divine maiesté,	avec grande gloire et Maiesté, pour se declarer estre le Iuge des vivans et des morts:
estant ce vieil	mettans en feu et en flambe ce vieil
monde consumé par feu:	monde pour le consumer.
Et lors comparoistront	Lors comparoistront
devant luy	personellement devant ce grand Iuge[22]
tous les hommes	toutes creatures,
	tant hommes que femmes et enfans,
qui auront este dés	qui aurons este depuis
le commencement du monde.	le commencement du monde
	iusques à la fin, y estans adiournez
	par la voix et cris espouvantables
	des Anges et des Archanges, et par
	le son de la trompette Divine.
Car ceux qui auront este morts au	Car tous ceux qui auront paravant
paravant,	esté morts, ressusciteront de la terre,
seront derechef unis	estans derechef l'esprit ioinct et uni
avec les mesmes corps	avec son propre corps
dont l'ame estoit separee:	auquel il a vescu.
Et ceux qui seront vivans	Et quant à ceux qui survivront,

---

22. Actually, the original text reads "iour," a misprint for "Iuge."

a l'heure de cest advenement,	lors ils ne mourront point comme les autres
seront changez	mais seront changez et muez
en un moment	en un iect d'oeil
changez, di-ie, quant a la qualite	
corruptible de leurs corps.	de corruptible en incorruption.

From this point onward, the two confessions differ greatly. Beza's confession goes on to state that the Lord will judge all people according to his Word, but the Belgic Confession refers instead to the people's consciences. Beza's confession continues by speaking about the believers, who will participate in the kingdom of God, not only in their soul but also in their body. This is followed by a brief passage on the evildoers, who will also be immortal and will undergo eternal suffering. The Belgic Confession, on the other hand, adds a section describing the comprehensiveness of the judgment. It goes on to explain that it will be horrifying for the evildoers, but a great consolation for the good and elect. These will see the judgment God brings on those who had persecuted them. The article ends with a description of God's recognition of those who did persevere during the persecution.

In short, in composing article 37, de Brès obviously consulted chapter VI of Beza's confession, for he more or less followed the first part. However, he completely rewrote the second half, particularly emphasizing the consolation the final judgment will bring. This was intended to comfort the believers in the Netherlands who were suffering under persecution.

Concluding Remarks

The preceding survey has shown that the influence of Beza's confession on the Belgic Confession is more pervasive than has been acknowledged up to now. Probably its lengthiest single contribution is found in article 37, while articles 19 and 20 also derived entire sections from this confession. In articles 10, 12, 13, 18, 22, 27, 29 and 33, full sentences from Beza were included. Smaller, isolated expressions were inserted in articles 1, 9, 10, 12, 14, 15, 16, 19 and 28. This means that about seventeen of the thirty-seven articles in the Belgic Confession show smaller or larger traces of Beza's confession.

Overall, however, the Gallican Confession must still be considered as the more influential source for the Belgic Confession. Not only was its structure followed, but a considerable part of its content was also included. Beza's confession was a secondary source. Actually, one gets the impression that Beza's confession was worked into an already existing structure. In other words, Guido de Brès probably wrote an outline for a confession based on the Gallican Confession and then decided to include material from Beza's confession as well. This is why many of Beza's statements were rephrased to fit existing articles.

This may also be the explanation for a remarkable feature in the earliest editions of the Belgic Confession. As has been mentioned before, initially two articles included the word "finally" in their opening statement. Article 36 began with the words "We believe finally," and article 37 used the same words in a different order: "Finally we believe." Article 36 is a reworking of the concluding articles 39 and 40 of the Gallican Confession, although the word "finally" does not occur there. Article 37, on the other hand, is a reworking of chapter VI of Beza's confession, which begins with the expression: "Finally we believe."[23]

A probable solution for the double use of the word "finally" suggests itself on the assumption that Guido de Brès initially made his confession on the basis of the Gallican Confession, adding the word "finally" to its concluding article dealing with the government. While he was still working on his draft, he acquired a copy of Beza's confession and decided to include a good number of ideas and phrases into his concept for a confession. The same confession inspired him to add a whole new final article on the return of the Lord and the last judgment, in which he unwittingly repeated the word "finally."

All of this does not allow us to determine exactly when the Belgic Confession was made. The Gallican Confession was published in 1559, after the Synod of Paris had been closed by the end of May. Beza's confession was published around the same time. The preceding investigation suggests that de Brès began working on his confession for the Dutch churches on the basis of the Gallican Confession, including sections from Beza's confession at a later stage. Since article 37 was obviously added after a first draft for the confession had been made, it is probable that de Brès was only able to consult Beza's confession late in 1560 or even sometime during the spring of 1561.

A second remark concerns de Brès' view on Calvin and Beza. The fact that in making the Belgic Confession he used these two sources indicates that he did not see a fundamental difference between the theological position of these two confessions. He may not have known that Calvin had provided the draft for the confession adopted by the French churches, but Beza's publication came with the name of the author.

It has been argued that at an early date, Reformed theology changed from a pastoral theology in Calvin to a scholastic system determined by election in Beza.[24] When comparing de Brès and Beza, it can be acknowledged that God's decree has

---

23. The final chapter 7 of Beza's confession contains a comparison between Roman Catholic and Protestant doctrines and does not belong to the confession proper. That is the reason why the beginning of chapter 6 was correct in its opening phrase: "Finally we believe . . ."

24. This issue is discussed by Richard A. Muller, "The Myth of 'Decretal Theology,'" *Calvin Theological Journal* 30 no. 1 (1995): 159-67 (esp. 162-63); and more in general in his articles "Calvin and the 'Calvinists': Assessing Continuities and Discontinuities Between the Reformation and Orthodoxy," *Calvin Theological Journal* 30 no. 2 (1995): 345-76 and 31 no. 1 (1996): 125-60.

a more prominent place in Beza's confession. This is particularly striking in the brief first chapter. Here he states that nothing happens by chance and without the very just ordination of God (I, 3). In the next chapter, dealing with the Father as Creator and Preserver, he says that God upholds and governs everything according to his eternal providence (II, 2). In the third chapter, he mentions that the Father has ordained from eternity to unite the Son to the human nature, in order to save his elect by him (III, 2). Later, when Beza is dealing with the creation of man, he states in the title that there should be saved and condemned people, and all for the glory of God. He further adds that there are second causes by which all things come to pass, while maintaining that God ordains what must happen and that there is no sin in God's counsel (III, 5). Guido de Brès does not follow Beza in repeatedly giving prominence to God's counsel and election. However, this is a difference in emphasis, not in theological position. This is evident in the article of the Belgic Confession dealing with providence (art. 12) and the originally much longer article on election (art. 16).

Finally, the question must be considered whether Beza may have seen the Belgic Confession and commented on it. In the previous chapter, a letter was discussed that partly dealt with the Belgic Confession. This letter was written by Calvin on behalf of the Genevan ministers. Since the date of the response has been omitted in the printed version of the response, it is impossible to determine whether Beza belonged to the group of pastors in whose name Calvin wrote the response.

At any rate, it is very likely that Beza saw the Belgic Confession at a later date.[25] In 1566, the synod of the Reformed churches in the Netherlands, meeting in Antwerp, revised their confession. They sent it to the brothers in Geneva so that, after having received their approval, it could be printed.[26] This approval must have been given, for the 1566 edition of the Belgic Confession was printed in Geneva. Because Beza was the moderator of the Genevan pastors from 1564 onward, it can be inferred that he saw the confession and approved its printing. This is telling, for the Dutch churches had made their own confession, which was different from both the Gallican Confession used by the Reformed churches in France and from Beza's confession which was used by the Hungarian church. However, this prevented neither Calvin nor Beza from approving the Belgic Confession as a useful summary of the Reformed doctrine.

---

25. Andrew Pettegree, *Emden and the Dutch Revolt: Exile and the Development of Reformed Protestantism* (Oxford: Clarendon, 1992), 141.

26. Junius, *Opuscula theologica*, 26. For the Latin text, see above chapter 2, footnote 29.

5

The Authority of the Confession

No other issue in connection with the Belgic Confession has been discussed more frequently than its authority. That is understandable, for this, more than anything else, determines its place and function within the Reformed churches from which it originated. Its authority was already in discussion before the Synod of Dort convened in 1618. And the main reason why this international synod was convened was to determine whether the Belgic Confession and the Heidelberg Catechism should serve as the adopted doctrinal statements of the Reformed churches.

The same issue continued to be debated afterwards. It was the impetus for the studies of Ens and Te Water in the eighteenth century.[1] It was the cause of a debate between Van Toorenenbergen and A. Kuyper in the nineteenth century, which began as an exchange in newspapers and continued in pamphlets.[2] In the early twentieth century, Knipscheer contributed to the discussion by publishing a book on the introduction and evaluation of the confessions in the Reformed churches in the Netherlands.[3]

Bakhuizen van den Brink touched only briefly on this issue. On the basis of the letter of Saravia, which has already received attention above, he stated that in its early years the confession did not function as an ecclesiastical document with binding character, but as a confession presented to the government. He did not see the need to spend much time on discussing this issue, for it was obvious that during the early years the confession did not have a binding character. He argued that at the time an

---

1. See in particular the discussion on the term "Forms of Unity" in the introductory chapter of J. Ens, *Kort historisch bericht*, 4-9, and the remark made by his brother in the introduction, x-xi. See also the foreword in W. Te Water, *Tweede eeuw-getyde*, xiv-xvi.

2. Rullmann provided a useful summary of this debate in his *Kuyper-bibliografie* (Kampen: Kok, 1929), 2:1-11. A. Kuyper wrote the brochure, *De Leidsche professoren en de executeurs der Dordtsche nalatenschap* (1879); Van Toorenenbergen responded with *Hoe een deel der Dordtsche nalatenschap verzaakt wordt* (1879), which was evaluated by Kuyper in his study *Revisie der revisie-legende* (1879). According to Rullmann, in this second study Kuyper made use of material prepared by Rutgers (*Kuyper-bibliografie*, 2:4).

3. Frederik S. Knipscheer, *De invoering en de waardering der gereformeerde belijdenisschriften in Nederland voor 1618* (Leiden: A. H. Adriani, 1907).

organized Reformed church did not exist in the Netherlands, as it was still at a preparatory stage.[4]

It is important to note at this point that the question of authority is to be discussed first of all as a historical question. The issue of how the confession functioned in the early years is to be distinguished from the situation today, and is not dependent on today's use of the confession. Churches and their synods have the right to determine how a confession should function in their own time. However, the question of how the confession functioned in the early years is to be resolved on the basis of historical data.

Focusing on the historical aspect of its authority, this chapter will deal with the situation prior to the Synod of Dort, which was convened in 1618. As this international synod met with the express purpose of investigating the confessional statements of the Dutch churches, including the Belgic Confession, discussion in a separate chapter is warranted. In this chapter, however, the period up to the Synod of Dort will be discussed. First, attention will be given to the period from the Synod of Antwerp, 1565, to the Synod of The Hague, 1586, the last national synod prior to the great Synod of Dort. This will be followed by a discussion of Saravia's statements concerning the authority of the confession. Only after this will the data concerning the status of the confession prior to 1565 be investigated. There is a practical reason for this unusual chronology. From 1565 onward, the trail of decisions is rather easy to follow, but the issue of the authority in the very early years of the confession is much more complicated and requires special attention.

Synod of Antwerp, 1565

A synod of the Reformed churches in the Netherlands met in Antwerp on June 10 and 11, 1565. Not much is known about this synod itself, but its decisions were officially recorded. The first decision concerns the Belgic Confession:

> At the beginning of each synod, the confession of faith of the churches in this country shall be read out, both to affirm our unity and to detect whether there is anything to change or to amend.[5]

---

4. Bakhuizen van den Brink, *De Nederlandse belijdenisgeschriften*, 9.

5. Bakhuizen van den Brink, *De Nederlandse belijdenisgeschriften*, 17: "Qu'au commencement de chaque Synode, on ait à faire lecture de la Confession de foy des Eglises de ce païs; tant pour protester de notre union que pour adviser s'il ni a rien à changer ou amender." See also Van Langeraad, *Guido de Bray*, 127. Willem F. Dankbaar incorrectly attributes this decision to Synod 1566; see his *Hoogtepunten uit het Nederlandsche calvinisme in de zestiende eeuw* (Haarlem: H. D. Tjeenk Willink & Zoon, 1946), 17.

This statement has caused some confusion, as can be seen in the way A. Kuyper and Knipscheer dealt with it. Kuyper is not too pleased with it, and he presents several arguments in an attempt to diminish its importance. He expresses agreement with a statement by Hoyer that no other Dutch synod ever made a similar decision, and adds that no other Walloon synod had done that either. The fact that this rule was not taken over by later synods should be taken as an indication that such a statement was soon recognized as untenable. This properly belongs to the period prior to 1565, before the Belgic Confession had been officially adopted. Kuyper adds that this decision was not taken by a national synod, but only by a small, irregular meeting of some Antwerp churches during persecution.[6]

Knipscheer, who wrote a study on the adoption of the Reformed confessions in the Netherlands, distances himself from Kuyper's view. Although Kuyper had correctly noted that the intention of the 1565 decision was different from the decision of the Synod of Dort, 1618-19, he had failed to explain it in its proper context. According to Knipscheer, the statement concerning the confession must be understood against the background of the fact that several confessions were made around the same time. For example, already the next year, Synod Antwerp had ordered another confession to be made which they intended to present at a meeting of the Dutch nobility. According to Knipscheer, it had never been the intention to adopt all articles of this particular confession to the letter. One of the reasons for Synod 1565 to recognize the Belgic Confession was to counter the unwanted influence of several other confessions.[7]

Knipscheer's own reasoning concerning the decision of Synod 1565, however, is as vulnerable as Kuyper's was. The fact that the next year another confession was made at the request of the same churches in no way proves that there was no inclination to accept all articles of the confession adopted in 1565.

Remarkably, both Kuyper and Knipscheer concentrated on the second part of the decision, while neglecting the first part. The regulation begins by stating that the confession is to be read to "affirm our unity." Synod declares that a unity exists between the churches represented at synod and that this unity is expressed in the confession. This shows clearly that the rule refers to the unity in the faith. This is confirmed in the formulation on the title page of the confession itself: "*Confession of faith, made by common accord by the believers who live in the Netherlands.*" This unity was already expressed in the first article of the confession, beginning with the extended introductory formula: "We all believe with the heart and confess with the mouth."

---

6. A. Kuyper, *Revisie der revisie-legende* (Amsterdam: J. H. Kruyt, 1879), 100-105.

7. Knipscheer, *De invoering and de waardering der Gereformeerde belijdenisschriften*, 51-52.

A commentary on the practice of reading out the confession can be found in a statement made by the synod of the French churches in 1603, when they sent a copy of their confession to the Dutch churches:

> As we read it again and profess it at each synod, so we have confirmed it again in the synod of our churches and have held it as valid in the name of all of us; now for the first time with the addition of an article about the Antichrist.[8]

The reading of the confession at synod was a means of expressing and reaffirming doctrinal agreement. The fact that additions and changes could be made to the articles did not undermine the function of the confession as an expression of the unity of faith.

The Diet of Augsburg, 1566

Chronologically the next issue to be investigated is whether the Belgic Confession was submitted to the Diet of Augsburg in 1566. If it could be proven that at this illustrious meeting the confession was presented as an official submission on behalf of the Dutch churches, its authority would be confirmed. This is an issue which has been discussed from an early time. Trigland mentioned that several representatives of the nobility, including Count Lodewijk, a brother of William of Orange, submitted a supplication, which was read out in full session. The count had not merely appealed to the confession of the Reformed churches, he had actually submitted it, together with the supplication and his speech.[9] Trigland does not mention his sources, but this view can be found as early as 1611, in an edition of the Belgic Confession published in Middelburg.[10]

The Dutch historian Van Toorenenbergen came back to this issue in a monograph written on the occasion of the tercentenary of the Belgic Confession. He argued that a copy of the first edition had been presented to emperor Maximilian, supporting this with a statement from the supplication which was presented at that meeting: "we sent this public writing together with this our letter."[11] The expression

---

8. Kuyper, *Revisie der revisie-legende*, 101-2: "Quam ut in singulis Synodis religimus et profitemur, ita in hac ecclesiarum nostrarum Synodo confirmavimus rursus et ratam habuimus omnium nostrorum nomine; addito quoque atque inserto nunc primum articulo de anti-Christo."

9. J. Trigland, *Kerckelycke geschiedenissen*, 146; the text has been printed in the Appendix, Document 9.

10. See Johan J. Van Toorenenbergen, *Eene bladzijde uit de geschiedenis der Nederlandsche geloofsbelijdenis ter gedachtenisviering bij haar eeuwgetijde . . . met de oorspronkelijke beschedien* (Den Haag: M. Nijhoff, [1862]), 17-18.

11. The Latin statement is: "hoc publicum scriptum hisce literis nostris adjunctum animis candidissimis I.M. tuae misimus," which was translated in the Dutch as: "wy hebben uit een vranc ende vry herte, ende oprechte genegentheden, aen uwe Keyserlijcke Majesteyt ghesonden dit

"our letter" can only refer to the supplication itself, and so the question remains what the "public writing" refers to. It is improbable that a confession of faith would be called a public writing. Rather, the statement refers to the address by the Dutch churches directed to the emperor, as Van Langeraad has shown.[12] In support of this identification he pointed to a statement at the beginning of the same supplication, where two submissions are mentioned. Here the hope is expressed that the emperor "will carefully consider what we have explained in this brief address to your Majesty, and this personal letter."[13] This shows that the document does not refer to the confession, but rather to the address to the king and the accompanying personal letter.

We must conclude that there is no indication that the Belgic Confession was ever submitted to Emperor Maximilian at the Diet of Augsburg. The letter to the emperor cannot be used as an argument to bolster the authority of the first edition of the Belgic Confession.

Synod of Antwerp, 1566

The Belgic Confession was revised at the Synod of Antwerp, which was convened in May 1566. This synod met while the persecutions in the Netherlands continued. Haemstede's *Book of Martyrs* recounts the stories of seven martyrs executed in the southern part of the Netherlands during that year. Given the situation, it is understandable that the meetings of Synod Antwerp were held secretly. Although it may be assumed that the normal practice of recording the decisions was continued, no official records have been preserved.

A note in Franciscus Junius' autobiography, published in 1595, provides us with some information concerning the way the synod dealt with the confession. Junius, who was only twenty-one years old when synod met, was designated to act as clerk of this synod. He wrote:

> At this time I sent the confession of the Dutch churches, after it had been revised according to the decision of the synod which had been held at the beginning of May, to the brothers in Geneva, in order that they would allow it to be printed with

---

algemeyn Schrift, vervoecht by desen onsen brief." See Van Toorenenbergen, *Eene bladzijde uit de geschiedenis der Nederlandsche Geloofsbelijdenis*, lxiv, cix.

12. Van Langeraad, *Guido de Bray*, 132.

13. The text was published in Van Toorenenbergen, *Eene bladzijde uit de geschiedenis der Nederlandsche Geloofsbelijdenis*, lix: "quae sperare nos jubet I.M. tuam non tantum hunc conatum nostrum, quem tum brevi hoc oratione eidem inscripta, tum vero privatis hisce literis exponimus bene consulturam." For the Dutch translation, see ci: "dat uwe Keyserlicke Majesteyt, niet alleen niet voor onghoet sal vinden dit ons voornemen, d'welck wy haer, soo door dese corte Redenen ende Vertooch aen haer ghedaen, als by desen besonderen Brief te verstaen gheven."

their approval, and that they would commend this our institution to God in their prayers.[14]

Junius' recollection provides two indications for the authority of the confession. First, he notes that the confession was "revised." Taken by itself, this expression can be understood in two ways. In the literal sense it means that the confession was looked over or reviewed, but in a more extended sense it means that the confession was changed. Junius' statement shows that Synod 1566 had followed up on the decision from the previous year to go over the confession at their yearly synod in order to see whether something needed to be changed.

The second interesting feature of Junius' statement is the fact that the word "institution" is used in connection with the confession. This word has been interpreted differently. Trigland took this as referring to a plan or intention, but Bakhuizen van den Brink translated it in the sense of instruction book.[15] However, this was also a common expression for an ecclesiastical decision,[16] and this meaning suits the present statement. Junius, therefore, referred to an official synodical decision to "revise" the confession. This confirms that the Belgic Confession already had authority within the churches at this time. The fact that synods had the opportunity to make changes to the confession does not take away its official standing in the churches, but rather confirms it.

Knipscheer does not altogether deny this authority, but he qualifies it by referring to the fact that the same Synod of Antwerp that revised the Belgic Confession requested Junius to provide yet another confession that was to consist of Scripture passages. The intention was to use this confession at a meeting of Dutch nobility.[17] In the opinion of Knipscheer, this decision proves that no one had in mind to adopt

---

14. Junius, *Opuscula theologica*, 26: "Quo tempore Confessionem Belgicarum Ecclesiarum de Synodi, quae ineunti Maio habita fuerat, sententia recognitam ad fratres Geneuenses misi, ut à se probatam excudi sinerent, si videretur utile, et institutum illud nostrum Deo precibus commendarent." Brandt was correct when he connected this decision with the second edition, but he incorrectly stated that Junius revised the confession, see his *Historie der reformatie*, 1:254. The text of the decision clearly indicates that the synod made the changes.

15. Trigland, *Kerckelycke geschiedenissen*, 145; Bakhuizen van den Brink translated the word as "leerboek," *De Nederlandse belijdenisgeschriften*, 17.

16. See Albert Blaise, *Dictionnaire Latin-Français des auteurs chrétiens* (Turnhout: Brepols S. A., 1954), s.v. "institution."

17. Knipscheer, *De invoering en waardering der Gereformeerde belijdenisschriften*, 52. The authorship of Junius has been questioned by F. J. Los, as Knipscheer indicates, 38 n. 1. This criticism is justified, for Junius stated in his autobiography: "Post Antuerpiam redij, ubi Synodus sub finem mensis eiusdem habebatur. In ea [read: eo] brevi scripto de fide ex disertis Scripturae verbis exarato, placuit ut duo ex nobis Centronum opidum (S. Trudonis vocant) peterimus, ubi principum aliquot ac Nobilitatis Belgicae conventus inductus" (*Opuscula theologica*, 26). Junius does not say that he made this confession, but that he together with someone else delivered it.

all the articles of the Belgic Confession according to the letter, and to follow it even to the "manner of speaking" as was required at a later date.

This reasoning is not convincing. Synod wanted a confession made consisting of passages from Scripture for the specific purpose of persuading the nobility of the scriptural basis of the Protestant position. This statement did not have any ecclesiastical purpose, nor did any synod give it ecclesiastical status. As biblical statements, they could stand by themselves. The decision concerning the confession for the nobility cannot be used to qualify the authority of the Belgic Confession, which had already been acknowledged one year ago during the previous Synod of Antwerp.

Actually, the fact that Synod 1566 made the effort to revise the confession is an indication that the Reformed churches wanted their faith to be expressed as clearly as possible. Trigland pointed out that this synod met during the Diet of Augsburg.[18] The members of synod may have seen a glimmer of hope that this diet would lead to more freedom of religion in the Netherlands, and for that reason decided to check over their confession carefully. At any rate, the fact that the confession was revised in 1566 does not weaken its authority. Rather, this event strengthens the position of the Belgic Confession. For the very reason that the confession had authority in the churches, it was synod itself which oversaw the revision.

Convent of Wesel, 1568

The name by which this meeting is known is indicative of its character. This was not a synod with the authority to make decisions concerning ecclesiastical matters, it was a meeting of ministers who came together in Wesel in Germany, in preparation of organizing the churches in the Netherlands. At the very beginning of the statement produced by this meeting, they declare that in their judgment a number of regulations are necessary or useful for their churches.[19]

Doctrinal issues are discussed in the chapter on the ministers and theological teachers. The second of four rules concerning doctrine mentions the confession:

Further, he shall be asked whether he agrees in everything with that doctrine which is maintained publicly in the church, according to the [statements] first submitted to the king of France by the ministers of the churches in that kingdom, which later, translated in the vernacular, was addressed and presented to the king of Spain and

---

18. Trigland, *Kerckelycke geschiedenissen*, 145.

19. See Petrus Biesterveld and Herman H. Kuyper, preface to *Kerkelijk handboekje, bevattende de bepalingen der Nederlandsche synoden . . .* (Kampen: Bos, 1905), xix. Trigland noted that at this meeting preparations were made for the time the churches in the Netherlands would be free; see the marginal statement in *Kerckelycke geschiedenissen*, 161.

the other magistrates in lower Germany, and which are finally also contained in the catechism.[20]

It is remarkable that the Belgic Confession is presented here as a translation of the Gallican Confession. As shown in our chapter 3, the Belgic Confession does follow the earlier Gallican Confession, but it is decidedly not a translation. However, the identification is not in doubt, for the rule refers to the confession which was offered to the king of Spain and the magistrates of the Netherlands. This can only be the Belgic Confession which was published with an address to the king and another one to the Dutch magistrates.

According to this regulation, the Belgic Confession has an authority similar to that of the Gallican Confession and the Heidelberg Catechism. As result, all those who teach in the church must agree in every respect with the doctrine expressed there.

What does Knipscheer make of this decision? He points out that the decisions of this synod are overall very mild, noting that Gaspar Van der Heyden and even the more abrasive Petrus Dathenus held some moderate views. This evidence is used to support his conclusion that the proponents of subscription to the confession did not see this subscription as threatening the free development of personal views of the believers.[21] It must be noted, however, that Knipscheer fails to discuss the decision of the Convent of Wesel itself. A careful look at the statement given above clearly shows that the Belgic Confession, together with two other doctrinal statements, is presented as a standard for the teaching in the church. The ministers present at this meeting determined that agreement with the Belgic Confession was to be a prerequisite for admission to the public ministry in the churches.

Synod of Emden, 1571

When another meeting was to be convened in 1571, it was still not safe to meet in the Netherlands. As a result, the delegates met in Emden, Germany, which had long been a safe haven for the Reformed from the Netherlands. However, the

---

20. Frederik L. Rutgers, ed., *Acta van de Nederlandsche synoden der zestiende eeuw* (1899; reprint, Dordrecht: J. P. Van den Tol, 1980), 14-15: "Deinde quaeratur ecquid per omnia consentiat cum ea doctrina quae in ecclesia publicè retinetus secundum ea quae Confessione fidei primum Galliarum Regi per ecclesiarum illius regni ministros oblata, deinde etiam in vernaculam linguam conversa Hispaniarum regi, coeterisque inferioris Germaniae magistratibus inscripta exhibitaque fuit, denique etiam Catechesi continentur." A Dutch translation can be found in Biesterveld and Kuyper, *Kerkelijk handboekje*, 7-8.

21. Knipscheer, *De invoering en waardering der Gereformeerde belijdenisschriften*, 53, 60.

meeting in Emden was not an unofficial meeting of ministers but, as the introduction of the Acts states, "a synod of the Dutch churches which are under the cross."[22]

This synod made several regulations regarding the confession. The first concerns the members of the synod itself: "To testify of the agreement in doctrine within the Dutch churches, it was resolved by the brothers to subscribe to the confession of the Dutch churches."[23] Added to this was a resolution to subscribe also to the Gallican Confession, in order to testify to their allegiance and connection with the French churches. The hope was expressed that the French churches would in turn subscribe to the Belgic Confession to witness mutually of their agreement.[24] As to the purpose of the subscription, the quotation shows that it was done to express consent with the doctrine. The Belgic Confession is here used as an expression of the unity of faith.

Knipscheer again qualifies this decision by pointing out that some members of this synod had brought up objections to a binding confession, because they were afraid of creating another papal system. But he also mentions that these people were persuaded to subscribe to the confession.[25] This incident does actually indicate that the Synod of Emden maintained the authority of the confession which had already been determined at Wesel.

The fact that the confession was used as a basic statement of faith can be confirmed from another decision by the same synod:

> Also the Dutch ministers who are absent from this meeting will be urged to consent to the same subscription. The same [rule] will be maintained for all others who in the future will be called to the ministry of the Word, before they enter the ministry.[26]

In this regulation, the decision to require subscription is extended to include both the ministers not present in Emden and also the future ministers. These regulations had a far reaching significance for the Dutch churches. They determined that these

---

22. The Acts of this synod can be found in Rutgers, *Acta van de Nederlandsche synoden*, 55; and in the edition by J. F. Gerhard Goeters, *Die Akten der Niederländischen Kirchen zu Emden vom 4.-13. Oktober 1571* (Neukirchen: Neukirchener Verlag, 1971), 14.

23. Goeters, *Die Akten der Niederländischen Kirchen zu Emden*, 14: "Ad testandum in doctrina inter ecclesias Belgicas consensum, visum est fratribus confessioni ecclesiarum Belgicarum subscribere." For this meaning of "visum est," see *Oxford Latin Dictionary*, s.v. "video," sub 24.

24. Goeters, *Die Akten der Niederländischen Kirchen zu Emden*, 14.

25. Knipscheer, *De invoering en de waardering der Gereformeerde belijdenisschriften*, 62-63.

26. Goeters, *Die Akten der Niederländischen Kirchen zu Emden*, 16: "Admonebuntur quoque ministri Belgici, qui ab hoc coetu absunt, ut in eandem subscriptionem consentiant. Idem et ab aliis omnibus praestabitur, qui in posterum ad ministerium verbi vocabuntur, antequam ministerium exercere incipiant."

churches would be confessionally Reformed.[27] The authority of the confession, already stated in the meeting at Wesel, 1568, was therefore confirmed at Emden in 1571.[28]

Provincial Synod of Dort, 1574

Following the two ecclesiastical meetings which had to be convened outside of the country, this was the first meeting in the Netherlands itself. Delegates from classes in the provinces of South Holland and Zeeland met for a two-week period in June 1574. Classis Walcheren brought the confession on the agenda with the following question:

> [It was asked] whether the Belgic Confession shall be examined and be made similar to the recently published French edition of Master Beza, and after having it translated by someone in Latin, have all ministers in the Netherlands subscribe to it.[29]

This question must be understood against the background of the fact that a revised French language edition had been published in Geneva in 1566, which was incorrectly attributed to Beza.[30] At that time, the Dutch editions did not yet include the changes made in the French text. The synod made the following decision: "One shall leave the Dutch confession of faith for certain reasons as it is. If some words need to be changed after the copy printed in Geneva, one should wait for the general synod."[31]

---

27. Jan Plomp, "De kerkorde van Emden," in D. Nauta et al., eds., *De synode van Emden oktober 1571* (Kampen: Kok, 1971), 97.

28. An evaluation of the relationship between the Synods of Wesel and Emden can be found in "Wezel (1568) en Emden (1571)," in D. Nauta, ed., *Opera minora: kerkhistorische verhandelingen over Calvijn en de geschiedenis van de kerk in Nederland* (Kampen: J. H. Kok, 1961), 53-56. This article can also be found in *Nederlands archief voor kerkgeschiedenis* 36 (1949): 220-46.

29. Rutgers, *Acta van de Nederlandsche synoden*, 212: "Oftmen de nederlandtsche confessie zal examineren ende de Fransche editie van Domino Beza laestmael uytgegaen ghelyckformich maeken daer naer de zelue door yemant inde Latynsche spraeke doen ouersetten ende alle dienaers der nederlantsche natie doen onderteeckenen."

30. For more about this revision, see chapter 6.

31. The text can be found in Rutgers, *Acta van de Nederlandsche Synoden*, 141: "Men sal de Nederlandsche belijdinghe des gheloofs om seeckere oorsaecken laten als sij is, ende soo daer eenighe woorden in te veranderen waren na het exemplair tot Geneuen ghedruckt, salmen wachten tot op den Sijnodum generalem." It is incomprehensible that Bakhuizen van den Brink wrote that we do not know how synod responded (*De Nederlandse belijdenisgeschriften*, 20).

Knipscheer agrees with this decision not to revise the confession, for the reason that, in his opinion, making changes would spoil this historical document.[32] However, this provincial synod itself gave a different reason for its refusal to update the Dutch text after the revised French edition. It did not object to revision as such, but it declared itself incompetent to take this on, as such a task rightfully should be undertaken by a general synod. This decision of the regional synod actually implies official recognition of the Belgic Confession, for the only proper way of changing the confession is by dealing with it at the level of a national synod.

The authority of the Belgic Confession can also be seen in several other decisions made by this provincial synod. It stipulated that, following their ordination, the elders and deacons should subscribe to the confession and the articles of discipline.[33] This means that subscription is extended to all those who have an office in the church. A similar decision was made concerning those ministers who were active in the churches without having been examined, officially called, or ordained. Synod decided that these pastors should be examined as if they had never served in a church, and, if found able to serve in the ministry, they should be "made to subscribe to the confession and the articles."[34] These decisions concerning elders and deacons, as well as unordained ministers, show that the Belgic Confession was to be used as the standard for the teaching in the Reformed churches.

National Synod of Dort, 1578

This synod is important for the Belgic Confession for the reason that it combined in one statement the decisions made previously concerning the confession. It first determined in general terms that in the churches in the Netherlands the Belgic Confession would be subscribed to in order to express unity in doctrine. Synod went on to specify to whom this applies: "As this shall be done by the ministers of the Word and the professors in theology, it also would be good that the same is done by the elders."[35]

The most remarkable aspect of this summary is the fact that the deacons are not included among those who have to express agreement with the Belgic Confession.

---

32. Knipscheer, *De invoering en de waardering der Gereformeerde belijdenisschriften*, 67.

33. Rutgers, *Acta van de Nederlandsche synoden*, 155.

34. Rutgers, *Acta van de Nederlandsche synoden*, 159-60. The "articles" referred to probably are the articles of the regional synod, as can be seen in the decision of June 16; see 134.

35. Rutgers, *Acta van de Nederlandsche synoden*, 247: "Om eendrachticheyt in der Leere te betuyghen achten wy datmen in allen Kercken der Nederlanden de belydenisse des gheloofs in seuen en dertich artykelen begrepen in dit Iaer 1578 herdruckt, ende den Coninck Philippo ouer vele iaren ouerghegheuen onderschryuen sal. Ende ghelyck dit van den Dienaren des woordts ende Professoren der Theologie ghedaen sal worden, soo ware oock goet dat het selfde van den Ouderlinghen gheschiedde."

This is all the more striking in view of the decision of Armentières 1562, which will be discussed later.

National Synod of Middelburg, 1581

Knipscheer uses several statements made by this synod to prove that the Belgic Confession was hardly known, let alone that it would have authority. He provides three arguments in support of his opinion.[36] First of all, he points out that some ministers at Synod Middelburg had asked: "What is this confession of 37 articles?" Further, synod had admitted that the Dutch copy of the confession had not been translated very clearly nor printed correctly. Moreover, synod itself had decided that ministers, elders, deacons, professors in theology, and schoolteachers should subscribe to the Belgic Confession. Knipscheer elaborates on this last point, arguing that this decision to demand subscription actually refers to some time in the future when a correctly translated and revised edition of the confession would be available.

This interpretation is questionable. One can begin by considering the actual text of the decision of Synod Middelburg:

> The Ministers of the Word, Elders and Deacons, and also the Professors in Theology (which is also proper for the other Professors) and the Schoolteachers shall subscribe to the confession of faith of the Dutch Churches.[37]

Taken in isolation, it is indeed possible to argue, as Knipscheer does, that the words "shall subscribe" refer to the future. However, in a synodical regulation it is more probable that the future tense is used to state a rule.

This is supported by the context of this decision. The quoted statement actually belongs to Middelburg's Church Order and can be found in the section dealing with doctrine and sacraments. The article that follows it declares that no one shall publish a book on religion before it has been seen and approved by ministers from his region or by the professors. This is followed by an article dealing with infant baptism, which states that the covenant of God shall be sealed with baptism to children of baptized Christians, as soon as they can be baptized. There is no indication that these articles present future wishes. Rather, these decisions, as well as the one concerning subscription, regulate current practices in the Reformed churches.

---

36. For the following, see Knipscheer, *De invoering en waardering der Gereformeerde belijdenisschriften*, 68-69.

37. The text can be found in Rutgers, *Acta van de Nederlandsche synoden*, 390: "De Dienaers des Woordts, Ouderlinghen ende Diaconen, item de Professeurs inder Theologie (twelck oock den anderen Professoren wel betaemt) ende de Schoolmeesters sullen de Belijdenisse des gheloofs der Nederlandtschen Kercken onderteijckenen."

This rule concerning subscription to the confession can be explained further against the background of a request mentioned by Knipscheer. The churches in the province of Brabant had asked synod to identify the 37 articles to which the ministers, elders and deacons had to subscribe.[38] The question was not so much whether the articles should be signed, but which articles needed to be signed. Synod responded by stating that they were the same ones that formerly had been submitted by the Dutch churches to King Philip.[39]

The reason why this came up may have been a problem with the printing of the confession, for the same decision notes:

> And since these [37 articles] have been very badly printed, Daniel de Dieu has been charged with translating these articles from the French into the Dutch. Then they will be printed, after having been checked over by classis Brabant.[40]

At first glance, it is not clear what this regulation means. If the text was badly printed, a better edition would be needed rather than a new translation. We will have to come back to this issue in the chapter dealing with the translations of the confession. At this point it is important to note, over against Knipscheer, that the issue discussed during Synod Middelburg did not concern the authority of the confession, but rather problems in the Dutch translation.

The national Synod of Middelburg, 1581, decided that a corrected version of the Belgic Confession should be made. This version, needed in order to maintain faithful subscription to the confession, was published in 1582. It can be concluded that the way this synod dealt with the Belgic Confession underlines the authority that had already been established.

National Synod of The Hague, 1586

The Belgic Confession was again on the agenda of the next synod, held in The Hague. This was the last national synod before the Synod of Dort was convened in 1618. In the list of the issues that the churches brought before synod, the confession is mentioned twice. The first occurrence follows the observation that it is not sufficient for the church to make good rules:

---

38. Rutgers, *Acta van de Nederlandsche synoden*, 420.

39. The whole decision reads: "Op de vraeghe, welck de 37 artijckelen zyn, die byden Predicanten, Ouderlynghen ende Diaconen onderteeckent moeten worden? Is gheandwoordt dat het selue syn, *Die eertijts bij de Neder-landtsche kercken den Conynck Philips ouerghegeuen syn.* Ende ouermidts de selue seer misdruct syn, is Daniel de Dieu last ghegeuen, de selue artijckelen wt den Françoijschen in Nederduijtsche sprake ouer te setten, Om daer naer vande Brabandtsche Classe ouersien, ghedruct te worden." See Rutgers, *Acta van de Nederlandsche synoden*, 443-44 (italics in the original).

40. The text was given above, in footnote 39.

[R]ather, also means should be devised by which everyone would be obliged in an ecclesiastical way to maintain these, in order that thus by the uniformity of the pure doctrine, ceremonies and church government, according to the Word of the Lord, the Christian catechism and the confession of the 37 articles of the Dutch churches, God's honor may be furthered and the kingdom of Jesus Christ may be extended everywhere in the Netherlands.[41]

This statement emphasizes the need for the churches to maintain the church order for the purpose of unity in the doctrine. In that context, the Belgic Confession is mentioned as one of the means to achieve this unity of the faith. The request does not ask for adoption of the confession, but takes for granted that it has already been adopted.

The second request, too, mentions the need for maintaining the confession, but in addition it is concerned about its text:

It is also desired that from now on the 37 articles mentioned before are not only printed uniformly without addition or deletion, but are also subscribed to by all who serve in churches and schools, for the maintaining of the pure doctrine against all sects.[42]

The churches desire a uniform text, for the purpose of maintaining the unity in the doctrine.

The summary of the decisions taken during the final session of the synod provides further information concerning the confession. It contains a request to the government to have the Church Order printed, together with the Liturgical Forms and the 37 articles, in order that these would be maintained everywhere.[43] This is clearly in response to the request that synod provide a good edition of the important

---

41. Rutgers, *Acta van de Nederlandsche synoden*, 541: " . . . maer datmen oock middelen raeme waer door op Kerckelicke wijse een ieglick tot onderhoudinge derselve gehouden werde, op dat alsoo door de ghelijckformicheijt der suijvere leere, ceremonien ende kerckenregieringe, volgende 's Heeren woordt, den Christelicken Catechismus ende de confessie der 37 artickelen der Nederlantsche Ghemeijnten, Godes eere ghevordert ende het Rijcke Iesu Christi al omme in dese Nederlanden verbreijdet mach werden."

42. Rutgers, *Acta van de Nederlandsche synoden*, 543: "Wort oock begheert dat de boven verhaelde 37 Artickelen niet alleene voortaen eenformelick sonder daertoe oft aftedoen, gedruckt worden, maer oock onderteekent worden bij allen Kercken ende Schooldienaren, tot onderhoudinge der suijvere leere teghen all Secten."

43. Rutgers, *Acta van de Nederlandsche synoden*, 619: " . . . ende versocht hebbende 't advijs van sijn Excell. op de Kercken-ordeninge voorss., hebben gherelateerdt aan de Synoode, datt sijn Excell. een ghoedt behaaghen hadde aan de selve, ende begheerde die te communiceeren mett den Heeren Staaten, ende volghens, die te laaten drucken, mitsgaaders de formulieren daar bij, ende de XXVII [read: XXXVII] Artijckelen, t'en eijnde die ooverall onderhouden werden."

documents of the church. Noteworthy is the additional request that some copies, with an accompanying letter, be sent to the queen of England.

A final piece of information is found in the letter synod decided to send to the classes, urging them to maintain the church order:

> First of all, you shall take good care that every minister among you who may not have done so yet, subscribe to the confession of faith of the Dutch churches, contained in 37 articles and reprinted in 1582, as a token of the concord in the doctrine of the truth with all faithful churches.[44]

The same letter also requires the ministers to subscribe specifically to the revised church order.

Knipscheer also deals with the statements of this synod, remarking that the fact that not all ministers had subscribed is indicative of opposition to the confession. He refers to the way synod itself dealt with Caspar Coolhaes and Herman Herberts. We can only discuss their cases in as far as they pertain to the authority of the Belgic Confession. The question to be considered is whether the decisions synod made in connection with these ministers in any way indicate that the authority of the confession was qualified or diminished.

To begin with Coolhaes, he was a prolific author, who had published six books in the years prior to synod.[45] He submitted a statement declaring that he considers as retracted everything in his writings that could be found in disagreement with the confession. He wanted it to be known that his books should be interpreted "in agreement with the declaration he made yesterday concerning the 37 articles of the common confession of these lands, with the exception of the issue of reprobation given in article 16."[46] In his own declaration on election and reprobation, Coolhaes states that those who are saved are not saved because of their own merit, but only by the grace of God who works the good will in the elect. Those who are lost are lost because of their own fault; God is not the cause of this.[47] It is unclear how

---

44. Rutgers, *Acta van de Nederlandsche synoden*, 620-21: "Voor allen sullen u l[ieden] goede achtinge daerop nemen, dat een ijgelick Dienaer onder u lieden die tselve tot noch toe niet gedaen en soude mogen hebben de Bekentenisse des geloofs der Nederlantschen kercken vervatet in 37 artijckelen, ende anno 82 herdruckt onderschrijve tot een teecken der eendrachticheit met allen wel gevoelenden kercken inde leere der Waerheit."

45. For a brief survey of Coolhaes' life, see the articles by Gerrit P. Van Itterzon, in *Christelijke Encyclopedie*, 2:296-98; and by Nijenhuis, in *BLGNP*, 4:100-102. For Coolhaes' objections and a list of his books, see Jakob Kamphuis, *Kerkelijke besluitvaardigheid* (Groningen: De Vuurbaak, 1970), 14-18, 83-84.

46. Rutgers, *Acta van de Nederlandsche synoden*, 560.

47. Rutgers, *Acta van de Nederlandsche synoden*, 561. Rutgers also mentions that on this declaration, Coolhaes was received as a member, not as a minister (560).

Knipscheer could conclude that this resolution would diminish the authority of the confession.

The second case concerned Herberts, the minister of Gouda, who did not feel bound to the confession and the catechism. Although he had stated agreement with these documents in 1582, he had never subscribed to them.[48] Later, new problems arose, particularly in connection with the teaching of article 16 of the Belgic Confession and answer 114 of the Heidelberg Catechism. Synod 1586 dealt with this issue and came up with a formula of agreement to which Herberts subscribed. The statement concerning the Belgic Confession was:

> He accepts as scriptural the general confession of faith, contained in 37 articles, and he is willing to subscribe to it with the other brothers at the next meeting of classis, provided it is understood that in article 16, dealing with predestination, God is not the cause of sin.

Herberts did subscribe to the confession, although he only did so after the letter to the king of Spain had been removed from this particular copy of the confession, because Herberts did not think the king had the right to judge doctrinal issues.[49]

These two cases indicate that the confession of election and reprobation was a thorny issue already many years before the Synod of Dort had to deal with it. At the same time, they prove that the Belgic Confession was functioning as a rule for doctrinal unity. The confession did not have a merely formal authority, but was maintained as a doctrinal standard within the Reformed Churches in the Netherlands.[50]

Saravia

In this context, Saravia deserves further attention. This theologian is not only the most important source for the early history of the Belgic Confession, but he was also actually involved in the problems with Herman Herberts concerning the ecclesiastical position of the confession. His biographer Nijenhuis used the events at Synod 1586 to argue that Saravia had a less strict view on the confession and its

---

48. De Groot, "Herman Herberts," in *BLGNP*, 3:178-81.

49. The text of this agreement can be found in Trigland, *Kerckelycke geschiedenissen*, 217; cf. Rutgers, *Acta van de Nederlandsche synoden*, 559. This issue is also discussed by Knipscheer, *De invoering en waardeering der Gereformeerde belijdenisschriften*, 75.

50. H. H. Kuyper provides information about subscription to the confession on a provincial level in *De post-acta of nahandelingen van de nationale synode van Dordrecht* (Amsterdam: Höviker & Wormser, 1899), 132-34 .

subscription than was prevalent in the seventeenth century.[51] Another reason for dealing with Saravia here is that in his crucial letter of 1612, addressed to Uytenbogaert, he also discussed the authority of the Belgic Confession. Bakhuizen van den Brink, going beyond Nijenhuis, suggested that the real intention of this letter was to show that the confession was not an ecclesiastical and, as such, binding document, but rather a confession for the government.[52]

What is known about Saravia's contribution at Synod 1586 hardly supports the idea that he was less strict on maintaining the confession. Following the discussion of Herberts' view, in which Saravia played an important role, an agreement was reached on a number of regulations. As already mentioned, Herberts was to subscribe to the confession with the proviso that it does not teach that God is the cause of sin. In addition, Herberts was to declare that he accepted the Heidelberg Catechism, with the understanding that a sentence in answer 114 stating that in this life even the holiest have only a small beginning of the required obedience, would be understood in comparison to the obedience they will have in eternal life. Further, since some issues in his book were formulated in a way that was unsuitable, unclear, and in need of further explanation, Herberts promised that he would publish a statement on them after having submitted it to several theologians, including Saravia. He also expressed regret that in his book he had accused fellow ministers unjustly. He promised to stay in agreement with all ministers of the Word of God, to seek reconciliation with his fellow ministers at ecclesiastical meetings and maintain concord with them.[53]

These regulations do not in any way indicate a weakening of the confession's authority. Rather, it was Herberts' views concerning the Belgic Confession and the Heidelberg Catechism that were subjected to regulations. He also had to clarify certain statements he had made in his book and to seek reconciliation. Obviously, synod's decision concerning Herberts restricted his teaching. An indirect confirmation of this is the fact that he did not adhere to the agreement. His excuse was that he had never received the points on which he had to give further explanation, which were to have come from Saravia.[54] This is a questionable excuse, considering the fact that his signature is the first under the written copy of the agreement.[55] However that may be, the case of Herberts cannot be used to attribute to Saravia a tendency to weaken the authority of the confession. Rather, it shows

---

51. Nijenhuis, *Adrianus Saravia*, 75.
52. Bakhuizen van den Brink, *De Nederlandse Geloofsbelijdenis*, 9.
53. Trigland, *Kerckelycke geschiedenissen*, 218.
54. Nijenhuis, *Adrianus Saravia*, 74.
55. The copy was quoted by Trigland in *Kerckelycke geschiedenissen*, 218.

how, in this specific situation, its authority was maintained with the support of Saravia.[56]

This requires us to take a careful look at Saravia's opinions as expressed in his letter to Uytenbogaert in 1612. We will concentrate on the section in which he discusses the authority of the confession at some length. It opens with a reference to the "Leiden debates." Since Saravia is obviously referring to a recent occurrence, he probably had in mind the disagreement surrounding the appointment of Vorstius as a professor at the University of Leiden, for this theologian had caused considerable debate with the publication of his book on God's attributes in 1610.[57] It is in this context that Saravia refers to the Belgic Confession and the Heidelberg Catechism:

> I see that in the debates in Leiden, this confession of faith and the catechism are invoked and pushed forward as if it were the very Word of God. Unreasonable persons rashly despise the Augsburg Confession, and those who want to be regarded as more moderate require that there is something in it they want changed. However, in their own confession they do not allow anything to be changed, as if it were the Canon of faith.[58]

Saravia expresses disagreement with people who treat the confession as if it has the same authority as the Bible. Indirectly, he acknowledged that, different from the Scriptures, the confessions can be changed. In other words, he maintains the distinction between Scripture and the confession as expressed in article 7 of the Belgic Confession itself. But nothing in his statement implies rejection or weakening of the authority of the confession.

This is followed by a historical note on the confession including the important information that Guido de Brès was its author, which has already been discussed. Making the transition from the historical background to the character of the confession, Saravia continues:

> But before it was published, [Guido de Brès] showed it to those Ministers of the Word of God he could reach, and offered to change, add, or delete whatever displeased them, in order to [ensure] it would not be seen as the work of one person. But none of those who were involved ever thought to publish it as the rule of faith, but to prove their faith from the Canonical Scripture.

---

56. Saravia's lengthy defense of the Reformed doctrine against Coornhert could also be mentioned here. In this debate, Saravia was the spokesman on the side of the Reformed ministers; see Nijenhuis, *Adrianus Saravia*, 85-91.

57. On Vorstius, see Cornelis Van der Woude's article in *BLGNP*, 1:407-10. The doctrinal issue is briefly discussed in N. H. Gootjes, *De geestelijkheid van God* (Franeker: T. Wever, 1984), 53-56.

58. The original text of this and the following quotations from Saravia's letter can be found in Appendix, Document 6.

Responding to those who did not want any change in the Belgic Confession, Saravia referred to the fact that the author of the confession himself was willing to make changes. In his statement, Saravia maintains Scripture as the only infallible rule for the faith. But nowhere does he state or imply that the Belgic Confession should not have any authority within the churches. The following statement confirms this interpretation:

> Nevertheless, in my opinion there is nothing in this [confession] which I would disapprove or want to change. If there are some for whom not all things are acceptable, they should, in my opinion, be heard, and they should be taught from the Word of God if what they find fault with is in agreement with the Word of God. No one who is willing to be instructed should rashly be counted among the unbelievers.

Saravia, obviously, does not share the opinion of the Remonstrants that the Belgic Confession contains unbiblical teaching. However, he does allow for people who would have problems in connection with the confession. In that case, they need further instruction from Scripture. In other words, such people should not be censured or dismissed quickly but first of all be taught the biblical doctrine.

This is followed by another passage that has sometimes been used to defend the claim that the confession at that time did not have a binding character:

> The articles do not all have the same weight. Possibly there are some, if some persons would disagree with these, they must be tolerated, and not for that reason be removed from the church. I have the same opinion concerning your catechisms, which I myself have taught in French as well as in Dutch churches. I disagree with these on the explanation of Christ's descent into hell.

Saravia goes on to explain that he has changed his understanding of the meaning of Christ's descent into hell, now following the view of the bishop of Winton rather than the interpretation of Calvin and Beza. He adds that he has written two books, yet unpublished, about this issue. Since these books do not occur in Saravia's bibliography, it appears that they were never published. As far as the Belgic Confession is concerned, Saravia's problems focused on the articles dealing with church government. He disagreed with the presbyterian system with its emphasis on the equality of the ministers as expressed in article 31 of the confession, preferring the episcopalian system.[59]

However, the letter does not contain any indication that Saravia did not acknowledge the authority of the confession as such. Although mentioning a

---

59. Nijenhuis, *Adrianus Saravia*, 222-37.

qualification on one specific issue each in the Belgic Confession and the Heidelberg Catechism, he maintained both as a rule for the teaching of the church. The qualification itself shows how in his opinion people who have problems with specific statements in the confession should be treated. They should be taught, and in some cases it should be possible to have a different interpretation of a creedal statement. But this does not undermine the authority of the confession. Rather, during the whole discussion he maintained it.

An indirect confirmation of this interpretation of Saravia's letter is the fact that it was never published by the Remonstrants during the height of their debate with the Reformed. The letter was written in 1612 in response to questions he had received, but Uytenbogaert, who was the original addressee, never published it during the doctrinal debates leading up to the Synod of Dort. As noted in our first chapter, the Remonstrants quoted from the letter what suited them, but they did not make public the whole letter. They did not even let it be known that it had been addressed to one of their leaders. In fact, it was not published until fifty years afterwards. This reticence is understandable, for on the crucial issue of the authority of the confession Saravia had not stated what the Remonstrants wanted to hear. Concerning the content of the confession, he had made it very clear that there was nothing he did not support, with the exception of one issue that was not in discussion between the Reformed and the Remonstrants.

Before 1565

The question of the authority of the confession prior to 1565 brings us to a confusing period in the history of a church suffering under persecution. It has been known for a long time that a provincial synod in 1563 made a decision concerning the Belgic Confession. This meeting was generally referred to as the Provincial Synod of Armentières.[60] The decision is remarkable both for what it does and does not stipulate:

> In places where the order of the church has not yet been established, the deacons as well as the elders will be elected by the general vote of all the people together with their pastors, but where the discipline has already been established, they will be elected to the council of the church together with the ministers and the deacons. They will be charged with their task, and they will sign the confession of faith adopted among us. Afterwards, they will be presented to the people, and if there is

---

60. Nicolaas C. Kist, "Synoden der Nederlandsch Hervormde Kerken onder het kruis," *Archief voor geschiedenis, inzonderheid van Nederland* 10 (1837): 152; Cornelis Hooyer, *Oude kerkordeningen der Nederlandsche Hervormde gemeenten (1563-1638) . . . Verzameld en met inleidingen voorzien* (Zaltbommel: Noman, 1865), 4; Van Langeraad, *Guido de Bray*, 122-23.

opposition, the issue will be discussed and examined by the consistory, and if they cannot come to an agreement, it will be transferred to the Provincial Meeting.[61]

It is noteworthy that synod did not discuss the content or the adoption of the confession itself. Rather, the rule concerns subscription to the confession that has already been adopted, in order to ensure that the elders and deacons fulfil their office in agreement with it. The formulation shows that the confession had already received the status of doctrinal rule in the churches, and in that context stipulates that office bearers must officially state agreement with it. This decision implies that the Belgic Confession was established in the Dutch churches before this synod made this statement.[62]

More must be said about this synod. The passage quoted above forms part of the decision made by a synod known as the Provincial Synod of "Bouton," which was the pseudonym for Armentières. It was therefore taken as a decision valid only in a limited area of Belgium.[63] Moreau, however, investigated the records of the synods in Belgium in 1563 and came to a different conclusion.[64] At first glance the records seem to suggest that five different synods were convened in 1563, although the later custom was to have two meetings annually. However, Moreau noted that three of the 1563 synods appear to have met on the same date (April 26), but in three different locations (Teur, Doornik and Armentières). A comparison of the records brought to light that many similar decisions were taken on that day. This led Moreau to conclude that these three documents actually contain the records of the same meeting, and that each report was made independently by a delegate from the area they represented. The synod itself was presumably held in Antwerp.[65]

Based on these data, the intriguing conclusion must be drawn that the Belgic Confession had already received official status in the southern part of the

---

61. Hooyer, *Oude kerkordeningen*, 12: "Es lieux où l'ordre de l'Eglise n'est point encore dressé, tant les Diacres que les Anciens seront esleus par la voix commune de tout le peuple avec leurs Pasteurs, mais où la discipline sera desja dressée seront esleus au Senat de l'Eglise avec les Ministres et les Diacres, ausquels on dira leur charge, et signeront la confession de foy arrestée entre nous, puis seront presentez au peuple, et s'il y a opposition, la cause sera debatue et vuidée au Consistoire, et s'ils ne se peuvent accorder sera renvoyée au Concile provincial."

62. Kist does not say enough when he remarks that the confession at least since 1563 was used and had authority ("Synoden der Nederlandsch Hervormde kerken," 152).

63. Van Langeraad, *Guido de Bray*, 123; Doede Nauta, *Hoogtepunten uit het Nederlandsche calvinisme* (Franeker: Wever, 1949), 17.

64. See Gérard Moreau, "Les synodes des églises Wallonnes des Pays-Bas en 1563," *Nederlands archief voor kerkgeschiedenis* 46 (1965-66). Bakhuizen van den Brink apparently missed this, for he states that the Belgic Confession did not have ecclesiastical authority in the early years, for the reason that at the time an organized Dutch Reformed church did not yet exist; see his *De Nederlandse belijdenisgeschriften*, 9.

65. Moreau, "Les Synodes des Églises Wallonnes," 10.

Netherlands prior to this ecclesiastical meeting of April 1563. Braekman has argued that there are several indications that a synod was convened in Antwerp in 1562.[66] The agenda of this synod is not known, but one of the issues to be discussed concerned the question of whether believers were allowed to resist a government that did not allow them to live as believers. No record concerning the Belgic Confession exists, but the possibility that the confession was adopted cannot be excluded.

There are, however, two indications that the confession may have been adopted even earlier. The first is found in a statement in the well-known letter by Saravia: "But before it [the confession] was published, he [Guido de Brès] showed it to those ministers of the Word of God he could reach, and offered to change, add, or delete whatever displeased them."[67] Since the Belgic Confession was published before the unrest in Doornik began in the fall of 1561, these ministers must have examined the confession at the latest in the early summer of 1561. It should be noted that Saravia's letter gives the impression that this was a personal request to individual ministers, but an official revision at a meeting of synod cannot be ruled out.

The second indication is found in the original title of the Belgic Confession, which reads: *Confession of faith, made with common accord by the believers who live in the Netherlands, who desire to live according to the purity of the gospel of our Lord Jesus Christ*. Below the printer's mark, 1 Peter 3:15 is written out. At first glance, the formulation appears to indicate that the confession had not been officially adopted, for the title page merely mentions an agreement among believers and does not refer to adoption by the churches or their synod.

However, seen against the background of the Gallican Confession, this title could very well indicate that the confession had been officially adopted. As noted before, two versions of the Gallican Confession exist. These were published under different titles. The earlier version, containing thirty-five articles, bears the title: *Confession of faith made by the churches which are dispersed in France, and abstain from the papal idolatries*. The version revised by the Synod of Paris, 1559, and containing forty articles, is entitled: *Confession of faith, made with common accord by the French who desire to live according to the purity of the gospel of our Lord Jesus Christ*, followed by the quotation of 1 Peter 3:15.[68]

The Belgic Confession obviously derived its title from the second version, and this was the official version adopted by synod. This shows that the formulation "made by common accord by the believers who live in the Netherlands" does not mean to suggest this is a personal confession. Although the believers are mentioned, the

---

66. Émile M. Braekman, "Anvers - 1562: Le premier synode des églises Wallonnes," *Bulletin de la société royale d'"histoire du protestantisme Belge* 102 (1989): 25-27.

67. See the letter of Saravia in Appendix, Document 6.

68. See the study by Jahr, *Studien zur Überlieferungsgeschichte*, 19-20. More editions are mentioned later, 94-95.

phrase "with common accord" was used for a confession that had been officially adopted.

In all probability, two ecclesiastical meetings were held in 1561. One was mentioned in the interrogation of Jan Den Meldere who spoke of a meeting of elders and ministers, outside of the country, at Sandwich in England.[69] However, this meeting could not have been the one alluded to in the title of the confession, since it was held in September or October. At that time the Belgic Confession was already being handed out in Doornik. The other meeting is mentioned in a letter by Godfried Van Wingen, dated February 14, 1561, who reported about a meeting of brothers who are in the ministry.[70] This date would fit, for it allows time for the confession to have been printed and distributed to the Reformed people by the fall. As records of synodical meetings from that period are lacking, it cannot be confirmed at this time exactly when and where the confession was discussed and approved. However, the available data suggest that the Belgic Confession was officially adopted early in 1561. Therefore, by the time a printed copy was discovered in Doornik in the fall of the same year, it was already the official confession of the Reformed in Belgium.

---

69. Braekman, "Anvers - 1562," 36.
70. Braekman, "Anvers - 1562," 36-37.

6

The Revision of 1566

Several sources indicate that the Dutch churches were aware that the Belgic Confession had been revised at an early date. The first of these is a question discussed at the regional Synod of Dort, 1574, regarding whether the Belgic Confession should be revised and made similar to the recently published French edition. Synod judged that this should be done by a general synod.[1] This must refer to the fact that the changes made in the French text had not yet been included in the Dutch text of the confession. Although aware of this fact, the delegates did not consider it proper for the churches in only one province to make the required changes in the Dutch text. As argued in the previous chapter, this decision implies that already at that time the Belgic Confession was seen as the confession of the Dutch churches in general.

A second indication can be found in a decision made by the regional Synod of Holland, during its meeting on March 24, 1582. The acts report: "The Belgic Confession of faith, now translated anew from the French copy, is presented. It is decided that the [delegates] of Delft will go over it and then have it printed."[2] Scrutinizing this text would not have been necessary if the decision had merely concerned a reprint of the first edition.

A third indication is a statement made by Franciscus Junius, who had been present at the Synod of Antwerp, 1566. In his autobiography he wrote that the confession had been revised at the decision of Synod 1566, and that he had sent a copy of this revision to Geneva.[3]

It appears, however, that copies of this revised French edition were scarce. This is suggested by the existence of an early manuscript copy. At the end of this manuscript the date is given as 1580, and the text does not present the 1561 text, but a different one. Although handwritten, this copy must have had official status since it was used for subscription by ministers. Among the first subscribers were

---

1. The text of these decisions can be found in chapter 5, footnotes 29 and 31.

2. Johannes Reitsma and Sietse D. Van Veen, *Acta der provinciale en particuliere synoden: gehouden in de noordelijke Nederlanden gedurende de jaren 1572-1620* (Groningen: J. B. Wolters, 1892), 1:112: "Is voorgebracht de Nederlantsche bekentenisse des geloofs, nu van nyews uut het Walsch exemplar overgeset ende is besloten, dat die van Delft die oversien sullen ende daerna drucken laten." See also Bakhuizen van den Brink, *De Nederlandse belijdenisgeschriften*, 23.

3. The text of this statement was given before, in chapter 5, footnote 14.

Pieter Loyseleur, also known as de Villiers, and Jean Taffin, who served respectively as chairman and clerk of Synod 1580.[4] It is noteworthy that a handwritten copy was used, for it suggests that at the time printed copies of the revision were extremely scarce in the northern provinces of the Netherlands. The scarcity of the revised French edition is confirmed by the fact that a printed copy did not surface until 1912, when the university library of Geneva obtained one.

The title on this printed copy is identical to that of the first edition, and the same text from 1 Peter 3 is quoted, but the printer's mark is different. It shows an arm holding up a palm branch,[5] a mark that has been traced to Jean Bonnefoy. He was a citizen of Geneva who printed the confession for Nicolas du Bar, a traveling bookseller living in Geneva. On July 2, 1566, he asked permission to reprint the Confession of Faith of the churches in Flanders. This was granted, on the condition that the place of publication and the name of the printer not be mentioned.[6] The manuscript copy of 1580 must have been copied from this edition, for the title page has been reproduced in detail, with the exception of the year of publication.[7]

Considering the situation, it is surprising that this revised text could be published so quickly. Junius mentions in his autobiography that the synod where the confession was revised had met at the beginning of May.[8] Within two months after the confession had been revised at the Synod of Antwerp, a request for it to be printed was presented and approved in Geneva.

What is the character of this revision? Thysius, in the preface of his book dealing with the doctrine of the Dutch churches, writes:

> Having been revised, not in the content itself, but actually in the manner and way of writing, more briefly and clearly expressed, it was sent to Geneva by order of the synod mentioned before, to be printed in that form in Geneva on the advice of the excellent teacher Theodore Beza and his fellow servants of the gospel; which has been done by the said Crespin in the year 1566 (just as the previous edition).[9]

Again it must be noted that this author was not fully acquainted with the early history of the confession. It is true that the confession was printed in Geneva, but not

---

4. Bakhuizen van den Brink, *De Nederlandse belijdenisgeschriften*, 18; cf. "Quelques notes," 304-7. The reproduction of the handwritten title page (opposite page 17 in Bakhuizen van den Brink's edition) shows that a deliberate attempt was made to reproduce an original printed copy.

5. For a reproduction of the title page, see Bakhuizen van den Brink, *De Nederlandse belijdenisgeschriften*, 16.

6. Bakhuizen van den Brink, *De Nederlandse belijdenisgeschriften*, 18.

7. Reproductions of the two title pages are shown side by side in Bakhuizen van den Brink, "Quelques notes," opposite page 305; and *De Nederlandse belijdenisgeschriften*, opposite page 17.

8. Junius, *Opuscula theologica*, 26; the text was given before, in chapter 5, footnote 14.

9. Thysius, foreword to *Leere ende order*; cf. Brandt, *Historie der reformatie*, 1:255. The text of Thysius' statement can be found in Appendix, Document 7.

by Crespin. However, Thysius' main interest appears to have been to emphasize that the confession was not substantially changed. In the context of the debates between the Reformed and the Remonstrants at the beginning of the seventeenth century, he wanted to prevent his opponents from using the revision as an indication that the confession from the beginning had been defective and in need of a substantial overhaul. Schoock, apparently following Thysius, comments that few things were changed in the articles of the confession.[10]

According to Los, however, the second edition is in places considerably different from the original text.[11] He can speak with authority on this issue because he published a book in which the first French and Dutch editions of the Belgic Confession were printed out side by side, with annotations to note the changes in subsequent editions. Bakhuizen van den Brink, who prepared a text edition with many variant readings, noted these changes, although he did not evaluate the overall character of this revision.[12]

The character of the 1566 revision became an issue with a report on the Belgic Confession submitted to the synod of the Christian Reformed Church in North America in 1979. The committee charged to present the churches with a new English translation had considered the confession in its original situation, concluding that the political and theological climate in the Netherlands had changed soon after the publication of the Belgic Confession. When de Brès wrote the confession, the Reformed churches were persecuted by the government and forced to operate underground. However, later a different movement arose in the churches, which was seeking official support, approval and even espousal by the government. This approach had been supported by Calvin for a long time. However, de Brès had not followed Calvin's call for a different policy towards the government. Rather, he had sent his confession to be printed in 1561, disregarding the negative advice of Calvin.[13]

According to this report, steps were soon taken to have this confession removed. The decision of Synod 1565 is to be seen in that light, for it provided the opportunity for future synods to change the confession. The actual revision took place at the Synod of 1566, where the Belgic Confession was changed considerably, now advocating that the government should reform the church. "As a result there were

---

10. Schoock, *De bonis vulgo ecclesiasticis dictis* (Groningen: Johannes Nicolai, 1651), 521; see Appendix, Document 10. H. H. Kuyper, apparently following them, stated that the revision was limited to linguistic improvements without dogmatic importance; see his "Guido de Brès," article 16.

11. Los, *Tekst en toelichting van de geloofsbelijdenis der Nederlandsche Hervormde Kerk* (Utrecht: Kemink & Zoon, 1929), 8-10.

12. Bakhuizen van den Brink, *De Nederlandse belijdenisgeschriften*, 19.

13. See "Report 33," in *Agenda for Synod 1979* (Grand Rapids: Christian Reformed Church Publications, 1979), 362-66. This reconstruction appears to be based mainly on the testimony of Schoock.

from this time on virtually two confessions, each with its own sponsor or its own place of publication (the revised version was printed in Geneva)."[14] According to this report, the second and following editions are to be taken as a weakened version of the confession, compromising the original Reformed witness.

In a discussion of this report, Jelle Faber pointed out several weaknesses in this reconstruction of the history of the Belgic Confession. That Guido de Brès would have had serious disagreements with Calvin is not plausible in view of the fact that he corresponded with Calvin and studied under him. Further, the Belgic Confession is very similar to the Gallican Confession, for which Calvin had provided the draft. In fact, Calvin can be called the spiritual grandfather of the Belgic Confession. Faber also noted that it had not been proven that a political and theological shift took place soon after the publication of the confession in 1561. In addition, he investigated the sources used to prove that Calvin attempted to have the government reform the Roman Catholic church and showed that this opinion rests on a misunderstanding of these sources. Rather, they show that Calvin urged the Nicodemites, as he called the people who agreed with the Protestant doctrines but continued their membership in the Roman Catholic church, to break away from it.

In Faber's view, the overall character of the 1566 revision is a shortening of the confession. Although not all changes were made in an admirable way, the decision to abbreviate the confession was in itself understandable, for at times de Brès' confession was too wordy and too personal in its expressions.[15]

The question of the character of this revision deserves to be investigated. A closer look at the differences will show that the synod did more than shorten the text. In the following, a comprehensive list of changes will not be given. Rather, the first ten articles will be surveyed in order to determine the general character of the revision. This will be followed by a closer look at three selected articles.

General Characteristics

The first characteristic of the second edition is that it corrected numerous misprints occurring in the first:

> In the original article 1 a comma was mistakenly placed, so that God was described as "a single and simple being, spiritual . . ." In the second edition, this comma was deleted. As a result, the adjective "spiritual" is now connected with the

---

14. "Report 33," 363-64; the quotation can be found on 364. The synod of the Christian Reformed Church did not follow the recommendation of this report to go back to the 1561 version, but decided that the revised text approved by the Synod of Dort should be the basis of the translation; see *Acts of Synod 1979* (Grand Rapids: Christian Reformed Church Publications, 1979), 126-27.

15. Jelle Faber, "Textus Receptus of the Belgic Confession," in *H. E. R. O. S. lustrumbundel 1925-1989* (Kampen: Van den Berg, 1980), 97-100.

noun "being," resulting in a clear statement: "a single and simple spiritual being which we call God."

In article 2, one wrong letter in the second sentence obscured the meaning of the statement. The first edition stated, "by (*par*) this is before our eyes as a beautiful book," which did not make sense. By correcting a single letter, the sentence was restored to what was undoubtedly the original intention: "for (*car*) this is before our eyes as a beautiful book."

In article 6, dealing with the apocryphal books, another clear example of a necessary correction occurs. Originally, the article ended with the statement that one should not use these books "to quote a testimony from these to prove something about the law (*Loy*) or Christian religion." The word "law" could be taken as referring to the Old Testament, but even then the formulation is questionable. The statement was corrected in 1566, so that it reads: "about the faith (*foy*) or Christian religion," which was probably the original intention.

A second characteristic is that Latin sentence structures were replaced by more common sentences:

This pattern can already be found in the first article, which was quoted before: "We believe . . . there to be a single and simple essence." The 1566 revision changed this into more colloquial language: "We believe . . . that there is a single and simple essence."

A similar Latinized sentence occurred originally in the middle of article 8: "Scripture teaches us the Father, the Son and the Holy Spirit to have each his distinct existence." In the second edition, this Latin sentence structure was replaced by a smoother expression: "Scripture teaches us that the Father, the Son and the Holy Spirit each has his existence, distinct by their properties." As an aside it must be noted that the last three words were added on this occasion, thereby further clarifying the meaning of the phrase.

In article 9, the doctrine of the Trinity is confirmed with a reference to the annunciation of Christ's birth. Originally, this was followed by the statement: "We see here the Father to be called the Most High." This statement was removed in 1566.

In the third place, as has been mentioned before, both Thysius in the seventeenth century and Faber in the twentieth stated that the 1566 edition was an abbreviated version of the confession. A survey shows that, indeed, several words and statements were removed by Synod Antwerp:

The last line of article 3 originally began with the exclamation "Voire" in the sense of "Indeed." This word was deleted in the second edition, presumably as not fitting in the context of a confession.

Several changes were made to article 7. In the first edition, the first line stated: "We believe that this Holy Scripture perfectly contains in itself the divine will . . ." The words "in itself" were removed; apparently they were seen as superfluous.

Later in the article, an elaborate warning was given: "Therefore everyone must watch out for adding to it or taking away from it, thus mixing human wisdom with divine wisdom." The second part of this sentence was removed in 1566. The reason may have been that this explanatory statement only applies to adding to Scripture; it does not apply to taking away from Scripture.

Still in article 7, originally the sentence that all people are liars continued with the statement, "and their wisdom cannot be subjected to God." This statement was deleted in 1566.

Yet another deletion occurs in the conclusion of article 7. The quotation from 1 John 4:1, "Test the spirits whether they are from God," was originally followed by the explanatory statement that "this shows that they can be known from their writings." As in previous instances, this deletion is probably a correction. The apostle John intended his statement concerning testing the spirits as a warning against false teachers. Contrary to the original meaning of this text, the first edition of article 7 appears to have used John's statement as a positive support for the authority of the apostolic writings.

To add one more example, the old article 8 used to reject the view that "the unity of God is divided into three Gods." In 1566, the rejection was restated as "God is divided into three."

The examples could easily be multiplied, but they confirm the general opinion that the revision of 1566 shortened the text of the confession in several places, particularly in article 7.

Fourthly, although this is not usually mentioned, in the 1566 revision a surprising number of additions were made. This can be noted as early as the first article of the confession, where the well-known closing statement that God is an "overflowing fountain of all good" was added in 1566. The additions include the following:

Article 5 originally used two expressions to describe the function of Scripture: we receive these books "for regulating and founding our faith." The revision of 1566 added to these a third function: "confirming of our faith."

The same article ends with a baroque expression urging the people to accept Scripture: "for even the blind are able to perceive that the things which are predicted there come to pass." This ending, included in 1566, replaced a plainer expression: "when they say something and thus it happens." This shows that Guido de Brès was not the only one able to invent colorful statements.

Article 6 provides another example where the original ending was shorter than the present ending. In the 1561 edition, this article on the apocryphal books concluded with the statement that the church "cannot adduce their testimony to prove a point of the law or of the Christian religion." This was changed and expanded in 1566, now stating that these books "do not have such authority and power that by a testimony from these one could confirm a point of the faith or of the Christian religion, let alone that they could diminish the authority of the others."

The original formulation of article 7 stated that custom may not be preferred[16] to the truth. This was expanded to "the truth of God." The addition prevents a possible misunderstanding by clarifying that a comparison is made between human custom and divine truth.

Further, the concluding statement of this article was strengthened. To the original statement "Therefore we reject," the words "with all our hearts" were added. And at the end of the biblical injunction "do not receive him in your house" the words "at all" were added.

A theologically significant addition was made in article 8. Following the statement that the Holy Spirit is the "eternal power and might," the traditional expression "proceeding from the Father and the Son" was added. As a result, the statement about the Holy Spirit is more comprehensive than that about the Father and the Son.

Other additions to article 8 include the insertion of "persons," "therefore," "nevertheless," and "for" in various places. There are many more besides these.

Different from the general opinion mentioned before, that this revision resulted in a shortening of the confession, it appears that there were numerous additions as well.

In the fifth place, a number of changes can be characterized as more or less substantial corrections:

The last line of article 2, dealing with God's Word, used to state that God "makes himself known to men as clearly as is necessary in this life and for their salvation." The final statement was expanded with a qualifying statement: "namely as clearly as is necessary in this life, for his glory, and for the salvation of his people." This addition appears to have been included in order to prevent the possible misunderstanding of universal salvation.

In article 7, the reference to Galatians 1:8 used to speak of "an angel from paradise." In the revision of 1566, the biblical expression is followed more closely: "an angel from heaven."

The same article originally stated, "One ought not to prefer the writings of men, however holy they may have been, to the divine Scriptures." This formulation could give the impression that the Roman Catholic doctrine elevated human writings above the Scriptures.[17] Synod 1566 corrected this by replacing the word

---

16. For this word, see the next category of changes.

17. Los stated that the Roman Catholic church actually regards human writings higher than divine, *Tekst en toelichting*, 120. However, this was not the official doctrine; see the decisions of the Council of Trent concerning tradition in Denzinger and Schönmetzer, *Enchiridion symbolorum*, #1501 and #1502, 364-65.

"to prefer" with "to equate." The new formulation also takes into account the statement of article 6 that the apocryphal books may be read for instruction.

A theological statement was corrected in article 8. This first article on the Trinity originally ended by stating that the three persons "are similar in truth and power, in goodness and mercy." In the revision, this was changed into "one in truth and power, in goodness and mercy." This formulation brings the statement of the confession closer to the text of the Athanasian Creed.

The intention of this survey was not to provide a complete list of all changes, but rather to allow us to characterize this revision. When Los, who in his book on the Belgic Confession reviewed all the articles concluded that the revision led to considerable changes in the text of the confession, he is undoubtedly correct. Synod 1566 did a comprehensive overhaul. At the same time, Thysius' opinion that the revision did not result in substantial changes in the content is also proven to be correct. The articles surveyed before do not support the view expressed by the committee of the Christian Reformed Church that the 1566 text means a fundamental change had taken place.[18] They also do not support Thysius' and Faber's view that the revised text was primarily a shortening of the original. However, Thysius was right to conclude that the revised version shows greater clarity.

Three Selected Articles

On several occasions, the revision went beyond making small repairs, for a number of articles were revised considerably. In the following survey, certain articles have been chosen that not only show how comprehensive the revision was, but also allow us to determine its intention. As the Acts of Synod 1566 have not been preserved, this may be the only way to gain further insight into the character of the revision. For this purpose, two short articles have been selected, followed by a longer article.

Article 15

In view of the fact that this is a rather brief article, the number of changes is surprising:

1. The order of the opening words was reversed. In the 1561 edition, the subject followed the verb, causing an unusual word order: "by the disobedience of Adam has been spread original sin." In the revision, this was straightened out: "by the disobedience of Adam original sin has been spread."

---

18. The report focused on the church's view of the government; for more on this issue, see our discussion of article 36 below.

2. Originally, this was followed by the words "over the human race." The revision added one word: "over the whole human race," thus stating the universality of original sin more explicitly.

3. Following an explanation of original sin, "by which even are infected the little children in the womb," the article continued with an awkward connection: "and produces in people all kind of sin." In the revision, the connection is clarified by the addition of one word: "and which produces in people all kind of sin."

4. The next section began with the words that "this whole evil itself is so vile." This is rephrased in the second edition: "therefore it is so vile and heinous before God." The slightly expanded phrase runs much more smoothly.

5. The spelling of the French word "suffissant" was changed to "suffisant."[19]

6. The article continued with an anti-Roman Catholic phrase, pointing out the lasting results of original sin: "and it is not abolished even by baptism." This statement was enlarged in 1566: "And it is not abolished even by baptism, nor entirely eradicated, seeing that, as from an evil well, bubbles[20] continually flow from it."

7. The sentence "however much [original sin] is not imputed to the children of God to condemnation by his grace and compassion" was expanded by inserting the words "but is pardoned." Now, not only the negative result of original sin is stated, but the positive grace of forgiveness, as well.

8. Another result of original sin is added. Following the statement that "the awareness of this corruption makes the believers groan," a phrase has been inserted in the revised version: "not in order that they would fall asleep, but . . ." Here, the negative aspect has been added.

Although the revision did not substantially alter the original meaning of article 15, several changes were made. An alternate spelling was used (5), unusual word order was straightened out (1), words were deleted (4) and also added (2, 3, 4, 7). The greatest change was the addition of whole phrases (6, 8). Overall, much more was added than deleted.

Particularly striking in this article is the comparison of original sin with a sulphurous wellspring bringing up evil. This sentence appears to have been included as a direct response to the statement on original sin, made in 1546 by the Council of Trent. To quote a crucial statement from this decision:

> If someone denies that through the grace of our Lord Jesus Christ, which is granted in baptism, the guilt of original sin is forgiven, or even asserts that what constitutes the true and real nature of sin is not remitted, but says that this is merely erased or

---

19. Los, *Tekst en toelichting*, 173.
20. The image is that of a sulphurous well, producing foul smelling, undrinkable water.

not imputed, he must be anathema. For God hates nothing in those who are born again.[21]

Although this pronouncement had been made as early as 1546, twenty years later Synod Antwerp decided to make its objection to this Roman Catholic doctrine explicit by expanding the article.[22] The Reformed saw a need to maintain that original sin not only continues to exist in baptized people, but that it also continues to have an evil influence.

Article 16

Synod 1566 did not make many changes in this article, but two of the changes that were made are rather substantial.

The explanation of God's mercy originally contained the statement that God rescues and saves the elect "without any consideration of their righteous works." This was followed by a sentence which did not run properly: "By leaving the others in their ruin and fall into which they had fallen, by so doing he shows himself a compassionate and merciful God toward those whom he saves."[23] Because of its awkward phrasing, the statement was virtually incomprehensible. An additional problem was that the confession had announced it would deal with the two issues of God demonstrating his mercy as well as his righteousness, while in fact the article only explains God's mercy.

It required only some minor changes for the sentence suddenly to make sense.[24] In connection with God's mercy, the revised text states that God rescues and saves the elect "without any consideration of their works." Further, the word "righteous" (*iustes*) should not to be connected with "works" (*oeuvres*). Rather, it should be taken as the beginning of the following statement: [God proves to be] "righteous (*iuste*) by leaving the others in their ruin . . ." A survey of the marginal texts leaves no doubt that this was the original intention of the statement.[25]

In addition, synod made an important change when it replaced the statement "the fall into which they had fallen" with "the fall into which they had thrown

---

21. The decision is part of the decree concerning original sin, promulgated by the Council of Trent in 1546. For the original text, see Denzinger and Schönmetzer, *Enchiridion symbolorum*, #1515, 367-68.

22. Los, *Tekst en toelichting*, 175.

23. The original text of 1561 stated: "sans aucun esgard de leur oeuvres iustes: en laissant les autres en leur ruine et tresbuchement ausquels ils sont tresbuchez, en ce faisant il se demonstre Dieu pitoiable et misericordieux vers ceux qu'il sauve . . ."

24. In the revision of 1566, the corrected statement read: "sans aucun esgard de leurs oeuvres. Iuste, en laissant les autres en leur ruine et tresbuschement ou ils se sont precipitez."

25. Los, *Tekst en toelichting*, 183.

themselves." This rephrasing not only avoided an unpleasant repetition of words, it also emphasized human responsibility for this fall into sin.

A third change was made in the second part of the article. Originally, it ended with a lengthy defense of the doctrine of predestination:

> By so doing, he shows himself a compassionate and merciful God toward those whom he saves, to whom he was not at all indebted. Likewise he makes himself known as a righteous judge by demonstrating his most righteous severity to the others. In the meantime, he does not do any injustice to them, for when he saves some of them it is not because they are better than the others, since they are all fallen into the same destruction till God separates them and rescues them according to his eternal and unchangeable decree established in Jesus Christ before the world was created. Understood like this, no one would be able to attain to this glory by himself, since by ourselves we are incapable of thinking any good unless God by his grace and pure goodness would precede us, so corrupt is our nature.

No record is available explaining the reason why synod removed all but the first sentence of this statement. Los refers to Van Toorenenbergen's opinion that the article was abbreviated for political reasons, in order to receive the support of the Lutheran noblemen in Germany. However, this argument does not convince him, for the much longer article on the Lord's Supper, which clearly opposes the Lutheran position, was not drastically shortened.[26]

The omitted section itself provides the reasons why it was removed. It begins by referring to God's mercy toward those whom he saves, something stated earlier in this article. This is followed by a sentence dealing with God's judgment, which is discussed in article 37. The question whether God does injustice to those whom he condemns had already been answered earlier in this article, in more or less the same words. And the final sentence is not germane to the issue of divine election; it could have been included in the second part of article 14.

The pruning of this article does not appear to have been the result of theological considerations. Rather, the reason why this lengthy section was removed will have been that it was too general and repetitious. It could be taken out without loss of content.

Article 36

As this article was changed considerably in 1566, it deserves to be investigated in greater detail. The character of the revision concerning the task of the government was discussed in "Report 33" on the Belgic Confession, mentioned

---

26. Los, *Tekst en toelichting*, 183; see also Faber's view concerning a political background of the revision, mentioned above (120 n. 15).

above. This revision was seen as a radical change in direction toward involving the government in the reformation of the church. In the first version, a single task of the government was mentioned: to punish evil men and to protect good people. In the revision of 1566 a double task was attributed to it: watching for the welfare of the civil state and protecting the sacred ministry.[27] Before investigating this specific issue, the changes made in this article (with the exception of differences in spelling) will be surveyed, in order to determine their intention.

1. Originally, the article began with the words "We believe finally," but in the 1566 edition the word "finally" was dropped. We can safely assume that this was done because this was not the last article of the confession.[28]
2. The original edition spoke of God "wanting the world to be governed by their laws and policies." In the revision, the word "their" was omitted. This may have been done to prevent the impression that God would agree with every rule made by governing authorities. Rather, the confession is concerned with the general principle that there should be laws, without considering specific laws.
3. In the expression "good order among the people," one word for people (*humains*) was replaced by another (*hommes*). There is no apparent difference in meaning.
4. The first edition stated that the sword was given "in the hand" of the magistrate, whereas the second edition used the plural: "in the hands."
5. In the 1561 edition, a double expression was used for the good people who are protected by the government (*les bons et gens de bien*). In the revision, this was reduced to a single expression (*les gens de bien*).
6. The first task of the government was originally formulated as "to restrain and guard the affairs of state." The statement was rephrased as "to watch and guard the public order." Later, an explanation for this rephrasing will be given.
7. The second task of the government was described as "to restrain and guard . . . the concerns of the church." This was abbreviated: "to uphold the sacred ministry."
8. In the next section, dealing with the duties of the citizens, a minor change was made. The 1561 edition spoke "of what state" everyone may be; the 1566 revision changed that into "of whatever state."
9. The sentence continued by stating that the citizens must be subject to "the Magistrate." The revision used the plural: "the Magistrates." This was probably done to correct a misprint, for the same word also occurs at the end of the article, where the plural was already used in the first edition.
10. The first edition stated that the people must "obey in all matters," but the synod added a word: "obey them in all matters." This addition brings the phrase in

---

27. "Report 33," 420; cf. 427.
28. On this issue, see our chapter 4.

line with the previous phrases, where the duties toward the government are mentioned.

11. The first edition mentioned the obligation of the citizens to pray for the government "in prayers." The 1566 edition added a word: "in their prayers," making the sentence somewhat smoother.

12. Originally, the first petition contained a request to God to direct the government "in their whole way." In the second edition, the plural was used: "in all their ways." The plural sounds more natural.

13. The second was a petition that we "would be able to live in good peace and tranquillity under them." This was rephrased to read that we "would lead a peaceful and quiet life in all piety and uprightness." This reformulation brings the sentence closer to the text alluded to, 1 Timothy 2:1, 2.

14. The rejection of errors at the end of the article was originally formulated in general terms, without mentioning the Anabaptists: "We detest all those who want to reject the Superiors and Magistrates." The revision added an explicit denunciation: "We detest the Anabaptists and other rebels, and in general all those who want to reject the Superiors and Magistrates." The Synod of 1566 wanted to make it completely clear that the Reformed were not to be confused with the rebellious Anabaptists who had tyrannized Münster thirty years earlier.

These changes are different in character. Some appear to be merely cosmetic, without causing change in meaning. For example, in several cases words were replaced (3, 8) and words in the singular were changed to the plural (4, 9, 12). The case where the formulation of the confession was brought closer to that of Scripture (13) is more substantial, but it is not a change in content.

In a few cases, the text was shortened. A word was omitted (1, 2), and one of two expressions with identical meaning was left out (5). On the other hand, several additions to the text of the confession were identified. Some consist of only one or two words (10, 11). A substantial addition is the explicit rejection of an Anabaptist teaching (14). Again, the perception that the revision of 1566 was primarily an abbreviation is not borne out by the data. In fact, the revised version of this article is longer by twenty-two words, when the changes made in the formulation of the task of the government (7, 8) are included.

At this point we need to come back to the general character of these changes, which became an issue as the result of Report 33. Here, the changes are attributed to magisterialization, a movement which intended to entrust the civil government with the task of reforming the church. This interpretation is based on the new formulation of the task of the government in article 36. In the original text of 1561, the single task of the government was to hold the sword, which should be used for the twofold purpose of punishing evil people and protecting good and devout people. The kingdom of God was served, be it only indirectly, by providing peace. Later, in 1566, this was reformulated so that the single task of the government also extended to the offices of the church. "The magistracy now has two duties—to 'watch for the welfare of the civil state' and 'to protect the sacred ministry.'"[29]

This interpretation is based on the translation of the 1561 text given in the report:

> The government's task of restraining and sustaining is not limited to the public order but it extends also to the affairs of the church with a view to the uprooting and destruction of all idolatry and false religion.[30]

However, when the statement in the first version is read carefully, it shows clearly that not even the first version assigned a single task, that of restraining, to the government. This can easily be seen when the original French text is translated more literally:

> And their task is not merely to restrain and to guard the affairs of state but also the ecclesiastical affairs, to remove and destroy all idolatry and false worship of God . . .[31]

Right from the first edition, this article assigned a twofold task to the government, one concerning the state and the other concerning the church. In other words, from the very first edition of its confession, the persecuted church in the Netherlands recognized a positive role for the state toward the church. In this respect, there is no difference between the original version of 1561 and the revision of 1566.

If the view on the government did not fundamentally change during the early years, how should the changes made in the revised edition be understood? The first task of the government was originally formulated as "to restrain and to guard the affairs of state." Read together, this statement does not make sense, for the verb "to restrain" cannot be combined with the object "the affairs of state." After all, the civil government can hardly restrain its own affairs.[32] The reason for Synod Antwerp, 1566, to rephrase this statement was simply the obvious fact that the sentence had not been properly formulated in the first edition. In their effort to improve the formulation, synod also replaced the words "the affairs of the state" with "the civil order." This resulted in a proper sentence: "And their task is not merely to keep watch and to

---

29. "Report 33," 421.

30. "Report 33," 405.

31. Bakhuizen van den Brink, *De Nederlandse belijdenisgeschriften*, 140: "Et non seulement leur office est, de reprimer et veiller sur la police, ains aussi sur les choses ecclesiastiques, pour oster et ruiner toute idolatrie et faux service de Dieu . . ."

32. The problem in this formulation also occurs in the original Dutch translation: "Ende haer ampt ende officie, en is niet alleenlick te bedwingen ende te waken over de Burgerlicke regeringhe ende policie . . ." (Bakhuizen van den Brink, *De Nederlandse belijdenisgeschriften*, 141).

guard over the civil order . . ."[33] The purpose of this rephrasing was not to change the theological meaning, but rather to clarify the expression in the earlier edition.

Another change was made later in the article, when the task of the government toward the church is explained. Originally, the previously used verbs still govern its task: " . . . but also [to keep watch and to guard] over the ecclesiastical affairs . . ." The revision of 1566 rephrased this: " . . . but also to maintain the sacred ministry . . ."[34] The reason for this change is rather obvious. The original formulation gave the impression that the duty of the government toward the state was basically the same as its duty toward the church, for the same verbs were used to characterize it.[35] This would subject the church to the power of the government in the same way as civil affairs are subject to the government. By changing the formulation to "maintaining the sacred ministry," the confession indicated that the government's duty towards the church is upholding the true preaching of the gospel. Rather than forbidding the worship services of the Reformed and even persecuting them, the government should support these churches. However, the confession did not go into specifics; no indication is given whether the government should maintain the ministry by financial support, by protection, by force, or in any other way.

In conclusion, the changes made in article 36 do not constitute a substantial change in meaning. Rather, the original formulation lacked clarity and could easily lead to confusion. In 1566, the task of the government and its role toward the church were expressed much more clearly. Overall, the revision of article 36 is in agreement with the character of the entire revision. This was not the result of a different theological direction. Rather, the aim was to clarify the issues and to improve the formulation.

---

33. Bakhuizen van den Brink, *De Nederlandse belijdenisgeschriften*, 140: "Et non seulement leur office est de prendre garde et veiller sur la police, mais aussi de maintenir le sacré ministère . . ."

34. The statement "ains aussi sur les choses ecclesiastiques" was replaced by "ains aussi de maintenir le sacré ministère."

35. Vonk, *De Nederlandse geloofsbelijdenis*, 2:654.

7

At the Synod of Dort

The Synod of Dort, 1618-19, was the first national synod of the Reformed Churches in the Netherlands held since 1586 and was of crucial importance for the Belgic Confession. Already during the theological discussions leading up to the synod, the content of the confession was much in dispute. The foreword in the Acts of the Synod of Dort blames in particular Jacob Arminius, originally minister of the church of Amsterdam. He is described as someone with a bold mind, who appeared to have an antipathy against the majority of the doctrines of the Reformed churches.[1] In 1602, Arminius had been appointed as professor of theology at the University of Leiden. Within two years it became known that in his teaching he rejected many doctrines adopted within the Reformed churches. He had even stated openly that he had many objections against the adopted doctrine, which he would make known eventually.[2] The foreword also mentions that two years later, the Regional Synod of Holland dealt with a submission concerning the doctrinal disagreement that had arisen at the University of Leiden. This synod had noted that in many areas of the country subscription to the confession by the ministers had been neglected or even refused. It ordered all ministers to subscribe.[3] The main reason for the Synod of Dort to be convened was the fact that the unity in doctrine, as expressed in the Belgic Confession and the Heidelberg Catechism, was lacking in the churches.

The disputes in the years leading up to the Synod of Dort need to be surveyed before the discussions concerning the Belgic Confession at the synod itself can be addressed. First, the role of Arminius, who died in 1609, ten years before the synod was convened, must be considered. This will be followed by a section dealing with the place of the Belgic Confession in the theological debates prior to the Synod of Dort. These will provide the background for a discussion of the way in which the synod dealt with the Belgic Confession.

---

1. *Acta ofte handelinghen der nationalen Synodi . . . tot Dordrecht, anno 1618 ende 1619* (Dordrecht: Isaack Iansz. Canin, 1621), 1v. This introduction to the Acts was written by Festus Hommius; see Willem Van 't Spijker, ed., *De synode van Dordrecht in 1618 en 1619* (Houten: Den Hertog, 1987), 11.

2. *Acta ofte handelinghen*, 2v.

3. *Acta ofte handelinghen*, 3r and v.

Jacob Arminius

On several occasions during his ministry, Jacob Arminius (ca. 1564-1609) was accused of deviation from the confessional basis of the Reformed Churches. He was generally acknowledged as a gifted theologian who had studied widely. Originally, he enrolled at the University of Leiden to study theology. He received permission to pursue further studies in Geneva, and from there he traveled to Basel, Zürich and Italy. On his return to the Netherlands in 1587, he became minister of the Reformed church of Amsterdam.

According to Bangs, the first conflict concerning the confession arose in 1596, when Arminius preached on Romans 7:14, a text dealing with someone who does not do what he wants to do, but does what he hates. He defended the position that this refers to the unregenerated man. Another minister who also worked in Amsterdam, Petrus Plancius, accused him of deviation from the Belgic Confession and the Heidelberg Catechism. Arminius admitted that his view on Romans 7 was different from that of some Reformed theologians, but he denied that it was contrary to the confession and the catechism.[4]

Bangs does not indicate with which section of the Belgic Confession Arminius would have been in conflict in his preaching on Romans 7. The Reformed chronicler Trigland also drew attention to these sermons and the ensuing debate, but he did not indicate that the confession and the catechism were part of it.[5] There is no proof that this debate should be taken as the beginning of Arminius distancing himself from the Belgic Confession.

However, two years later, in 1593, Arminius had progressed to Romans 9 and in his preaching was dealing with predestination. This led to complaints in the consistory that Arminius differed from his colleagues in the explanation of Scripture and on certain points of doctrine. He defended himself by saying that he had never taught anything against the confession and the catechism, adding that he wanted to continue in this way.[6] He only admitted that he explained Romans 9:18 differently from the way it was used in the margin of the confession.[7]

A few months later, his sermons were again brought up for discussion in the consistory. There it was remarked that these had caused misunderstandings, and Arminius was kindly admonished to state openly that he agreed with the doctrine of

---

4. Carl Bangs, *Arminius: A Study in the Dutch Reformation* (Nashville: Abingdon, [1970]), 141-46. His information is taken from the biography of Arminius, written by Caspar Brandt, *The Life of James Arminius*, trans. John Guthrie (Nashville: E. Stevenson and F. A. Owen, 1857), 67-71; for Arminius' defense, see 83-85.

5. Trigland, *Kerckelycke geschiedenissen*, 283. He mentions that an authenticated extract from the protocol of the church of Amsterdam is the source for his information.

6. See Trigland, *Kerckelycke geschiedenissen*, 284, quoting from the reports of the consistory, and Brandt, *The Life of James Arminius*, 89, who also used the manuscripts of Arminius.

7. Bangs, *Arminius*, 148.

the confession and the catechism. On May 20, 1593, the first clear indication of Arminius distancing himself from the confession was recorded. He declared that he had nothing against the catechism and the Belgic Confession and that he had never taught anything against these, but rather had accepted these in all doctrines. However, he made one reservation. At this point in time he was unable to explain article 16 of the Belgic Confession. Nevertheless, he expressed willingness to adhere to the statements made in this confession.[8]

There is no record of further disagreements concerning the confession during the next ten years. The problems surfaced again after Arminius had become a professor at the University of Leiden, in 1603. From this period, two events in particular need to be briefly mentioned.

In 1604, Arminius drew up *Theses Concerning Predestination*, to be discussed in his lectures. He defined election as "the decree of the good pleasure of God in Christ, by which he resolved within himself from all eternity to justify, adopt and endow with everlasting life, to the praise of his own glorious grace, believers on whom he had decreed to bestow faith."[9] This is substantially different from article 16 of the Belgic Confession, which describes election as a result of God's mercy for sinners: "God has shown his mercy by rescuing and saving from perdition those whom in his eternal and unchangeable counsel he has elected by his pure goodness in Jesus Christ our Lord." Where the confession defined the object of salvation as those whom God has chosen, Arminius' main statement is that God decided to save believers. Actually, his definition refers to two decisions made by God. The first is to save believers, the second is to bestow faith. The first decision was made from eternity, but it is not indicated when the second, fundamental decision is made. Although this disputation did not lead to action on the side of the church or the university, it provoked Gomarus to organize his own disputation on election.

Arminius came back to this issue several years later. In October 1608, he was invited to appear before the States of the province of Holland to state his views on the Belgic Confession and the Heidelberg Catechism. He presented a lengthy declaration in which he first of all dealt extensively with the supralapsarian position. After comparing this with the doctrine formulated in articles 14 and 16 of the Belgic Confession and in question and answer 20 of the Heidelberg Catechism, he concluded that supralapsarianism does not agree with the confessions.[10]

Later on in the same statement, Arminius explained his own views on God's decree of election. This decree has its foundation in God's foreknowledge. By it, God

---

8. Trigland, *Kerckelycke geschiedenissen*, 284, taken from the report of the consistory.

9. Disputation 15.2 in *The Writings of James Arminius*, trans. James Nichols and W. R. Bagnall (Grand Rapids: Baker, 1956), 1:565; cf. Trigland, *Kerckelijcke geschiedenissen*, 289, quoting the Dutch translation made by Johannes Uitenbogaert. On this event, see Bangs, *Arminius*, 262.

10. Declaration of Sentiments, I.1.vi.1; see *The Writings of James Arminius*, 1:220-21, and Bangs, *Arminius*, 312.

"knew from all eternity those individuals who through his prevenient grace would believe, and through his subsequent grace would persevere." God also knew by foreknowledge "those who would not believe and persevere."[11] He added that this view was in agreement with the statement on election in article 16 of the Belgic Confession, and with answers 20 and 54 of the Heidelberg Catechism.[12]

However, a comparison with article 16 of the Belgic Confession shows a distinct difference between the confession and the statements of Arminius. This article states that God saves from perdition "those whom, in his eternal and unchangeable counsel, He has elected and chosen in his pure goodness in Jesus Christ our Lord, without any consideration of their works."[13] While the confession states that God saves those whom he has elected, Arminius maintained that God elected those whom he knew would believe in response to his grace.

Arminius must have been aware that his view did not square with the formulation of the confession. His statements quoted above show that he actually qualified the meaning of article 16 by stating that those whom God had elected were the believers, and the others the unbelievers.[14]

The *Remonstrance* and the Conferences at The Hague and Delft

After Arminius' death in 1609, the discussion on the confession widened. This was the result of the *Remonstrance* (1610), a document which caused Arminius' adherents to be called "Remonstrants." It consists of four sections, two of which directly concern the Belgic Confession. The first section presented a request for a revision of the existing confessions of the Dutch churches, the Belgic Confession and the Heidelberg Catechism. The third section contained five statements in which the subscribers to the document summarized their own position on five confessional issues. These statements dealt with election, the extent of the atonement, the forgiveness acquired by Christ's death, the possibility of resisting the Holy Spirit in

---

11. Declaration of Sentiments, I.5.iv.6; see *The Writings of James Arminius*, 1:248.

12. Declaration of Sentiments, I.5.iv.6; see *The Writings of James Arminius*, 1:248-49.

13. Declaration of Sentiments, I.5.iv.6; see *The Writings of James Arminius*, 1:248.

14. Arminius' problems with the Reformed doctrine as presented in the Belgic Confession were not limited to article 16 of the confession. Richard A. Muller concludes after a lengthy survey of his theology that Arminius' system was different from Reformed theology: "Arminius argued, in a manner quite foreign to the Reformed, whether infra- or supralapsarian, that the divine rule of the created order is limited and that this limitation provides the only conceivable ground of human freedom"; *God, Creation and Providence in the Thought of Jacob Arminius* (Grand Rapids: Baker, 1991), 281. See also Eef Dekker, *Rijker dan Midas: Vrijheid, genade en predestinatie in de theologie van Jacobus Arminius* (Zoetermeer: Boekencentrum, 1993), especially 128-31, 178-231; and his article, "Was Arminius a Molinist?" *Sixteenth Century Journal* 27 no. 2 (1996): 337-52. Both Muller and Dekker explain Arminius' doctrine of election against the background of the theology of the Jesuit Luis De Molina.

producing faith, and uncertainty concerning the perseverance of the saints.[15] This list of issues indicates that the difference between the Reformed and the Remonstrants was wider than election itself. The real issue concerned the relationship between God and humans in general, as it was expressed in the confession and the catechism.

This is confirmed by the reports of the ensuing discussions. The first debate was held in 1611 and is known as the Conference at The Hague. The five points were successively dealt with in written statements and discussed. For our purpose, only the disagreement concerning the Belgic Confession needs to be surveyed. The issue of election as explained in the first article of the *Remonstrance* led to extensive discussions. The Reformed claimed that the Remonstrants took election to mean merely God's eternal and unchangeable decree to save believers and to condemn unbelievers. This was not in agreement with Scripture and the Reformed confessions. They referred not only to article 16 of the confession, but pointed out that article 37, as well, taught that God has elected specific persons. Furthermore, the reason why God decided to elect them is not that he saw in advance that they would believe, but because of his own good pleasure and mere grace.[16]

The next issue concerned the question for whom Christ died and obtained forgiveness. The Remonstrants had stated that he died for all people, so that by his death he obtained salvation and forgiveness of sins for all. The Reformed responded by pointing not only to article 16 but also to article 21 of the Belgic Confession. Here, the meaning of the name Jesus is explained as Savior, for he would save his people from their sins.[17] The Reformed emphasized that according to the confession, Christ's saving work concerns his people. The Remonstrants, in turn, appealed to article 17 of the same confession to prove that this limitation was not intended. Here the confession speaks in general terms, not only when it deals with the first humans who had fallen, but also when it says that God sought the man, comforted him and promised his Son for salvation.[18]

Concerning the third and fourth articles of the *Remonstrance*, the debate focused on the ability of the human will to believe in God. The Reformed participants in the debate presented statements taken from articles 14 and 24 of the Belgic Confession,

---

15. The text of the five statements can be found in Schaff, *Creeds of Christendom*, 3:545-49; Bakhuizen van den Brink, *De Nederlandse belijdenisgeschriften*, 288-93. A brief introduction was provided by Donald N. Sinnema, *The Issue of Reprobation at the Synod of Dort (1618-1619) in Light of the History of This Doctrine* (Ph.D. diss., Toronto School of Theology, 1985), 156-58.

16. *Schriftelijcke conferentie, gehouden in 's Gravenhaghe inden Iare 1611. tusschen sommighe kerkendienaren: Aengaende de Godlicke praedestinatie metten aencleven van dien* (Den Haag: Hillebrant, 1617), 53. These statements also refer to texts from Scripture and statements in the Heidelberg Catechism, but our focus is on the Belgic Confession.

17. *Schriftelijcke conferentie*, 115.

18. *Schriftelijcke conferentie*, 123. The Reformed responded that the promise of Gen. 3:15 applies to the seed of the woman, and maintained that the Remonstrant articles are in disagreement with "our confession and catechism" (*Schriftelijcke conferentie*, 144).

and from questions and answers 5, 8, 9, 21 and 65 of the Heidelberg Catechism, to prove their point that faith and conversion are not partly attributed to the human free will, but rather are exclusively dependent on the grace of God and the working of the Holy Spirit.[19] The Remonstrants rejected this appeal to the confessional standards, pointing out that no confession of any Reformed church states that conversion is worked irresistibly by God. To prove this, they referred to several confessional statements, including article 14 of the Belgic Confession and question and answer 8 of the Heidelberg Catechism.[20]

The fifth doctrinal statement of the *Remonstrance* dealt with perseverance. It stated that those who had been incorporated in Christ by true faith, by the power of the Spirit would have sufficient strength to persevere. However, the question of whether it was possible for people who by true faith had been incorporated in Christ to desert Christ and return to the world was not clear to them. This issue needed to be investigated further before they would be able to teach this with assurance.[21] The Counter-Remonstrants, in their submission, not only discussed Bible texts in support of the perseverance of the saints, they also listed statements from the confession and the catechism. They pointed to a sentence in article 29 of the Belgic Confession concerning those who belong to the church and to passages in the articles on baptism (art. 34) and the Lord's Supper (art. 35).[22] The Remonstrants countered that none of the articles of the confession dealt explicitly with this issue and that a doctrine of perseverance can only be derived from it by consequence. The same applies to the quotations from the catechism. They also listed statements from several confessions that denied that it was impossible for a believer to lose the Holy Spirit.[23] The ensuing discussion did not resolve anything. While the Counter-Remonstrants insisted that the perseverance of the saints is taught in the confessions, the Remonstrants maintained that this is not taught but can only be inferred.[24]

The outcome of this written debate confirmed the Counter-Remonstrants in their opinion that the doctrinal differences concerned several issues already dealt with in the confessions. They asked for a national synod to examine the objections against the doctrine contained in the confession and the catechism.[25] The Remonstrants went on record stating that there was no confessional issue between the two parties, with the exception of article 16 on predestination.[26]

---

19. *Schriftelijcke conferentie*, 189.
20. *Schriftelijcke conferentie*, 198-99.
21. Bakhuizen van den Brink, *De Nederlandse belijdenisgeschriften*, 289.
22. *Schriftelijcke conferentie*, 293. They added even more passages from the Heidelberg Catechism.
23. *Schriftelijcke conferentie*, 305-7.
24. *Schriftelijcke conferentie*, 338-39, 386-87.
25. *Schriftelijcke conferentie*, 404.
26. *Schriftelijcke conferentie*, 409.

The extent of the differences between the Reformed and the Remonstrants was explored at a later conference, held at Delft in 1613. The Remonstrants had asked for toleration on the disputed five points. The Reformed wanted a national synod to be convened in order to deal with the doctrinal differences, but from the side of the government no permission was forthcoming. As a national synod could not be convened, a conference was organized to determine whether the existing differences on the doctrine of the confession and the catechism were limited to the five points.

At this conference, the Reformed demanded that the Remonstrants state their agreement with six other doctrines.[27] These concerned Christ's satisfaction, justification, faith, original sin, assurance of salvation and perfection.[28] Most of these statements were taken from the Heidelberg Catechism, but some of them came from the Belgic Confession. In the section on saving faith, a sentence from article 22 is mentioned, and in the section on original sin, article 15 is quoted.

This conference did not lead to an agreement on these issues. However, it allowed the Reformed to make the point that the doctrinal divide between them and the Remonstrant party was wider than the five disputed issues. Several other confessional issues were at stake as well.

Festus Hommius' *Specimen controversiarum* (1618)

On September 29, 1617, the States General of the United Provinces of the Netherlands finally decided by majority vote to call a general synod of the Reformed churches. This synod was to consist of national delegates, supplemented by delegates from several foreign Reformed churches. Their task was to decide whether the opinions of the Remonstrants were still within the scope of the Reformed doctrine.

In preparation for this synod, Festus Hommius, since 1602 minister in Leiden and afterwards clerk of the Synod of Dort, published *Specimen controversiarum* (1618), in which the Belgic Confession was the focal point.[29] The book was written in Latin since it was first of all intended for the foreign delegates. In this publication, the text of every article of the confession is printed, followed by quotations from dissenting theologians.

---

27. These six issues were taken from a resolution made by the States of Holland, determining that these points should be taught in the churches and in the schools. See Trigland, *Kerckelycke geschiedenissen*, 644.

28. These statements can be found in Trigland, *Kerckelycke geschiedenissen*, 644-46; see also Jan D. De Lind van Wijngaarden, *De Dordtsche leerregels*, 2nd ed., (Utrecht: G. J. A. Ruys, 1905), 52-59.

29. The full title gives a clear indication of its purpose: *Specimen controversiarum belgicarum. Seu confessio ecclesiarum reformatarum in Belgio, cujus singulis articulis subjuncti sunt articuli discrepantes, in quibus nonnuli ecclesiarum Belgicarum doctores hodie a recepta doctrina dissentire videntur*. This book was also published in Dutch.

Hommius did not restrict himself to Remonstrant views. He included many quotations from the writings of Conrad Vorstius and Henricus Welsing, who did not belong to the Remonstrants but were influenced by Socinianism. Vorstius was professor at a theological school in Steinfurt but after the death of Arminius had been called to the University of Leiden. However, fierce opposition caused by his book on the doctrine of God had prevented him from taking up this position.[30] Welsing, a minister in a local church, had published a book by Faustus Socinus with an introduction in which he recommended it to his readers.[31]

In the early articles of the Belgic Confession, Hommius mentions hardly any Remonstrant objections. For articles 1 through 3 he focuses on Vorstius. No objections are mentioned in connection with articles 6, 7, 12, 17, 18 and 26. Opposition to the doctrine of the Belgic Confession is found particularly in those articles that deal with the relationship between God and humans. The way Hommius deals with the doctrine of providence as expressed in article 13 is representative of his approach. The Belgic Confession states that God rules and governs all things he has created according to his holy will, in such a way that in this world nothing happens without his ordinance. By way of contrast he adds the distinctions Arminius had made in his teaching: "What God wills that happens he effectively brings about; what he wills not to happen, he effectively prevents; what he neither wills to happen nor wills not to happen, he permits to the creature."[32]

In connection with article 14, dealing with the results of the fall, Hommius quotes several statements made by Remonstrants at the Conference of The Hague, to show that they did not acknowledge that the will is totally depraved. Concerning original sin, discussed in article 15, Hommius quotes a number of statements denying that original sin is so evil in God's sight that it is sufficient to condemn the human race.[33] As especially article 16, dealing with election, was in contention between the Reformed and the Remonstrants, it could be expected that he would particularly focus on this article. However, Hommius does not treat this topic in any different way. He simply lists Remonstrant quotations stating that God decreed to save those who believe,[34] which is different from the way article 16 formulates election. The

---

30. Cornelis Van der Woude remarks that the Remonstrants agreed with Vorstius on several issues but did not want to be identified with him because of his Socinian ideas; see "Vorstius, Conradus," *BLGNP*, 1:407-10.

31. Hommius, introduction to the reader in *Specimen*, 6.

32. Hommius, *Specimen*, 35: "Quod Deus vult ut fiat, hoc efficaciter effecit. Quod vult ut non fiat, hoc efficaciter impedit. *Quod neque vult ut fiat, neque vult ut non fiat*, hoc permittit creaturae." The italics are in the original, presumably added by Hommius.

33. Hommius, *Specimen*, 54-55.

34. Hommius, *Specimen*, 60-61.

issue of election is treated similarly in connection with article 37, which mentions the number of the elect.[35]

Many more differences between the Reformed confessions and the Remonstrants are listed in the section dealing with the work of salvation. In connection with article 23, Slatius, a maverick who was later disowned by many Remonstrants,[36] is quoted as saying that God did not require Christ's satisfaction for our sins. Arminius had presented this in the form of questions: Was God's justice satisfied in Christ, and was the law satisfied by Christ?[37] Even more objections are brought up in connection with the articles on justification. A central issue is the question of whether our righteousness rests on the obedience of Jesus Christ, apprehended by faith, as article 23 states.[38] In the section dealing with good works, article 24, Hommius quotes the Remonstrants as saying that doing good works is a prerequisite for justification, rather than maintaining the formulation of the Reformed confession that good works follow faith and justification. On a related issue, the Remonstrant leaders questioned the statement that even the best works of believers are tainted with sin.[39]

Another contentious issue was the character of the Old Testament, in connection with article 25. Remonstrant leaders such as Arminius and Episcopius are quoted as having stated that the promises of the Old Testament differ qualitatively from those of the New Testament, and that the Old Testament laws were mostly carnal but the New Testament laws spiritual.[40]

In the section on the church, as expressed in articles 27 through 32, several Remonstrant objections against the marks of the true church are mentioned. In their view, it is not possible or even necessary to list certain marks to recognize the true church. In connection with the articles on church government, the quotations given advocate the right of the government to control the church. The government should appoint office-bearers and maintain church discipline.[41]

The Remonstrant quotations Hommius brings together in the section on the sacraments appear not to deal with the sacraments themselves, but more particularly with the issues of assurance of faith and certainty of election. To give an example, a statement of Arminius is quoted, questioning whether a believer, without receiving a special revelation, can be certain he will not defect from the faith.[42] In the background, however, there is a different view on the nature of the sacraments. A statement made by Episcopius is quoted to the effect that the purpose of baptism is

---

35. Hommius, *Specimen*, 142.

36. Arie Th. Van Deursen, "Slatius, Henricus," *BLGNP*, 1:345-46.

37. Hommius, *Specimen*, 74, 76.

38. Hommius, *Specimen*, 83.

39. Hommius, *Specimen*, 94-95.

40. Hommius, *Specimen*, 97-100.

41. Hommius, *Specimen*, 114, 117-18, 119.

42. Hommius, *Specimen*, 127.

merely to signify divine grace and our profession.[43] This means that baptism is not recognized as a seal on the remission of sins by Christ's blood. Similarly, the Lord's Supper is not seen as a sign of the communion in the benefits of Christ, but as a profession of the communion and a commemoration of Christ's death.[44]

The main purpose of Hommius' book is to prove to the foreign delegates at the Synod of Dort that the disagreement between the Reformed and the Remonstrants was not limited to a single issue such as election. He wanted to show that the Arminian position in fact represented a different doctrinal conviction from that expressed in the Reformed confessions. The fact that after the Synod of Dort the Remonstrants came with an altogether different confession[45] can be seen as a confirmation of Hommius' thesis.

Remonstrant Questions at the Synod of Dort

The international Synod of Dort was solemnly constituted on November 13, 1618, and Johannes Bogerman was elected to chair the meetings. Two days later, synod adopted a letter in which several Remonstrant leaders were summoned to present their objections to the Reformed doctrine as summarized in the Belgic Confession and the Heidelberg Catechism.[46]

About a month later, the Remonstrants handed in their remarks on the Belgic Confession.[47] This lengthy submission appears to have been made by a committee consisting of Episcopius, who had succeeded Arminius as professor at the University of Leiden, and three ministers: Poppius, Corvinus and Dwinglo. Their list of objections was followed by a statement signed by eleven Remonstrant ministers, in which they expressed their opinion that these statements are worthy to be considered for a revision of the confession.[48] The form in which the Remonstrants presented

---

43. Hommius, *Specimen*, 125.

44. Hommius, *Specimen*, 126, 134.

45. This was their *Belijdenisse oft verklaringhe van't ghevoelen der leeraren die in de gheunieerde Nederlanden Remonstranten worden ghenaemt*, which was published in 1621.

46. *Acta ofte handelinghen*, 1:10 (November 15, 1617). All references to the *Acta* are to the 1621 Dutch language folio edition of the Acts. Since the Acts have been published in several editions and in different languages, the date on which an event occurred will be added in parentheses.

47. *Acta ofte handelinghen*, 1:164 (December 21, 1618). For the discussions that preceded this, see Hendrik Kaajan, *De groote synode van Dordrecht in 1618-1619* (Amsterdam: De Standaard, 1918), 144-48, and H. H. Kuyper, *De post-acta*, 318-22.

48. These objections can be found in the *Acta et scripta synodalia Dordracena ministrorum Remonstrantium in foederato Belgio* (Herder-Wiici: Ex officina typographi Synodalis, 1620), 86-102. The Dutch translation can be found in [Bernardus Dwinglo], *Historisch verhael van 't ghene sich toegedragehen heeft binnen Dordrecht in den jaeren 1618 ende 1619*, published together with *Oorspronck ende voortganck der Nederlantsche kerckelijcke verschillen tot op het nationale synodus* (n.p., 1623), 71-76. This record was published anonymously, but the author is presumably Bernard Dwinglo, who at the time was minister in Leiden. He acted as the unofficial clerk of the Remonstrants, recording the

their objections will have surprised the delegates at synod, for all objections were formulated as questions. This allowed the Remonstrants to bring forward their objections without having to state their own opinion.

The response to their submission was negative. One of the members of the British delegation, Hales, who regularly wrote reports to the king of Great Britain, mentioned that many at synod were astonished that the Remonstrants, who had threatened the churches for so many years with discoveries of falsehood and error in their confession and catechism, "should at last produce such poor impertinent stuff. There is not, I perswade my self, any writing in the world, against which wits disposed to wrangle, cannot take abundance of such exceptions."[49] In a similar vein, H. H. Kuyper would later speak of insignificant remarks.[50]

The submission begins with several general questions. For example, the third question concerns the issue of whether all parts of the doctrine discussed in the catechism and the confession are such that every Christian must believe these for salvation. If the answer is positive, would an implicit faith be sufficient? If the answer is negative, how can doctrines necessary for salvation be distinguished from doctrines not necessary for salvation? In this question, a statement taken from Lord's Day 7 of the Heidelberg Catechism is used against the catechism itself and against the confession. There is no need to deal with all these questions, but in view of later developments, the thirteenth question should be mentioned: "Should it not be considered whether the testimonies from Scripture cited in the text of the confession, were quoted correctly?"[51]

The question concerning article 1 provides a good example of the way the remarks on the confession are presented:

We want to be considered whether this is not an incomplete enumeration of the divine attributes, since some attributes are not listed while the knowledge of these is extremely necessary, since they are the basis of faith, love, hope, trust and fear of God, for example, omnipotence, mercy, severity, anger, hatred etc.[52]

---

proceedings during the sessions. On Dwinglo, see H. Kaajan, "Dwinglo," *Christelijke encyclopedie,* 2:525.

49. John Pearson, ed., "Mr. Hales Letters from the Synod of Dort," in *Golden Remains of the Ever Memorable Mr. John Hales,* 2nd rev. ed. (London: Th. Newcomb, 1659), 55 (letter dated December 17/27, 1618). Other delegates such as Gisbertus Voetius and Johann J. Breitinger also judged the objections insubstantial.

50. H. H. Kuyper, *De post-acta,* 321.

51. *Acta et scripta,* 87: "An non attendendum sit, num testimonia S. Scripturae in Confessionis textu allegata, recte ad propositum allegata sint." Cf. *Historisch verhael,* 71r. For more on this issue, see below (157).

52. *Acta et scripta,* 88: "Expendi velimus, an non sit imperfecta proprietatum divinarum recensio, quandoquidem quaedam proprietates non recensentur, quarum tamen cognitio perquam necessaria

These objections do not in any way touch on the doctrinal differences debated between the Reformed and the Remonstrants. It is true that at that time the article did not contain a comprehensive list of God's attributes, and several attributes, including God's omnipotence, were not mentioned. However, in view of Arminius' statements concerning God's providence quoted earlier, it is surprising to see the Remonstrants appear as the champions of God's omnipotence. It is also remarkable that the Remonstrants make a point of the fact that God's mercy is not mentioned here, for this was brought up in the article on election (art. 16).

In connection with article 2, five objections are brought up. The first concerns the title of the article: "In what way God is known." Should this not be: "By what means one comes to the knowledge of God," as it was in the 1561 edition? The second question asks why preservation is not mentioned among the means to know God, as in the first edition. The third question, dealing with the addition "which are sufficient to convict all men and to make them inexcusable," questions the correctness of making this the first and main purpose of general revelation. Is this not rather an accidental result of the abuse of this knowledge? In the fourth question it is pointed out that God's Word not only makes known God, but also Jesus Christ our Savior, and asks whether the difference between the knowledge from creation and the knowledge from God's Word is not expressed incompletely. The fifth question concerns a phrase in the final sentence. Should the words "to the salvation of his people" not be replaced with "to the salvation of the people," as the first edition had stated?[53]

These questions do not amount to much. The first and the second only concern matters of formulation. The third question overlooks the fact that the article begins by stating the positive main purpose, namely that we know God through his work, before it goes on to say that this revelation by itself is sufficient to convict people. The fourth goes beyond the specific purpose of article 2; this issue is taken up later in the confession. Only the fifth question could be connected to the discussion between the Remonstrants and the Reformed. But the question itself only deals with the purpose of special revelation, without determining the extent of salvation. In view of this, the response of Hales and others that the objections were "poor, impertinent stuff" appears justified. On closer inspection, however, the questions are often revealing. Several of the questions presented by the Remonstrants give insight into their convictions, as will be demonstrated in the following examples.

Six questions were presented in connection with article 13, dealing with providence. The statement of the confession that in this world nothing happens

---

est, utpote quae sunt fundamentum fidei, charitatis, spei, fiduciae, timoris Deo debiti, v.g. *Omnipotentia, Misericordia, Severitas, Ira, Odium* etc." Cf. *Historisch verhael*, 71r.

53. *Acta et scripta*, 88: "An loco istorum verborum, suorum salutem, non videantur reponenda quae in veteri extant exemplari, salutem hominum." Cf. *Historisch verhael*, 71r and v.

without God's ordinance is called ambiguous. The question is raised whether this statement means that God himself has decreed to do something and to direct events in such a way that it must happen necessarily, or whether he has decreed to permit it, considering that the confession elsewhere says that God is neither responsible for nor the author of evil. In addition, can the statement of this article that God is not the author of the sins that are committed be true if providence is taken in the first sense? This leads straight to the next question, dealing with the following sentence of article 13. The confession denies that God is the author of the sins committed by people. The Remonstrants ask whether it is not better to excuse God from these sins, and whether the statement should not be rephrased by adding that creatures committing sin are not simply instruments of God but are themselves the main workers of evil.[54] The questions indicate clearly that the Remonstrants actually disagree with the doctrine of God's providence as expressed in article 13. However, they do not come with an alternative, such as the solution of Arminius quoted by Hommius. They do not go beyond asking questions.

The Remonstrants present nine questions on article 14, dealing with the creation and fall of human beings. Concerning the depravity of the will, they point out that the confession speaks of small sparks of the excellent gifts humans had received. This leads to the question whether some traces of goodness, justice and holiness remain after the fall. To this is added the question whether the only reason for these traces is to make humans inexcusable.[55] In effect, the Remonstrants question whether the confession does actually teach a doctrine of the total depravity of the will.

Remarkably, no question is brought up in connection with original sin as discussed in article 15. Even more remarkable is the fact that only two questions are raised in connection with article 16 on election, but the first of these touches the core of the debate. The question is asked whether those who are elect are merely specific persons, or specific persons who are endowed with faith.[56] Already before, Hommius had pointed out that the latter view was that of the Remonstrants.[57]

In article 21, dealing with Christ our high priest, the only question is why Christ's prophetic and royal office are not mentioned.[58] This is a trivial question, in view of

---

54. *Acta et scripta*, 91-92; cf. *Historisch verhael*, 72-73.

55. *Acta et scripta*, 92: "An quod in lapsu homini religuum mansit recte describatur. Nam cum dicitur, *nihil homini relictum praeter exiguas scintillas excellentium donorum*, quorum ante facta erat mentio, puta bonitatis, iustitiae et sanctitatis; Queritur, An homini sciintillae aliquae istius iustitiae et sanctitatis sint relictae; et an heac verba, ad inexcusabiles reddendos homines, exprimant unicum et proprium finem, cui relictae scintillae in seruisse possint : Item qua ratione et qua efficacia homini omnem excusationem adimant." Cf. *Historisch verhael*, 73r, question 7.

56. *Acta et scripta*, 92-93: " . . . ut intelligantur particulares personae que tales, vel particulares quidem, sed fide circumscriptae . . ." Cf. *Historisch verhael*, 73r.

57. Hommius, *Specimen controversiarum*, 60-61. See also above.

58. *Acta et scripta*, 93; cf. *Historisch verhael*, 73v.

article 27 of the confession and Lord's Day 12 of the Heidelberg Catechism. Other questions in the section concerning Christ and his work are more weighty. The sixth question in connection with article 22 asks whether the statement at the end of the article that Christ imputes to us all his merits and the holy works he has done for us should not be reconsidered.[59] This question presumably refers to the theology of Piscator, an issue that will come up later in this chapter.[60] The same issue is mentioned in connection with article 23. Quoting the statement in the confession concerning the obedience of Christ crucified, the Remonstrants suggest that this obedience only consists in Christ's cross and suffering; the obedience he showed during his life does not form a part of it.[61]

Concerning the discussion of good works in article 24, the question is asked where Scripture teaches that it is not possible for us to do good works without stain of sin and worthy of punishment.[62] This is another of the list already mentioned by Hommius. The issue of whether a qualitative difference exists between the Old and the New Testament surfaces in connection with article 25, when the question is asked whether the statement "we still use the testimonies taken from the law and the prophets" is fitting.[63]

The section dealing with the articles on the church contains several questions touching the content of the confession. The only question on article 27 concerns the last sentence, that the church is joined and united with heart and will in one Spirit by the power of faith. The Remonstrants asked whether this can be maintained in view of the fact that Christians disagree on many doctrines.[64] Several questions concerning article 29 concentrate on the issue of the true church: Can it be known? Are Lutheran churches, which have a different doctrine of the Lord's Supper, true? Are the churches in Switzerland, where church discipline is not exercised, true churches?[65]

In the section of the confession dealing with church government, a number of questions concern the issue of whether God has prescribed one form of government for all churches and whether the confession was made to fit the situation of the Dutch churches.[66] This was a touchy issue at the Synod of Dort, where representatives of churches with different forms of church government were together.

---

59. *Acta et scripta*, 94; cf. *Historisch verhael*, 73v, question 6.
60. On Piscator, see H. H. Kuyper, *De post-acta*, 334-36.
61. *Acta et scripta*, 94; cf. *Historisch verhael*, 74r.
62. *Acta et scripta*, 95; cf. *Historisch verhael*, 74r, question 3.
63. *Acta et scripta*, 95; cf. *Historisch verhael*, 74v.
64. *Acta et scripta*, 95; cf. *Historisch verhael*, 74v.
65. *Acta et scripta*, 96; cf. *Historisch verhael*, 74v, 75r, questions 1 and 2.
66. *Acta et scripta*, 97; cf. *Historisch verhael*, 75r. This was the first question for both articles 31 and 32.

Remarkably, the issue of election is brought up again in connection with the articles on baptism and the Lord's Supper. Article 34 states that God commanded "all those who are his" to be baptized. This provoked the Remonstrants to ask whether this concerns those who by an exact and absolute decree of God have been predestined. Should the baptismal formula not be phrased conditionally: "I baptize you if you are elected for eternal life?" On the other hand, if "all those who are his" are to be taken as the believers, the minister cannot baptize anyone with assurance, for faith is hidden in the heart.[67] In article 35, election is brought up in connection with the phrase that only the elect have a spiritual and heavenly life. The question is asked whether the elect are different from the believers, mentioned later in the article. These questions apparently want to convey the impression that the doctrine of election is confusing or irrelevant.[68]

In connection with article 36, several questions are brought up concerning the statement that the government was instituted because of the depravity of the human race. Further, about the expression that the government has to maintain the ministry of the Word to prevent and remove all idolatry and false worship, the question is asked whether the government does not have the highest authority in these matters, without being bound by a judgment of the church.[69]

This is only a partial survey of the questions, but it should be enough to show that the objections brought in against the Belgic Confession were not all of the same quality. Many are relatively unimportant, such as the remarks concerning the absence of words such as omnipotence (art. 1) and preservation (art. 2). Other questions focus on proper formulation; for example, the question on the heading of article 2. However, several questions deal with important doctrinal issues, such as providence (art. 13), the difference between the Old and the New Testament (art. 25) and the question on the place of the doctrines in the church (art. 27). A number of issues debated between the Reformed and the Remonstrants are also touched on, in the questions about the depravity of man and the possibility of good works (arts. 14 and 21), election (arts. 16, 34 and 35) and the role of the government (art. 36). Although all remarks were presented in the form of questions, the fact that the Remonstrants disagreed with the teaching of the Belgic Confession comes through loud and clear.[70] The judgment by Hales and others that the Remonstrant objections were insignificant does apply to a number of questions, including some dealing with

---

67. *Acta et scripta*, 98: "Queritur, quo sensu ista verba accipi debant, 'omnes qui sui sunt.' Si n[on] tales intelligantur qui praeciso et absoluto Dei decreto Praedestinati sunt, Minister non poterit Baptizare nisi sub hac conditione, 'Baptizo te si ad vitam aeternam electus es.'" Cf. *Historisch verhael*, 75v, question 2.

68. *Acta et scripta*, 98; cf. *Historisch verhael*, 75v, question 2.

69. *Acta et scripta*, 98-99; cf. *Historisch verhael*, 76r, questions 2 and 3.

70. See also Van 't Spijker, *De synode van Dordrecht*, 111.

article 16, but not to many others. In most cases, their questions left no doubt that they actually disagreed with the teaching of the confession.

The Approbation of the Belgic Confession

The Synod of Dort dealt with the Belgic Confession on two separate occasions. First, a decision was made on the main issue of whether the Dutch churches were justified in using the Belgic Confession as the standard for the preaching and teaching in the church. This discussion took place in the presence of the foreign delegates, and it was decided to uphold this normative function of the confession. At a later point in time, when the foreign delegates had returned to their own countries, the text of the Belgic Confession was revised.

After the Canons of Dort had been drawn up and ratified, the synod continued by dealing with the existing confessions of the Dutch churches, the Belgic Confession and the Heidelberg Catechism, which had caused the original debates between the Reformed and the Remonstrants. During the meeting of April 29, 1619, the commissioners of the government conveyed the desire of the States General of the Netherlands that the confession and the catechism would be read and examined in the presence of the foreign delegates. They requested all members of the synod, the national as well as the foreign delegates, to declare freely whether they had noted anything regarding the doctrines and the substance of the doctrine that would appear to disagree with the truth of God's revealed Word or with the confessions of other Reformed churches.[71]

Two qualifications were added. The foreign delegates need not concern themselves with the formulation of the confession or with the articles on church government, for these were to be dealt with at a later date by the national delegates alone.[72] The reasons for excluding these two issues were not recorded, but they are not hard to guess. The actual formulation could not be determined at this stage because the issues were discussed in Latin, while the languages of the officially adopted versions of the confession were French and Dutch. Latin translations did exist, but they had never acquired official status.[73] The articles on church polity were excluded because the English church had a different structure from the one presented in the Belgic Confession.[74] This confession describes the presbyterian form

---

71. For the report on the proceedings, see *Acta ofte handelinghen* 1:345 (April 24, 1619). The text can be found in Appendix, Document 8.

72. *Acta ofte handelinghen*, 1:345.

73. See below, chapter 8.

74. The delegates of Hessia stated that these articles were excluded because of the English delegates; see H. H. Kuyper, *De post-acta*, 323. The Acts actually only mention articles 31 and 32, but article 30 was probably included, for Balcanqual reported that the three articles on church polity were excluded (Pearson, *Golden Remains*, 161). For the issue, see Willem Nijenhuis, "The Controversy

of church government, but the English church had an episcopalian structure. In fact, the leader of the English delegation was a bishop.

The official Acts of the Synod of Dordrecht summarized the statement of the British delegation, which was given in the morning session of the following day, April 30, 1619. They had carefully scrutinized the Belgic Confession. Notwithstanding the objections of the Remonstrants, they had found everything in the confession to be in agreement with God's Word. Most of the Remonstrant objections could be directed to all confessions of the Reformed churches. At this point, the meeting had to be interrupted to allow the delegates to attend the funeral of a fellow member who had passed away. In the afternoon, when synod resumed meeting, the other foreign delegates stated that there was no doctrine of the confession that disagreed with the truth of Holy Scripture. On the contrary, everything in it agreed with this truth and with the confessions of the other Reformed churches. The delegates urged the Dutch theologians to stand by this orthodox, pious and straightforward confession till the day of Christ's return.[75]

However, this is a simplified version of the actual events. In fact, the British delegates had brought up the issue of church government, disregarding the previously given directive by Bogerman. The leader of the British delegation, the bishop of Llandov, had objected to the equality of the ministers as expressed in the confession. Two other members of this delegation, Davenant and Goad, had stated that they approved of the Belgic Confession, with the exception of the articles on church government. In addition, remarks had been made concerning other articles. For example, in connection with article 9, Davenant had mentioned that it is impossible to derive the three divine Persons from their works. Another British delegate, Ward, had urged the synod to restore the words "and as many holy works" in article 22, as they had been omitted in the 1612 edition.[76]

Other delegations added their own remarks. In view of the fact that so many different versions of the confession existed, the request was made that one carefully prepared version be made, to function as the authentic text. The Bremen delegates proposed that God's omnipotence be expressly stated among God's attributes in article 1. In addition, they submitted a clarification of the first sentence of article 8. Furthermore, concerning article 15 they asked whether the church fathers had ever stated that in the view of the Pelagians original sin spread by imitation. Bogerman did respond to the remarks of the different delegations, but he appears to have ignored the church political issue. On the basis of the statements made by the delegations he concluded that the Belgic Confession had been approbated by the whole synod. He

---

Between Presbyterianism and Episcopalianism Surrounding and During the Synod of Dordrecht 1618-1619," in *Ecclesia Reformata: Studies on the Reformation* (Leiden: Brill, 1972), 215-20.

75. *Acta ofte handelinghen*, 1:346.

76. H. H. Kuyper, *De post-acta*, 326-28.

promised that an official text would be determined in the final sessions, after the foreign delegates had left.[77]

The complete text of the confession is included in the Acts of the Synod of Dordrecht under the heading of April 30, 1619. This gives the impression that the synod in the presence of the foreign delegates determined the text of the Belgic Confession as it was published in the Acts. In fact, however, on that day all that the delegates agreed on concerned the teaching of the Belgic Confession. The actual formulation of the confession was left to be discussed and determined by the national delegates.

The Revision of the Belgic Confession

After the foreign delegates had returned to their countries, the national delegates continued to finish what was left of the agenda. Some delegations appear to have realized that content and form cannot simply be separated. The theologians of Geneva had given Bogerman some annotations on the confession before they left. And the delegations of the Palatinate and of Hessen had each left a written advice with him.[78]

On May 13, 1619, the first session after the departure of the foreign delegates, it was decided to compare the Latin, French and Dutch versions of the Belgic Confession. This was necessary because discrepancies between the existing copies had been noted. An authorized text of the confession had to be made to be used in the future. The committee was to consider particularly the editions adopted by the French and Dutch churches.[79] This committee consisted of Thysius, Faukelius, Colonius, Hommius and Udemannus, most of whom had already done work on the text of the Belgic Confession. Faukelius had published a standard Dutch text of the Belgic Confession in 1611, Thysius had compared the first and second Dutch editions of the Belgic Confession, and Hommius had published Latin versions of the confession in his *Specimen*.[80] Colonius had been asked by Synod Vlissingen to check several editions of the confession.[81]

Synod finalized the Dutch text of the three final chapters of the Canons of Dort just over a week later, on May 21. The official records do not mention it, but at this

---

77. H. H. Kuyper, *De post-acta*, 326-30.

78. Bogerman mentioned this during session 172 (May 23, 1619); see H. H. Kuyper, *De post-acta*, 223.

79. The decisions taken during the final, national sessions of the Synod of Dort were not included in the original Acts of 1620 and 1621. They were published much later, in 1668 (Latin) and 1669 (Dutch). H. H. Kuyper republished them with explanatory remarks in his *De post-acta*. The passages dealing with the Belgic Confession can be found in Appendix, Document 8.

80. H. H. Kuyper, *De post-acta*, 337.

81. Bakhuizen van den Brink, *De Nederlandse belijdenisgeschriften*, 21.

point the chairman proposed to close the national part of the synod on the next day, for some theologians could be assigned to finish the revision of the Belgic Confession afterwards. This proposal was not well received, and many members protested that the revision of the confession should be finalized first. They asserted that synod itself should investigate and determine whether the changes made by the committee were appropriate. Gomarus, in particular, argued that making changes in the confession should not be left to a few people, but should be done by synod itself. He added that this applied particularly to article 22, where the phrase "and as many holy works he has done for us" had been omitted in the Genevan edition of the confession in the *Harmonia confessionum* published in 1612.[82] Bogerman's proposal to close the synod did not receive much support, with the result that the delegates continued to meet. The revision of the text of the Belgic Confession was placed on the agenda for the next day.

The issue at stake was the extent of Christ's saving work on our behalf. The confession stated in article 22 that "Jesus Christ and all his merits, as many holy works he has done for us," is our righteousness. This was a disputed issue. The German Calvinist theologian Piscator had denied that Christ's obedience to God's commandments was an integral part of his salvation work. The English and French churches had already rejected Piscator's teaching on this point. A Dutch regional synod had been approached with the request to join in this condemnation, but they had refused to do so for the reason that it properly belonged to a general synod to judge this issue. At the Synod of Dort, the delegates from Hessen and the Palatinate were supportive of Piscator, and the chairman, Bogerman, was inclined to defend this view.[83]

The order in which the articles were discussed on the next day proves the sensitivity of the issue concerning article 22. In the morning session, the text of articles 1 through 21 was read, and reasons for the changes were duly presented.[84] When the reading resumed in the afternoon session, it started with article 23 to the end of the confession. Finally, article 22 was read. Bogerman, as chairman, stated that the theologians of Geneva had left with him remarks on the confession, and the theologians of Hessen and the Palatinate had given him written advice. After these were read to the delegates, Bogerman proposed to replace the phrase "and as many

---

82. Voetius, who was present at synod, included a record of the events in his *Politica ecclesiastica*, 4 vols. (Amsterdam: Johannes Jansonius à Waesberge, 1676), 4:54-57, where he dealt with the confession of the church. This quotation is slightly lengthier than the formulation mentioned in footnote 76.

83. H. H. Kuyper, *De post-acta*, 338-44; Gerrit P. Van Itterzon, *Johannes Bogerman* (Amsterdam: Ton Bolland, 1980), 105-7.

84. See Appendix, Document 8.

holy works he has done for us" with the words "Christ's obedience," in order to accommodate the wish of the theologians who had left.[85]

The written advices have been preserved.[86] The Genevan theologians did not deal with the issue of article 22 at all. Rather, they stated in general terms that those who teach in the church should do so according to the Belgic Confession, the catechism and the articles made in Dort. The theologians of the Palatinate submitted eight rules for maintaining orthodoxy and peace within the church. The final, lengthiest rule concerns the issue of Christ's active obedience. They requested the Dutch brothers not to go beyond certain limits or to destroy the unity, but in their teaching to be content with the general formulation and explanation of Scripture as found in Romans 5:28 and Philippians 2:6. Only the letter of the Hessian theologians dealt exclusively with the issue of Christ's active obedience. In their opinion, the difference concerns expression rather than content, for both sides acknowledged that our righteousness is not based on our merits but on Christ's obedience. They therefore requested the delegates to tolerate some disagreement on this issue. All should teach in agreement with Scripture that Christ's obedience is imputed to us for righteousness. This obedience must be explained as Christ being obedient to death on the cross.

Remarkably, none of these statements given to Bogerman had requested the national delegates to change the text of the confession or the catechism. It appears that Bogerman's proposal to rephrase the text of article 22 went beyond the advices left by the three delegations and was in fact his own. This was already noted by the Dutch theologian Ellard Van Mehen (also called Menius), who stated that the Palatinate theologians only wanted to prevent condemnation of their opinion but were agreeable to retaining the text of the confession.[87]

Without exception, all delegations rejected Bogerman's proposed change during the meeting of the next day. In a vote, his proposal was defeated with only two votes in favour. It was even decided to expand the original statement "and the many holy works as he has done for us," with the explanatory words "and in our place." Only one other delegate voted with Bogerman against this formulation.[88] With this revision, the Belgic Confession was reconfirmed by the Synod of Dort as the authoritative confession of the Reformed Churches in the Netherlands.

The question must now be answered as to how this revision affected the confession. It is not necessary to go over all the changes; this has been done

---

85. See Appendix, Document 8.

86. The text of these letters can be found in H. H. Kuyper, *De post-acta*, 513-16.

87. His statement was included in the declaration by the delegation of the province of South Holland, quoted by Voetius, *Politica ecclesiastica*, 4:57.

88. Voetius, *Politica ecclesiastica*, 4:55; H. H. Kuyper, *De post-acta*, 344. Bakhuizen van den Brink's statement in *De Nederlandse belijdenisgeschriften*, 27, that the text of article 22 was not changed is incorrect.

meticulously by Kuyper.[89] We want to look at the kind of changes made. How comprehensive were they, and how did they affect the confession?

This is all the more pressing because these changes were characterized differently during the following centuries. In the seventeenth century, Voetius argued against Seldenus that the changes made at this synod were not substantial. He supported this by appending a list of the changes.[90] In the eighteenth century, Reverend Van der Os used the changes made at Dort to argue that the confession can be abandoned when God gives more light. De Moor responded to this in a lengthy discussion. After having reprinted the list of changes given by Voetius, he concluded that the revision of Dordrecht had not resulted in a substantial change in the confession.[91] H. H. Kuyper returned to this issue at the end of the nineteenth century, providing the most comprehensive survey and evaluation of the changes. On that basis he supported Voetius, in opposition to Van Toorenenbergen, who had stated that the Synod of Dort made an important revision of the confession.

Kuyper's careful study presents a convincing argument that the revision at Dort did not mean a change in doctrine from the earlier versions of 1561 and 1566. The data he provides allow us to gain further insight into the character of this revision. A general survey shows clearly that the revision was not limited to the disputed issues or the remarks of the Remonstrants; rather, it was a general overhaul. It is not necessary to repeat Kuyper's comprehensive list. Some representative examples will suffice to provide a clear indication of the extent of the changes made.

The first category contains a relatively large number of changes, which are the direct result of the objections presented by the Remonstrants:

> Concerning article 1, they had remarked that a number of attributes of God, such as his omnipotence, mercy, severity, anger and hatred, had not been mentioned. As stated before, this objection was not altogether fair, since several of these attributes were mentioned in other articles. Presumably because God's omnipotence was not mentioned anywhere else, synod decided to state this explicitly: "who is almighty."
>
> In article 2, the first means of knowing God was his work in this world, expressed by two synonymous words: "the created, *led* and *governed* world." When the Remonstrants pointed out that the preservation of the world was not mentioned, synod decided to replace one of the synonyms and to include the

---

89. H. H. Kuyper, *De post-acta*, 365-88. Separate from this discussion, Bekker also dealt with the changes in the text of the Belgic Confession in *De leere der gereformeerde kerken*, 2-40. This book consists of sermons on the Belgic Confession, one of several collections of sermons Bekker published at the end of his life because his orthodoxy was suspect after the publication of his book on sorcery, *De betoverde weereld*.

90. Voetius discussed the issue in *Politica ecclesiastica*, 4:61-67; for the list of changes, see 67-74.

91. Bernardus De Moor, *Commentarius perpetuus in Johannis Marckii Compendium* (Leiden: Johannes Hasebroek, 1768), 6:359-85, concluding that no real change had taken place.

idea of preservation: "by the creation, *conservation* and government of the whole world."

Still in article 2, the confession stated originally that God "makes himself known to us more clearly and evidently in his holy and divine Word." The expressions "clearly" and "evidently" are obviously used synonymously, and the Synod of Dort decided to change the formulation to "more clearly and fully" in the Dutch text.[92] This change shows awareness of the fact that general and special revelation not only differ in clarity, but that special revelation also goes beyond general revelation. In this case, too, the synod made the improvement in response to a Remonstrant question.

Since the revision of 1566, article 8, dealing with the doctrine of the trinity, stated that God is a single essence, eternally distinct in three Persons. The Remonstrants asked whether God is distinct in three Persons, as the first edition had expressed it, or whether God's essence is distinct in three Persons, as it was formulated in 1566. This question caused synod to rephrase the whole sentence, stating that God is "one single essence, in which there are three persons, really, in truth and eternally distinct." A similar change was made in article 9.

A statement in article 18 was refined. The Remonstrants had pointed out that the Anabaptists did not deny that Jesus Christ assumed human flesh, but that he assumed this from his mother. The synod added the words "from his mother" to this article.[93]

This brief survey shows that the changes were not of the same nature. In articles 1 and 2, additions were made to the content of the article, but the changes in articles 8 and 18 concern formulation.

Another category that can be identified consists of instances where the text of the confession was brought closer to a statement from the Bible:

In describing the inspiration of Scripture in article 3, the expression "the holy men" was expanded to "the holy men of God." Later in the same article the name "the Spirit of God" was replaced by "the Holy Spirit." These changes, which do not contribute a new element to the article, can only be explained from a desire to follow the formulation of 2 Peter 2:21 more closely.

In article 10, dealing with the Son of God, the expression "the proper image of the substance of the Father" was adjusted after Hebrews 1:3: "the engraved image of the person of the Father."

---

92. Remarkably, this addition was not included in the French text. See Bakhuizen van den Brink, *De Nederlandse belijdenisgeschriften*, 72-73; H. H. Kuyper, *De post-acta*, 356. Kuyper writes that the expression "more clearly and fully" was already found in the Latin version of 1612, but there appears to be no evidence for this.

93. H. H. Kuyper, *De post-acta*, 369.

In article 13, dealing with God's providence, one example of God's care was formulated wrongly. Originally, the confession stated that "a small hair of our head is numbered." This was revised after Matthew 10:29: "not one of the hairs of our head (for they are all numbered) . . . can fall on the ground without the will of our Father."

In the original description of Christ's suffering in article 21, it was stated that "he sweat blood and water." This statement undoubtedly resulted from a confusion of two different events: his suffering in Gethsemane and the flow of blood and water when the soldier pierced him to see whether he had died (John 19:34). In view of Luke 22:44, this was rephrased as "his sweat became as drops of blood, falling on the earth."

Perhaps we can include in this category an occasion where the text of the Belgic Confession was changed to bring it closer to the formulation of the Heidelberg Catechism. In the early editions of article 33, the sacraments were described as "symbols and visible signs." This was changed by Synod of Dort to make it conform to Lord's Day 25, answer 66: "For they are visible signs and seals."

In the third place, the Synod of Dort also made a number of corrections in the text. Some of these concern mistakes that had found their way into previous editions:

In the 1566 revision of article 2, the word "whole" had been inserted: "the creation, preservation and government of the whole world." The word had been left out in the 1611 edition, but synod, following earlier editions, restored it.

A more important change was the official insertion of the name of Arius among those who rejected the doctrine of the Trinity in article 9. His name had appeared in Dutch editions as early as 1563, but it had been omitted later. The Synod of Dort included Arius again. However, it is questionable whether his name is correctly included among those who denied the Trinity.

Among the biblical statements concerning the human nature of Jesus Christ in article 18 was the expression that he is "of the seed of Abraham and David." However, mentioning David at this point did not make sense for two reasons. Not only had Christ's descent from David been mentioned before, but the confession also continued by speaking only about Abraham. David's name was correctly removed.

In the explanation concerning Christ's sacrifice in article 21, it used to say that he sacrificed himself "on the altar of the cross." This was rephrased to read: "on the wood of the cross." Voetius later wrote that this change was made after reasons had been given,[94] but these reasons have not been preserved.

Article 26 originally stated that Jesus Christ "has been made man, joining together God and man." The revision of 1566 had already changed the phrasing, but, as the result of unintentionally omitting the human nature, the result was an

---

94. Voetius, *Politica ecclesiastica*, 4:53.

incomplete sentence: "joining together the divine nature." In later editions, the statement was rephrased in various ways. The revision of Dort used the formulation in a private Latin edition of 1612 as the basis for its statement: "uniting together the divine and human nature."

Fourthly, there are a number of cases in which synod added to the text of the articles:

The list of the canonical books in article 4 originally mentioned mostly categories, such as "the five books of Moses" and "the four books of the Kings." In the revised version of 1619, the individual books are listed.[95] Similarly, in article 6, dealing with the apocryphal books, the names of these books were now written out.

In article 9, a very small addition was made. The statement that we know the three Persons "from the works" was changed to "from their works." Somehow, this was not implemented in the French text, but it was in the Dutch text. The Latin text is even more explicit: "from the works of these Persons."[96]

In the same article, a qualification is inserted in the statement concerning the knowledge of the Trinity in the Old Testament by the addition of the word "somewhat." As a result, the concluding statement concerning the Old Testament basis for the doctrine of the Trinity now reads: "what for us is somewhat obscure in the Old Testament."

In article 14, the phrase "contrary to this" was inserted. The reason is obvious when the whole sentence is considered: "Therefore we reject all teaching contrary to this about the free will of man."

In article 19, the word "dying" was added in the confession of Christ's death: "What he, dying, committed into the hands of his Father."

In article 22, the words "of our sins" were added: "to acquit us of our sins."

These changes were not all original for the Synod of Dort. For example, the change made in article 14 was already made by Hommius in his book, and the change in article 22 can be found in the Latin text of 1612.

Overall, the changes made by the Synod of Dort are very limited and not significant. This is understandable in view of the fact that synod now consisted only of the Dutch delegates. The revision was not meant to make substantial changes in a text that had already been approved by the full synod, including the foreign delegates.

In view of this, it is unlikely that a minor change in article 29 would have doctrinal significance. The original text stated that the sects claim "to be of the

---

95. The book of Habakkuk has been omitted in the Dutch version of the confession. This was no more than an oversight, for it was mentioned in the French and Latin editions.

96. H. H. Kuyper, *De post-acta*, 361.

church." In the revision this was rephrased to read that the sects claim "to be the church." Kuyper applauded this change as a very valuable correction, for the reason that sectarianism causes people to claim that they alone are the church, rather than being a part of the church.[97] However, this interpretation can hardly be based on such a minor change, and it does not agree with the general character of this revision.

Fifthly, it should be mentioned that the textual references were omitted in the editions published at the order of the Synod of Dort. This is probably the direct result of one of the questions presented from the side of the Remonstrants. They had asked whether the marginal references were all quoted correctly. Rather than going over these texts, checking and if necessary debating them, synod decided simply to leave them out. However understandable in the historical situation, this decision is regrettable for two reasons. The marginal texts had been part of the confession from its first edition. Removing them was breaking with the good tradition to indicate on which biblical data the teaching of the church was founded. Moreover, as a result of this decision an inconsistency occurs in the confessional documents of the Reformed churches. The same synod that removed the supporting texts in the case of the Belgic Confession, retained these in the edition of the Heidelberg Catechism, and actually added texts in the Canons of Dort.

Finally, one more aspect of this revision must be mentioned. There are slight differences between the Dutch and the French texts. This is remarkable, for during the final sessions both versions were read aloud article by article.

> As stated before, the tautological expression in article 2 "more clearly and evidently" was replaced by an expression that goes beyond it in meaning: "more clearly and fully." However, in the French text, the words "and fully" were not included, so the notion that God has revealed more in his special revelation is not expressed.
>
> Since 1566, article 15 contained the remarkable comparison of a water spring to explain the influence of original sin: "seeing that bubbles continually flow from it as from an evil well." The Dutch version of Dordrecht formulated this in a somewhat less picturesque way: "since sin always flows from it as water welling up." However, the French text was left unchanged.
>
> Article 21 contains a slight inconsistency. When quoting 1 Corinthians 2:2, the French text speaks of "Jesus and him crucified," but the Dutch text has "Christ and him crucified."

---

97. H. H. Kuyper, *De post-acta*, 380. The change is minor, for the Dutch text first stated: "alle secten welcke segghen, datse van de Kercke zijn," which was changed at Dordrecht to read: " . . . datse de Kercke zijn." A more probable reason for changing the formulation is the fact that later in this article the same expression was used in a different context.

In article 34, the French text states that one "must be baptized one time." This used to be followed by the words "with a single baptism," but they cannot be found in the Dordrecht text. This omission may have been an oversight. However, the Dutch text states: "someone who aspires to enter eternal life, should be baptized only once with a single baptism, without evermore repeating it." In view of the redundant phrasing of the Dutch text, it is also possible that the omission in the French text is intentional.

In the final article, a word was left out at the end of the French version. It now reads "Therefore we await that great day with desire" rather than "with great desire," as in earlier editions. This, too, may have been done intentionally in order to avoid repeating the word "great." However, the Dutch text of Dort maintains the double use of "great."

These discrepancies are not significant. In some cases, it was the Dutch version that was edited somewhat more carefully, on other occasions it was the French version. It appears that the revisors were not obligated to achieve complete uniformity in the text, but were allowed some freedom in expression.

The Publication of the Confession

As the result of the Synod of Dort, several editions of the Belgic Confession were published. As this had been an international synod, the Latin *Acta* were published first, in 1620. This was undoubtedly also done in recognition of the contribution of the foreign delegates. In the Latin edition, the full text of the Belgic Confession is printed following the report on the proceedings of April 30, 1619, the day on which all delegates had approved the Belgic Confession.

The text printed in these Acts was not the same one the foreign delegations had seen and approved. They had judged the confession in the Latin version as published in the *Syntagma Confessionum* (1612).[98] The revision of the confession that took place after the foreign delegates had left resulted in many changes in the text. This required a new Latin version to be made for the Latin *Acta*. The translation was made by Festus Hommius,[99] one of the clerks of synod, who had previously published a Latin version of the confession in his *Specimen*.

This Latin text of the confession was never officially approved. The content had been approved by the international synod, but the text itself had not been scrutinized by the foreign delegates before they left, nor was this done later by the national

---

98. Bakhuizen van den Brink, *De Nederlandse belijdenisgeschriften*, 25. He adds that this Latin text was very similar to that of the *Harmonia confessionum* of 1581.

99. Bakhuizen van den Brink, *De Nederlandse belijdenisgeschriften*, 27.

delegates.[100] It is a translation of the Dort version of the Belgic Confession for the international Reformed community that had participated at the Synod of Dordrecht.

The approved French text, as revised at Dordrecht, was printed in 1619 by Nicolas Vincent and Françoys Borsaler. The approved revision of the Dutch text was first published by the same Borsaler, also in 1619. Both Vincent and Borsaler were associates of the publisher Isaack Canin, who in 1621 published the Dutch version of the Acts of the Synod of Dordrecht.[101] Just as in the Latin *Acta*, the Dutch text of the confession was inserted in the Dutch *Acta* as part of the events recorded under April 30, 1619, when the confession had been approved, although the actual text was made later. But unlike the Latin text, the text of the Belgic Confession printed in the Dutch Acts was one of the two officially approved texts.

---

100. H. H. Kuyper, *De post-acta*, 345-46; see also 224-25.
101. Bakhuizen van den Brink, *De Nederlandse belijdenisgeschriften*, 39.

8

Translations

The original language of the Belgic Confession is French, but in the course of time it was translated into several languages. Some of these translations are predictable, others unexpected. It is obvious that a Dutch translation needed to be made, for at the time the Netherlands was a bilingual country, consisting of both French-speaking and Dutch-speaking provinces. However, the existence of a Greek translation is a surprise, all the more so because there are two. The purpose of surveying these translations is not so much to determine their quality. Rather, this survey will focus on the background and function of each translation, in order to understand the influence of the confession.[1] We will discuss the translations by language.

Dutch Translations

Generally speaking, in the southern provinces of the Netherlands where the Belgic Confession was first discovered, the vernacular was French, while in the northern provinces Dutch was spoken. However, the language division was not so clear cut. For example, in the southern port city of Antwerp, a congregation of Dutch-speaking Reformed people had been established next to a French-speaking congregation. The need for a Dutch translation was soon apparent, and a Dutch translation was made.

During the disputes concerning the Belgic Confession in the seventeenth century, the year of publication of this translation was given as 1563.[2] This date can still be found in Ens' study on the confessions, originally published in 1733.[3] Le Long mentions that he had found a Dutch edition dating from 1562, but he neglected to

1. For that reason, translations made for scholarly purposes will not be included.

2. According to Van Langeraad, *Guido de Bray*, 103, this was already stated by Thysius, in his *Corpus Doctrinae*, 8. See also Trigland, *Kerckelycke geschiedenissen*, 144; Brandt, *Historie der reformatie*, 1:254.

3. Ens, *Kort historisch berigt*, 78.

indicate where this copy could be consulted.[4] The issue was finally decided in the nineteenth century, when Van der Linde reported in 1864 that a Dutch edition of 1562 had been discovered.[5] It is not clear whether this is the same copy already mentioned by Le Long.

This edition was first mentioned in a proclamation by Johan van Ligne, Count of Aremberg. This proclamation, dated April 7, 1562, states that some sectarians had disseminated a small book to instigate rebellion among the subjects of the king and to bring them to their side. The title of this booklet is given as: "Confession of faith, made by common accord by the believers who are dispersed in the Netherlands, who desire to live according to the purity of the holy gospel of our Lord Jesus Christ."[6] This closely resembles the title printed on the extant copy of the Dutch translation. Apart from a few insignificant spelling variations, the only difference is the use of a slightly different word for "confession." On the title page of the printed edition the word "Belydenisse" was used, but the proclamation refers to the "Belijdinge."[7] The proclamation gives the date of publication as 1562, adding that the name of the printer had been suppressed. Undoubtedly, the Belgic Confession is meant here.

The early date of the Dutch translation is surprising. The original French edition was not printed before the spring of 1561, and it was not mentioned before October 1561. Within six months of the first appearance of the French version of the Belgic Confession, it was reported that a Dutch translation had been discovered.

Similar to the original French edition, the Dutch translation was published anonymously; neither the name of the author nor that of the translator is mentioned. Two ministers in particular have been mentioned as possible translators: Hermanus Moded and Godfried van Wingen.[8] As no direct proof exists for the involvement of these theologians, we need to consider whether it is probable that one or both made this Dutch translation.

---

4. Te Water, *Tweede eeuw-getyde*, 47-48, following Le Long, *Kort historisch verhaal van den eersten oorsprong der Nederlandschen gereformeerden onder 't kruis* (Amsterdam: S. Schouten en zoon, 1751), 84, 86-88.

5. Los, *Tekst en toelichting*, v-vi, 5-6.

6. Van Langeraad, *Guido de Bray*, 96 n. 3: "Also sommige Sectarissen, om beter te moegen verwecken eenyge beroerten ende remotien onder goede Ondersaeten van Conincklijke Maiesteyt ons Aldergenaedichste Heere, ende die selve te trecken toe haerluyder quade opinie, souden hebben doen verspreyen zeecker boecxken, geintituleert: *Belijdinge des geloofs*, gemaict mit een gemein accordt, doir die Gelovige, die in de Nederlanden over al verstroyt zijn, dewelcke nae die zuyverheyt des heylighen Evangeliums ons Heeren Jesu Christi begeeren te leven, gedruckt in den jaere ons Heeren Jesu Christi duysent vijffhondert twee ende 't sestich, wesende de naem van den Drucker des voirscreven boecxkens gesupprimeert . . ."

7. This is probably a mistake, for no 1562 Dutch copy with the title "belijdinge" is mentioned in the survey by Van Langeraad, *Guido de Bray*, 153-55.

8. Van Langeraad, *Guido de Bray*, 97; Bakhuizen van den Brink, *De Nederlandse belijdenisgeschriften*, 23.

Moded was born in Zwolle, a city in Overijssel, a province in the northeast of the country.[9] He had enrolled as a student at the University of Cologne in Germany (1550), where he received a master's degree (1553). After having taught at that same university for a number of years, he became critical of the Roman Catholic church and escaped to the Netherlands. In 1560, he became a minister of the Dutch-speaking Reformed congregation at Antwerp. Between 1561 and 1566 he was one of the leaders of the Reformed in Flanders, and he was one of the delegates at the Synod of Antwerp in 1566. He wrote several books, all in his native language, Dutch.

In connection with the Belgic Confession, his name is mentioned twice in the older literature. Saravia wrote that he and Moded belonged to the first authors of the confession. As discussed before,[10] Saravia did not present himself as one of the original drafters of the confession or its translation. Rather, he was referring to the fact that he had promoted it. When he in the same statement mentioned Moded as another author, he meant that Moded, too, had supported the confession, presumably at the Synod of 1566.

Much later, in 1762, Te Water misunderstood Saravia's statement and presented Moded as one of the original authors of the confession. He supported this with a quotation from one of Moded's publications: "With which agrees the confession which we, Reformed in the Netherlands, have submitted to the king of Spain, by me, served under the cross, in the year 1561."[11] Te Water interpreted the word "served" as meaning that Moded had "read again, checked and approved" the Belgic Confession in 1561,[12] which is a rather imaginative way of explaining the word. In fact, his interpretation is based on a misunderstanding of the text. The word "served" does not refer to him serving the confession, but rather to the fact that Moded served the Reformed people in the Netherlands. We can conclude that Moded's original statement does not refer to any involvement on his part in making the confession. He said no more than that he served as a minister to the Reformed churches, which had submitted the Belgic Confession to the king of Spain.

According to Los, Godfried Van Wingen is generally seen as the translator of the confession in Dutch.[13] He does not present any proof for this statement, but it may

---

9. For a general survey of Moded's life, see Kaajan, "Moded," 4:227; Van Itterzon, "Moded, Herman," 3:267-71.

10. See the discussion of this passage in chapter 2.

11. Te Water, *Tweede eeuw-getyde*, 11, where he quotes from Moded's book, *Tegen de Wederdoop*, 270: " . . . waer meede dat accordeert de belydinge, die wy Gereformeerden van de Nederlanden den Coninck van Spaengien hebben overgegeeven, by my, onder 't Cruyce beneerstigt, in 't Jaer 1561."

12. Te Water, *Tweede eeuw-getyde*, 12: " . . . dit moest ik hier aenmerken, op dat men zyne uitdrukkinge niet verkeerdelyk zoude opvatten als hadde hy die belydinge in de maent January des Jaers 1561 *beneerstigt*, dat is, herleezen, overzien, en goetgekeurt, willende hy alleen zeggen dat zulks van hem gedaen is in den jaere 1561, wanneer *Guido de Bres* zyn opstel aen meer andere beroemde mannen heeft overgegeeven ter onderzoekinge."

13. Los, *Tekst en toelichting*, 6.

go back to a remark in Van Langeraad's study on Guido de Brès,[14] which in turn refers to a book published by Outhovius in 1723. However, Outhovius does not say that Van Wingen was the translator; rather, he calls him a maker of the confession.[15] This statement cannot be used to attribute the translation to Van Wingen.

Godfried Van Wingen was originally from Luik, in the southern part of the Netherlands.[16] After having lived in England, he went to Emden in northern Germany where he was involved in Bible translation. In 1559 he worked in Flanders, but by the end of the year he was in London. During 1561, he was in Belgium, England and Germany. At the beginning of 1562, he had to flee from Flanders back to England. Thysius, in the preface of his book on the doctrine and church order of the Dutch churches, praised Van Wingen as someone who was sent by the church of Emden for the upbuilding of the Reformed congregations in Flanders on account of his extraordinary learning in theology and ability in Greek and other languages.[17] Thysius' statement shows great appreciation for Van Wingen, but it does not mention that he contributed to the Dutch text of the Belgic Confession.

With the information presently available, it is not possible to state with certainty who made the first Dutch translation of the Belgic Confession. If a choice must be made between Moded and Van Wingen, it is more likely that the latter made the translation because he was in the area at the right time and had experience with translating.

The Dutch translation of the first edition of the Belgic Confession was often reprinted in the early years. Already in the year after the initial publication, a virtually identical edition was printed, followed by editions in 1564 and in 1566, before the synod where it was revised convened.[18] Remarkably, even after the official revision of the French text in 1566 the Dutch editions continued to reproduce the text of the first edition, for this text was reprinted in 1573, 1576, 1578 and 1580. In the Dutch *Book of Martyrs*, the same Dutch text of the confession was printed under the events from the year 1562,[19] although it is also possible that this was done for historical reasons. However, the question arises as to why the Dutch editions after 1566 did not present a translation of the revised text, but rather continued to publish a Dutch version of the first edition.

---

14. Van Langeraad found a handwritten note on the title page of a 1566 Dutch translation of the Belgic Confession, stating that Godfried van Wingen was the translator; *Guido de Bray*, 97 n. 3.

15. Gerardus Outhovius, *Ter waerschuwinge aan alle Kristenen* (Emden: H. Van Senden, 1723), 217: "mede in 't jaar 1561 de opstelder was van die brave Neerlandsche Geloofsbelijdenisse." This remark may go back to Schoock's statement on the Belgic Confession.

16. The date and year of birth of Van Wingen are unknown. He was already teaching in the early 1550s and died in 1598; see Van Itterzon, "Godfried van Wingen," 3:403-5.

17. Te Water, *Tweede eeuw-getyde*, 13-15; Van Langeraad, *Guido de Bray*, 97-98.

18. Los, *Tekst en toelichting*, 5; Bakhuizen van den Brink, *De Nederlandse belijdenisgeschriften*, 23.

19. Van Langeraad, *Guido de Bray*, 154; the reprints are listed in the footnote.

The reason may well be that the Reformed churches were waiting for an official translation of the revised French text. At the provincial Synod of 1574, the churches of classis Walcheren submitted a proposal to have a Latin translation made for subscription by the Dutch ministers. This request concerned the authority of the confession, but it was preceded by the question of whether the Dutch version should not be made to agree with the recent French edition of Master Beza.[20] At the time, the Dutch churches obviously were well aware of the fact that the functioning Dutch text of the confession was outdated. However, synod decided to leave the confession unchanged: "If some words in it ought to be changed after the copy printed in Geneva, this should wait for the general synod."[21] Although the revised text had been adopted, the provincial synod did take it upon itself to adjust the Dutch translation accordingly, but considered this to be a task for the churches in general.

In the end, however, the Dutch text of the confession was not adjusted at a general synod. In 1578, the national Synod of Dort regulated the subscription to the confession, but it did not update the Dutch text or even appoint a committee for this purpose.[22] At the national Synod of Middelburg in 1581, a question concerning the confession led to the decision that Daniel de Dieu should translate it from French into Dutch.[23] Although the second clerk of this synod, Herman Van de Corput, wrote several letters reminding de Dieu of this decision, he did not receive any answer. In a letter dated January 25, 1582, he reported this to Arent Cornelisz, who had been chairman of the synod, adding the wish that a French edition of the revised text might be available when synod met, in case the Dutch edition had not been printed yet.[24] This statement implies that he did not know where to obtain the original French text of the revised edition. This caused Van Tielt to travel to Antwerp, where he not only obtained a copy of the revised text of the confession, but also learned the name of its author.[25] The synod mentioned by Van de Corput was a regional synod of the whole province of Holland. At that time, the churches of the northern and southern parts of this province met separately, and only occasionally had a combined meeting for the whole area. As a combined meeting was slated for March of that year, Van de Corput wanted the updated Dutch translation of the confession to be presented at that synod.

---

20. Rutgers, *Acta van de Nederlandsche synoden*, 212.

21. Rutgers, *Acta van de Nederlandsche synoden*, 141.

22. Rutgers, *Acta van de Nederlandsche synoden*, 247.

23. Rutgers, *Acta van de Nederlandsche synoden*, 372: "Daniel de Dieu sal oversetten de confessie des geloofs der nederlantschen kercken, uut den francoys int nederduytsch."

24. Hendrik Q. Janssen and J. J. Van Toorenenbergen, eds., *Brieven uit onderscheidene kerkelijke archieven*, Werken der Marnix-vereeniging, series 3, vol. 2 (Utrecht: Kemink & Zoon, 1878), 184; see also Los, *Tekst en toelichting*, 26-27.

25. See the discussion in chapter 2 and my article, "The Earliest Report," 86-94.

Van de Corput was present as a delegate when this provincial synod met. On the day after the opening, he wrote another letter to Arent Cornelisz, urging him to provide a translation:

> Concerning the Confession of Faith, since no answer is coming from Brussels, you will do a good work by translating and sending it right away. If possible, have someone else make a neat copy so that we can deal with it more quickly, also that they do not see at first glance that it is your work. Do your utmost, and also send the French text.[26]

This statement shows that the initiative came from Van de Corput, who as clerk felt responsible for the implementation of Synod Middelburg's decision. Since de Dieu, the appointed translator, had failed to do the work synod had assigned to him, in Van de Corput's estimation no one was in a better position to take on the translation than the chairman of that synod. At the same time, Van de Corput did not want it to be known that it was Cornelisz who had translated the confession. The reason is presumably that he wanted to prevent a debate on the propriety of involving a different translator, for this could interfere with the adoption of the Dutch text by synod.

The text of the Dutch translation was presented to the Synod of Haarlem 1582, as the minutes of March 24 mention this new translation. It was decided that those belonging to classis Delft would check it over and have it printed.[27] This report does not give any indication that the translation had been carefully scrutinized and approved in a public meeting of synod. This is confirmed by the fact that the decision was taken on the day before synod closed, when both the morning and afternoon had been devoted to making a record of the proceedings. However, Hendrik Van de Corput and Arent Cornelisz could be satisfied, for synod had made the principal decision to recognize the presented version as the Dutch translation of the 1566 revised text. What remained to be done was to obtain the approval by classis Delft. Regrettably, the first volume of the records of this classis no longer exists, and the second volume begins with November 5, 1582, after the new translation had been

---

26. Janssen and Van Toorenenbergen, eds., *Brieven uit onderscheidenen kerkelijke archieven*, 194: "Aengaende de bekentenisse des geloofs, nadien van Bruessel geen antwoirt coomt, sult ghy een goet werck doen die oversettende ende van stonden aen seyndende, ende, cont ghy, laet die by eenen anderen ende wat nettelick afschrijven, opdat wy te eer daer mede veerdich syn, opdat sy oyck prima facie nyet sien dat het uw werck is; doet hier inne d'beste ende seynt mede de walsche copie." See also Los, *Tekst en toelichting*, 27-28.

27. Reitsma and Van Veen, *Acta der provinciale en particuliere synoden*, 1:112: "Is voorgebracht de Nederlantsche bekentenisse des geloofs, nu van nyews uut het Walsch exemplar overgeset ende is besloten, dat die van Delft die oversien sullen ende daerna drucken laten."

dealt with. For that reason it is not possible to determine whether anything was changed at the direction of classis.[28]

This Dutch edition has several characteristic features compared to the previous editions of the confession. It opens with a foreword for the Christian reader, in which the biblical origin of confessing the faith is explained. Following this, the Belgic Confession is explained against the background of the fact that the orthodox fathers in the early Christian church wrote symbols and confessions and presented these to the government. Concerning the articles themselves, brief summaries of the content of each article are added to make it easier to find and remember the articles.[29] The Dutch text of the articles themselves is affected in two ways. First of all, the changes made in 1566 are now included in the Dutch translation of the confession, resulting in many differences compared to the first Dutch edition. Furthermore, in many instances the original Dutch text is changed with respect to expression and spelling without affecting the meaning.

The third Dutch edition of the Belgic Confession was made by the great Synod of Dort after the foreign delegates had left.[30] It was first printed in the Dutch version of the official Acts. Later, it was included in many church books, following the Psalms and the Heidelberg Catechism. The first comparison between the Dort text of the Belgic Confession and the earlier editions was produced by Balthasar Bekker, as mentioned before. In the introduction of a publication of his sermons on the Belgic Confession, he presented a lengthy survey of the differences between the first Dutch text of 1562 (which he mistakenly dated as 1563), the text of 1582 and the text determined by the Synod of Dort.[31]

During the following centuries, the text of the Belgic Confession was not touched. That changed in the twentieth century, when objections to the formulation concerning the task of the government in article 37 led the 1905 Synod of the Reformed Churches in the Netherlands to decide to delete the words "to prevent and destroy all idolatry and false worship of God." However, the desire was expressed to print these words in a footnote, adding the reason why these words were deleted.[32]

After the Second World War, several newly translated versions of the Dutch text of the Belgic Confession were published. The initiative came from Bakhuizen van den Brink who wrote a report in 1950 on the text of the confessions for the Liturgical

---

28. Los, *Tekst en toelichting*, 29-30.

29. These changes are mentioned in the introduction "To the Christian Reader" added to the 1583 edition, which can be found in Van Langeraad, *Guido de Bray*, 148-49 n. 2.

30. See chapter 7.

31. Bekker, *De leere der gereformeerde kerken*, 2-40, preceding the foreword.

32. *Acta der Generale Synode van de Gereformeerde Kerken in Nederland gehouden te Utrecht 1905*, 81-82. For an overall discussion of this issue, see Klaas Van der Zwaag, *Onverkort of gekortwiekt? Artikel 36 van de Nederlandse geloofsbelijdenis en de spanning tussen overheid en religie* (Heerenveen: Groen, 1999), particularly 333-44.

Committee of the Nederlands Hervormde Kerk.[33] In view of the changes in the language since the seventeenth century, the general synod of the Nederlands Hervormde Kerk decided in 1955 to publish an updated version.[34] Realizing that an official text should be determined in cooperation with others using the same confession, they contacted other churches.[35] In 1962, a committee was organized consisting of representatives from several churches including Bakhuizen van den Brink, and chaired by W. F. Dankbaar. This committee presented its updated version in 1971, based on the 1619 Latin and Dutch texts of the confession. This text was officially published in 1983 in an edition containing revised versions of the three ecumenical creeds and the Reformed confessions.[36]

The response to this edition varied in the various churches. The general synod of the Nederlands Hervormde Kerk[37] did not adopt this translation as its official text, but received it in gratitude, in the expectation that this text would function in the churches. The general synod of the Gereformeerde Kerken decided in 1980 to adopt this text and to recommend it for use in the churches. The general synod of the Christelijke Gereformeerde Kerken decided to recommend this translation as a reliable rendering of their confession after a number of changes would be made.[38] The Gereformeerde Kerken (vrijgemaakt) had already concluded as early as 1958 that it was advisable to make a new version, but it took until 1975 before its general synod dealt with a far-reaching proposal for a new translation. At that time, a reorganized and reformulated text of articles 1 through 9, based on the translation principles of Eugene A. Nida and Charles R. Taber, was presented to the 1975 Synod. However, synod decided not to follow this approach.[39] At General Synod 1978, a committee

---

33. This report was later published as "De tekst van de Belijdenisgeschriften en van de Liturgische Formulieren der N. H. Kerk," in *Nederlands archief voor kerkgeschiedenis* 40 (1954): 207-50. The call for a new translation of the confession coincides with the work for a new Dutch translation of the Bible, resulting in a new translation of the New Testament in 1939, and of the Old Testament in 1951; see Cornelis Houtman, *Nederlandse vertalingen van het Oude Testament* (Den Haag: Boekencentrum, 1980), 44-46.

34. *De Nederlandse belijdenisgeschriften* (Den Haag: Boekencentrum, 1983), 5-6.

35. See the letter sent by the general synod of the Nederlands Hervormde Kerk, in *Bijlagen bij de Acta van de Generale Synode, 1955-56* (Kampen: Kok, n.d.), 141.

36. *De Nederlandse belijdenisgeschriften*, 17-45.

37. Since the names of these churches, when translated, are identical, I have chosen to retain the Dutch names. The "Nederlands Hervormde Kerk" is the continuation of the national Reformed church which existed in the Netherlands since the sixteenth century. The "Gereformeerde Kerken" is the result of the 1892 union of two church federations which separated from the "Nederlands Hervormde Kerk" earlier in the nineteenth century. The "Christelijke Gereformeerde Kerken" was originally established by those members who did not agree with this union. The "Gereformeerde Kerken," popularly known as "vrijgemaakt," emerged as a separate church from the Gereformeerde Kerken around 1944.

38. *De Nederlandse belijdenisgeschriften*, 5-6.

39. *Acta van de Generale Synode, Kampen 1975* (Kampen: J. Boersma, n.d.), 87-93 and 377-82.

submitted a different proposal. Recognizing the value of the text given by the Dankbaar committee, it decided to review and, if necessary, correct this translation. Synod did not adopt this version but presented it to the churches for their perusal.[40] A rephrased text was submitted to the next synod, documenting the changes that had been made. After discussion at synod, during which further changes were made, this text was adopted in 1982.[41] The unfortunate result of this complicated process of updating is that several newly formulated Dutch texts of the Belgic Confession exist side by side, all more or less going back to the Dankbaar text.

German Translations

The first record of a German translation of the confession can be found in Trigland's book *Kerckelijcke geschiedenissen*. Having discussed the original French text, which he dates to the year 1562, he states:

> And right the next year, namely in the year 1563, [it was] published in Dutch, further translated in German and printed in Heidelberg, as I who write this have seen a copy, as there are still some available of the previously mentioned edition of the year 1563.[42]

This information was repeated by later authors such as Brandt, Te Water and Ens, who state that the Dutch as well as the German edition were published in 1563.[43]

Van Langeraad goes beyond this tradition by mentioning two German editions. In addition to the 1563 edition, another edition exists that was printed by J. Mayer in 1566. He based this on information found in a nineteenth-century antiquarian catalogue.[44] The existence of this edition has now been confirmed, for a German edition of 1566 with exactly the same title is available in microfiche format.[45] However, to date a 1563 German edition has not been found. This requires us to look carefully at the original information on this edition, as given by Trigland.

In his statement, Trigland begins by referring to the Dutch translation published in 1563. This is followed by the remark that the confession was translated into

---

40. *Acta van de Generale Synode, Groningen-Zuid 1978* (Haarlem: Vijlbrief, n.d.), 201-2 and 269-307.

41. *Acta van de Generale Synode, Arnhem 1981* (Haarlem: Vijlbrief, 1981), 71-93 and 363-82.

42. The text can be found in the Appendix, Document 9, first paragraph.

43. Brandt, *Kerckelycke geschiedenissen*, 1:254; Te Water, *Tweede eeuw-getyde*, 163; Ens, *Kort historisch bericht*, 78.

44. Van Langeraad, *Guido de Bray*, 155, footnote (continuation of 153 n. 1), referring to an 1873 catalogue published by M. Nijhoff.

45. The title of this edition is *Bekanntnusz Christliches Glaubens. Der Niderlendischen Kirchen / so in Flandern und Brabant / Das Evangelium Jesu Christi einhelliglich angenommen. Ausz jrer Sprach trewlich verteutscht.*

German and printed in Heidelberg. About this German edition he says no more than that he saw a copy, adding with respect to the previously mentioned version of 1563 that some copies are extant. This final part of the sentence is ambiguous, for the impression is given that he saw copies of a 1563 German edition. However, a careful reading shows that Trigland did not actually say that there was ever a 1563 German edition. Rather, he makes a distinction between a German translation—for which he provides no date—he has seen, and extant copies of the 1563 Dutch edition. In conclusion, in all probability there is only one early German translation of the Belgic Confession.

Although the publication of this version dates from 1566, it contains a translation of the first edition. That can be seen clearly in article 16, which presents the original full version, not the shortened version of 1566. Other characteristics confirm this, such as the absence of the final statement in article 1 ("and an overflowing fountain of all good") and the presence of the ridiculing statement of article 34 ("otherwise we should always have our head in the water").

The German translation appears to be based on the Dutch translation, rather than the French original. This can be seen, for example, by comparing a statement from article 3.

French: "but the holy people, being driven by the Spirit of God, have spoken."
Dutch: "but the holy people, driven by the Spirit of God, have spoken this."
German: "but the holy people, driven by the Holy Spirit, have spoken this."[46]

While the French text appears to make a general statement on God's speaking, the Dutch makes the connection with the Word of God explicit. The German edition follows the Dutch version. At the same time it must be noted that the German text deviates from the other two by referring to the "Holy Spirit," rather than the "Spirit of God," returning to the expression used in 2 Peter 1:21.

Another comparison of different versions of the same article shows the same pattern:

French: "[God] has commanded his servants, the Prophets and Apostles to write his oracles in writings."
Dutch: "[God] has commanded his servants the Prophets and Apostles to put his revealed Word in writing."

---

46. French: " . . . mais les saincts hommes estans poussez par l' Esprit de Dieu, ont parlé."

Dutch: " . . . maer de heylighe mannen, door den Gheest Gods gedreven, hebbent ghesproken."

German: " . . . sonder die heilige Menner Gottes / getrieben durch den heiligen Geist, habens gesprochen."

German: "[God] has commanded his Servants and Prophets and Apostles to draw up his revealed Word in writing."[47]

The word "oracles" used in the French text, was replaced by a more common expression "revealed Word" in both the Dutch and the German text. At the same time, the formulation of the German text gives the impression that three categories of prophets are mentioned. This somewhat independent character of the German translation is confirmed in the final words of this article:

French: "For that reason, we call such writings holy and Divine Scriptures."
Dutch: "Therefore we call such scriptures Holy and divine Scriptures."
German: "Therefore we call such scripture the Holy Scripture."[48]

A very interesting feature of this translation is that headings have been added to the articles. At the beginning of the first article, the number is included in the heading: "The first article about God." From the second article onward, the number is given in Roman numerals, followed by a summary of the content. To give some examples: "How Holy Scripture is divided" (art. 4); "About the righteousness of faith" (art. 23); "About the sacraments: what and how many they are" (art. 33). Remarkable is the heading belonging to article 31: "About the calling of a minister," although the article itself deals with the calling of all three offices. This edition proves wrong the general opinion that the headings were first introduced in the Dutch translation of 1583.[49] Whether the idea to include headings in this Dutch translation was taken over from the German edition cannot be determined. However, the Dutch titles of the 1583 edition have not been taken simply from the German, as can easily be noted when they are compared.[50]

---

47. French: " . . . il a commandé e ses serviteurs les Prophetes & Apostres de rediger ses oracles par escrits."

Dutch: " . . . heeft God . . . synen Dienaren den Propheten ende Apostelen gheboden sjn geopenbaerde Woort by gheschrift te stellen."

German: " . . . hat er seinen Dieners und Propheten und Aposteln gebotten / sein geoffenbaret wort in Schriffen zuverfassen."

48. French: "Pour ceste cause nous appellons tels escrits Escritures sainctes et Divines."

Dutch: "Hierom noemen wy sulcke Schrifturen Heylighe ende Godlicke Schrifturen."

German: "Darumb nennen wir solche Schrifft/ die heilige Schrifft."

49. See, for example, Los, *Tekst en toelichting*, 35; Bakhuizen van den Brink, *De Nederlandse belijdenisgeschriften*, 23.

50. In the Dutch edition, the title of article 1 is, in translation: "That there is one God"; of article 4: "Canonical books of Holy Scripture"; and of article 33: "About the sacraments." A remarkable feature is that articles 5 and 6 do not have headings; rather, the words "Canonical" and "Apocryphal" are printed in the margin.

The German edition lacks several sections present in the original editions: the sonnet, the letter to King Philip, and the remonstrance for the magistrates. The reason for their omission is probably that these sections would not function in the different political situation of Germany, where the prince of the Palatinate was actively involved in the organization of the church and the maintenance of the Reformed doctrine.

The German translation was printed in 1566 by Johannes Mayer in Heidelberg, the same printer who had published the first three editions of the Heidelberg Catechism, and who, together with the publisher M. Schirat, had published the Latin translation of the catechism and the Church Order of the Palatinate.[51] The publication of the German translation of the Belgic Confession by the same publisher can be taken as an indication of doctrinal agreement between the Reformed in the Netherlands and the Reformed in the Palatinate.

Another German translation of the Belgic Confession was prepared and printed in the nineteenth century. Its background is the Reformation movement in Elberfeld, led by Herman F. Kohlbrugge. As a result of his influence, the confessional statements of the Reformed churches in the Netherlands were adopted. It appears that he and his congregation were unaware of an existing German translation. That was the reason why a new German translation of the Belgic Confession was made, to be adopted within these churches. Their translation of the confession, together with translations of the other confessional statements of the Dutch churches, was published in 1850 and republished in 1882.[52]

Later in the same century, two small groups of Reformed churches in Germany united. They had close ties with the Secession churches in the Netherlands, having received the support of Hendrik de Cock and Albert C. Van Raalte, leaders in the Secession churches.[53] One group was concentrated in the county of Bentheim. When they incorporated as a Reformed church, calling themselves the Oldreformed Church, they declared next to the Word of God to hold to the Heidelberg Catechism and the thirty-seven articles of the Belgic Confession.[54] The other group was located farther north, in Emden. In 1860, they adopted the Heidelberg Catechism, the Belgic

---

51. Nauta, "Die Verbreitung des Katechismus, Übersetzung in andere Sprachen, moderne Bearbeitungen," in *Handbuch zum Heidelberg Katechismus*, ed. L. Coenen (Neukirchen: Neukirchener Verlag, 1963), 40.

52. For the history of this translation, see Los, *Tekst en toelichting*, 83-84; the text is printed in this book, 434-62. Los also comments on several instances where the German translation is rather free or follows the first edition (84-85).

53. Gerrit J. Beuker, "German Oldreformed Emigration: Catastrophe or Blessing?" in *Beaches and Bridges: Reformed Subcultures in the Netherlands, Germany and the United States*, ed. G. Harinck and H. Krabbendam (Amsterdam: VU Uitgeverij, 2002), 103; see also his *Umkehr und Erneuerung: Aus der Geschichte der Evangelisch-altreformierten Kirche in Niedersachsen 1838-1988* (Bad Bentheim: A. Hellendoorn KG, 1988), passim.

54. The text can be found in Beuker, *Umkehr und Erneuerung*, 442-43.

Confession and the Canons of Dort, and joined the Oldreformed Church in Bentheim.[55] No indication is given as to which text of the Belgic Confession was used; presumably it was the Dutch text, since this was the language used during the worship service and for church business.[56] However, during the 1880s, growing German nationalism required that one language be spoken in the different states which together formed Germany. The Reformed churches in Ostfriesland and Bentheim were forced to adopt German next to Dutch in the 1890s, and they became exclusively German-speaking in 1915.[57] This resulted in a German translation of the Belgic Confession, published at the beginning of the twentieth century.

At the end of the nineteenth century, many members of these German churches had immigrated to America. A considerable number joined the Christian Reformed Church, under its umbrella establishing their own German congregations.[58] The worship services were originally conducted in Dutch, but the pressure to use German became stronger because the new immigrants had received their education in German, and back in their native land they had conducted the worship services in German as well. On the occasion of the fiftieth anniversary of the Christian Reformed Church, the complaint was raised that the knowledge of the confessions and the liturgy was decreasing in the congregations where German was used.[59] In this context, the request made by classis Ostfriesland for a German translation of the confessions, the liturgical forms and the church order can be understood. Actually, as early as 1902 a committee had been appointed to look into a German text, but to date no results had come out of this. Synod 1906 charged the committee to present a German translation.[60]

In its report presented to Synod 1908, the committee stated it had started working on a German translation when it found out that the churches in Bentheim and Ostfriesland were in the process of translating the same documents. In the meantime, the German translation had been published. As it was cheaper to import the books from Germany than to produce them in America, the committee had

---

55. For this statement, see Beuker, *Umkehr und Erneuerung,* 176-77.

56. Wayne Brouwer, "The German Element in the CRC: European Background," *The Banner* 115 (April 11, 1980): 11.

57. Herbert J. Brinks, "Ostfrisians in Two Worlds," in *Perspectives on the Christian Reformed Church: Studies in its History, Theology and Ecumenicity,* ed. Peter De Klerk and Richard de Ridder (Grand Rapids: Baker, 1983), 24-27.

58. Henry Beets, *De Christelijke Gereformeerde Kerk in Noord Amerika: Zestig jaren van strijd en zegen* (Grand Rapids: Grand Rapids Printing Company, 1918), 268-71.

59. W. Bode, "Onze Duitsche gemeenten," in *Gedenkboek van het vijftigjarig jubileum der Christelijke Gereformeerde Kerk 1857-1907* (Grand Rapids: Semi-Centennial Committee, [1907]), 73-74.

60. *Acta der Synode 1906 van de Christelijke Gereformeerde Kerk* (Grand Rapids: Christelijke Gereformeerde Kerk, n.d.), 18 (art. 35).

decided to order 250 copies in Germany. Synod approved this action.[61] The German translation used within the Christian Reformed Church in North America had its origin in Germany.

Latin Translations

Several Latin translations of the Belgic Confession were published.[62] Most of these date from the seventeenth century, but one goes back to the sixteenth century. Johann Cazimir, a son of Frederick III of the Palatinate, had not succeeded his father as prince of the Palatinate, so that he only governed over a relatively small dukedom. In an attempt to safeguard the Reformed religion there, he organized an international meeting in Frankfurt and mobilized other Reformed nations to send delegates.[63] At this meeting, a decision was made to unite the Reformed churches of Europe by drawing up an international confession.[64] In 1578, an incomplete draft for this confession was sent to Geneva for their approval, but here the plan ran aground. On behalf of the Genevan ministers, Danaeus wrote a response, praising the confession as scholarly in style and correct in method. However, they had decided to follow the advice of the French that the best course of action was to bring together in a harmony the teaching of the confessions adopted in the different nations: "Thus the work has already begun for compiling a *concordia*, which contains nothing but the very words of the several confessions, only reorganized under several chapters."[65]

The Belgic Confession was among the confessions included in this collection. The content of the confessions was organized topically in nineteen sections, dealing with issues ranging from Scripture to the civil government. In fifteen of the sections, the Belgic Confession was quoted. Although spread out over the book, the content of this confession was included in its entirety.[66] On several occasions, annotations were added to the text of the confessions. This applies to four articles of the Belgic Confession (arts. 19, 29, 33 and 35), but all are explanatory in character. To give an example, article 35 states that the operations of the Holy Spirit are incomprehensible. The note explains that both the work of the Holy Spirit and the effects, which exceed our senses, are incomprehensible.

---

61. *Acta der Synode 1908 van de Christelijke Gereformeerde Kerk* (Grand Rapids: Christelijke Gereformeerde Kerk, n.d.), 50 (art. 71).

62. A general survey was given by Bakhuizen van den Brink, *De Nederlandse belijdenisgeschriften*, 24-25.

63. Bakhuizen van den Brink, "Het Convent te Frankfort 27-28 September en de Harmonia Confessionum," *Nederlands archief voor kerkgeschiedenis* 36 (1941): 246-49.

64. Bakhuizen van den Brink, "Het Convent te Frankfort," 265.

65. The text can be found in Bakhuizen van den Brink, "Het Convent te Frankfort," 272.

66. Bakhuizen van den Brink, "Het Convent te Frankfort," 274-80. See also the introduction to the English translation, Peter Hall, ed., *The Harmony of Protestant Confessions* (1842; reprint, Edmonton: Still Waters Revival Books, 1992), ix-xviii.

This first Latin version of the Belgic Confession was made after the second Dutch edition of 1566. The publication does not provide information concerning the translation. However, it is mentioned in the Acts of the general synod of the Dutch churches, which was convened in Middelburg in 1581:

> Salvart has written from Geneva, and sent a sample of the harmony of the confessions. The Belgic Confession will be included. A gratuity of 72 kgg. has been awarded to him, which has been raised and has been deposited with Arent Cornelisz. This will be given to him when a printed copy will have been sent to the synod. Taffin has written him concerning this.[67]

Although it is unclear who made this Latin translation,[68] the purpose of the book in which it was included was evidently to show the extent of the doctrinal agreement among the Reformed confessions. This would strengthen the position of the Reformed churches, particularly in Germany. It was presumably for this reason that several German confessions were included: the confessions of Augsburg, Saxony and Württemberg. They provided in their *Harmonia confessionum* evidence of being in confessional agreement with the beginning of the Reformation in Germany and with the Reformed churches in other nations by including both the Augsburg Confession as well as the confessions of many other Reformed churches in Europe. Regrettably, shortly thereafter the Reformed in Germany were excluded from the religious peace among the German states by the introduction of the *Book of Concord*.

The same Latin version of the Belgic Confession was included in the *Corpus et Syntagma confessionum* of 1612.[69] This publication of confessional statements had a different structure in keeping with its purpose. The articles were not divided over a number of dogmatic topics, as in the *Harmonia confessionum*, but the confessions were presented as a whole. The specific purpose of this edition was to prove the agreement of the Reformed confessions with the patristic doctrine. This was achieved by adding

---

67. Rutgers, *Acta van de Nederlandsche synoden*, 364: "Salvardus heeft geschreven van geneven, ende een specimen oft beghinsel gesonden vande harmonie der confessien, sal de nederlantsche confessie daer mede inne gevuecht worden, is hem vande Synode een gratuiteyt toegevuecht 72 kgg., de welcke te wege gebracht is ende rust onder Arnoldo cornelii, sal hem gegeven worden als eenich gedruct exemplaer aenden Synode gesonden sal seyn, hier aff heeft Taffinus aen hem geschreven." The older opinion that Salnar was the editor, still supported by Los (*Tekst en toelichting*, 65) must be abandoned.

68. Bakhuizen van den Brink is of the opinion that Salvart, as the editor of this collection, made it himself (*De Nederlandse belijdenisgeschriften*, 25). His preference for Salvart is based on the decision of Synod 1581 to remunerate him, mentioned in the previous footnote. However, the synodical decision did not specify the reason why Salvart received this money.

69. Bakhuizen van den Brink corrected a previously popular view that this *Corpus* is a second edition of the *Harmonia confessionum*; see his *De Nederlandse belijdenisgeschriften*, 27.

a section showing how the teaching of these confessions agrees with statements of the fathers.[70]

The third Latin edition of the Belgic Confession appeared in Festus Hommius' publication *Specimen controversiarum*, already mentioned in the previous chapter. In the introduction of this book made for the political leaders of the Netherlands, he explains the role of the confessions in the churches. All those who want to function in a public office of teaching must subscribe to it.[71] According to Hommius, some teachers in the churches had publicly stated deviant views without officially notifying the churches and without first allowing them to judge the issues. As a national synod was going to be convened to which theologians from neighboring kingdoms and states were invited, it would be useful for them as well as for the whole synod "if I would publish in Latin a clear proof of several controversies by which our churches are now disturbed."[72] Hommius obviously intended this edition to be used by the foreign delegates at the forthcoming Synod of Dort.

As stated before,[73] Hommius wanted to prove that the Remonstrants deviated from the received doctrine of the church in many more articles than election alone, and that they came close to the errors of the Socinians.[74] This explains the format of the book, in which a Latin translation of the articles of the Belgic Confession is frequently followed by a list of quotations containing deviant views from those expressed in the confession. The translation is based on the text of the then current second edition, as can be seen from the inclusion of the words "and an overflowing fountain of all good" in article 1. The statements present in the first edition, but left out in the second, have been placed between brackets in the text.[75]

The fourth Latin edition, produced by Hommius for the Latin *Acta* of the Synod of Dort, differed from the text he had published in his *Specimen*. He did not simply take into account the changes made by the Synod of Dort, he actually translated the confession anew.[76] A few examples will provide some insight into what he did:

---

70. This purpose is expressed in the second part of the lengthy title: "Quibus annectitur, in omnibus Christianae Religionis Articulis, Catholicus Consensus, ex Sententiis Veterum qui Patres vocantur, desumptus" (Bakhuizen van den Brink, "Het Convent te Frankfort," 278).

71. Hommius, *Specimen controversiarum*, praefatio, *4r.

72. Hommius, *Specimen controversiarum*, praefatio, **r: " . . . existimavi me illis [the foreign delegates] & toti Synodo utilem navaturum operam, si specimen aliquot Controversiarum, quibus Ecclesiae nostrae hactenus sunt turbatae, Latinè exhiberem, ut ex eo aliquâ ex parte cognoscant, quibus de controversiis in hac Synodo potissimùm erit agendum."

73. See chapter 7.

74. Hommius, *Specimen controversiarum*, Ad lectorem, **2v.

75. Hommius, *Specimen controversiarum*, Ad lectorem, **3v.

76. Bakhuizen van den Brink, *De Nederlandse belijdenisgeschriften*, 27; he praises Hommius' work as an excellent translation.

The Latin text of article 3 used to speak of God's infinite care and solicitude. The latter word is left out, presumably because it has the negative connotation of anxiety or apprehension.

In article 5, the word "all," which was omitted in the previous Latin translation, is restored: "We receive all these books only for holy and canonical . . ."

A much larger restoration of the text took place in article 6, for the list of the apocryphal books, which had been omitted in the previous version, is again included.

In the earlier version of article 8, God was called "a single and eternal essence," but Hommius' translation leaves out the words "and eternal." This last example in particular provides insight into the character of his translation. The addition of these two words in article 8 had not produced a wrong statement, for the expanded expression was in agreement with the Reformed doctrine. The fact that these words were deleted is indicative of Hommius' intention to provide a faithful Latin rendering of the Dutch text.

This is confirmed by another example from article 8. The earlier Latin text stated that the Trinity does not cause "that God is divided into three parts." The word "parts," which had not occurred before and could only lead to misunderstanding, is left out in Hommius' translation.

This text is printed as the standard Latin text of the Belgic Confession.[77]

Greek Translations

In a publication of 1723, Gerardus Outhovius reported about a Greek translation of the Belgic Confession. He mentioned that Jacob Revius, minister at Deventer, had published a Greek translation of the confession, together with a Greek translation of the Heidelberg Catechism prepared by Fridericus Sylburgius (1526-1596). He quoted a statement from the poet Moonen that Revius' translation had made the Greeks aware of the faith of the Netherlands. However, when Outhovius in 1710 met Dionysius, bishop of Thessalonica, and presented him with a copy of this confession, the bishop was very surprised.[78] This raises the question of why the confession would have been translated into Greek, and whether it had any influence in the Greek church.

It is true that the seventeenth-century Dutch theologian and poet Revius made a Greek translation of the confession. In 1623, he published a Greek version of the Belgic Confession, together with an existing Greek translation of the Heidelberg Catechism, which had been made by Fridericus Sylburgius and first published in 1567. This edition was used in the schools, presumably to increase the students'

---

77. This text can be found in Müller, *Die Bekenntnisschriften der reformierten Kirche*, 233-49, and in Bakhuizen van den Brink, *De Nederlandse belijdenisgeschriften*, 77-145.

78. Gerardus Outhovius, *Ter waerschuwing aan alle Kristenen*, 221-22.

knowledge not only of Greek but also of the confessional statements. The liturgical forms were not included, but several personal prayers had been added.[79]

Remarkably, this version found its way to Constantinople, where the reformation-minded Cyril Lucaris (1572-1638) was patriarch of the Greek Orthodox Church. From a letter written in September 1627 by Cornelis Haga, the Dutch consul in Constantinople, it can be derived that Cyril had stated he fully agreed with it as conforming to the pure Word of God. As only the confession and the catechism are mentioned, this letter must refer to the first Greek edition of the confession.[80] This edition was reprinted in 1635.[81]

The same version of the confession was published in 1627 as part of a more comprehensive publication. Not only were Greek and Latin translations of the Belgic Confession and the Heidelberg Catechism included, but also translations of the liturgical forms and the church order. In fact, this was a bilingual version of Thysius' book on the doctrine and order of the Dutch churches, which had been published in 1615.[82] This edition was also sent to Constantinople. Revius himself reported to the Dutch ambassador that he had sent several copies, one with a personal message for Cyril.[83] At his request, the States General decided to send 200 unbound copies to Constantinople at their own expense.[84]

Two years later, in 1629, Cyril published his own confession of faith.[85] This was a Reformed confession, made with the intention to further the reformation of the Greek church in a Calvinistic direction. In a letter to Leger, Cyril stated that his own confession is in agreement with the confessions of the evangelical churches, but the

---

79. Egbert J. W. Posthumus Meyjes, *Jacobus Revius* (Amsterdam: Ten Brink & De Vries, 1895), 131-32, 140-41, and appendix A, iv.

80. Revius wrote: "Gratissimum fuit Reverendiss. Patriarchae Cyrillo examplar illud Confessionis et Catecheseos Ecclesiarum nostrarum, quibus, ut puro Dei verbo consentaneis, Praesul ille doctissimus assentitur" (Posthumus Meyjes, *Jacobus Revius*, 138).

81. Nauta, "Die Verbreitung des Katechismus," 45.

82. Posthumus Meyjes, *Jacobus Revius*, 130-35; for more information on Thysius' book, see our chapter 2.

83. Posthumus Meyjes, *Jacobus Revius*, 139.

84. Posthumus Meyjes, *Jacobus Revius*, 138-39.

85. On the date of publication, see Keetje Rozemond, "De eerste uitgave van de belijdenis van Cyrillus Lucaris," *Nederlands archief voor kerkgeschiedenis* 51 no. 2 (1970-71): 199-208. The Latin and Greek text of this confession can be found in Ernst J. Kimmel, *Libri symbolici ecclesiae orientalis* (Jena: Carolus Hochhausenius, 1843), 24-44. On its history, see Richard Schlier, *Der Patriarch Kyrill Lukaris von Konstantinopel: Sein Leben und sein Glaubensbekenntnis* (Marburg: Druckerei Bauer, 1927), 32-34, 48-51; George A. Hadjantoniou, *A Protestant Patriarch: The Life of Cyril Lucaris (1572-1638) Patriarch of Constantinople* (Richmond: John Knox, 1961), 91-109; Johannes A. Meijer, "De oosterse Confessie van Cyrillus Lukaris," in *Bezield verband*, ed. J. Douma, J. P. Lettinga and C. Trimp (Kampen: Van den Berg, 1984), 134-39.

only confession he mentions by name is the Belgic Confession.[86] This raises the question as to whether Cyril's confession shows traces of being influenced by the Belgic Confession.

A general survey proves that neither the structure of Cyril's confession nor its basic thoughts are derived from the Belgic Confession:

Concerning the structure, the first article of Cyril's confession opens with a brief phrase about God: "We believe one true God almighty and infinite," immediately followed by the confession of the Trinity. This is different from the Belgic Confession, which deals with God and his many attributes in the first article, and postpones discussing the Trinity till articles 8 and 9.

Another difference is that Cyril's formulation of the doctrine of the Trinity stays close to the council decisions from the patristic period, rather than reflecting the formulation of the Belgic Confession. This is noticeable, for example, when it says about the Holy Spirit that he is "proceeding from the Father through the Son" (art. 1).

A similar difference can be detected in the article on the work of creation. Cyril's confession states that "the Trinitarian God, Father, Son and Holy Spirit, is the creator of the visible and invisible things" (art. 4). The Belgic Confession does not refer to the Trinity at this point, and it uses a different expression for the world: "We believe that the Father through the Word, that is, through his Son, has created out of nothing heaven and earth and all creatures" (art. 12).

To give yet another example, the presentation of the doctrine of the church is also different. Cyril's confession opens this article with the statement: "We believe that the so-called catholic church contains the believers in Christ altogether, those who have died and are now in the fatherland, as well as those who are sojourners on the way . . ." (art. 10). This does not resemble the formulation of the Belgic Confession on the catholic church: "We believe and profess one catholic or universal church, which is a holy congregation and assembly of the true Christian believers . . ." (art. 27).

And yet, several similarities indicate that Cyril did consult the Belgic Confession:

Two examples can be found in article 3, dealing with election and reprobation. In the section on election, Cyril says that election is "without consideration of their work." And his article concludes with the statement: "For the Lord is merciful and righteous." These two expressions can already be found in article 16 of the Belgic Confession.

Another derived statement can be found in the last line of article 4 of Cyril's confession: "For this ought to be a sure rule that God is not the author of evil,

---

86. Schlier, *Der Patriarch Kyrill Lukaris*, 44 n. 155: " . . . nella dottrina Evangelica, conforme la confessione Belgica, la confessione mia, ele altre delle chiese Evangeliche, che sono tutte conformi."

nor can he with good reason be declared guilty." The Belgic Confession had already expressed this in similar words in its article 13, for after having stated that nothing happens without God's ordinance, it continues: "although God is neither the author, nor guilty of the sins which occur."

The last line of Cyril's article 5 on providence provides another example. Remarkably, this article does not really explain what providence is, but focuses on preventing misunderstanding: "We should rather adore than investigate this," and "in this matter we feel that silence in humility should be embraced, rather than saying many things that are not edifying." This statement not only explains why the positive statement is very brief, it also contains traces of article 13 of the Belgic Confession.

To give one more example, article 13 of Cyril's confession discusses justification by faith and explains: "When we say 'by faith,' we mean the correlate of faith, namely the righteousness of Christ, which faith embraces and makes its own." This is very close to a statement in article 22 of the Belgic Confession.

These are indications that Cyril's confession was influenced by the Belgic Confession. However, it must be added that the borrowed phrases do not constitute a large part of his confession. Cyril must have known and used the Belgic Confession, but the content of his confession was not determined by the confessional statements of other churches but by the need of the Greek church.[87]

A few years after completing his confession, Cyril Lucaris lost much of his influence because his protector, the ambassador of England, had left. Cyril was forced into exile, first in 1634, and again in 1635. He was restored to his position in the spring of 1637, but somewhat later he was again taken prisoner. In the summer of that same year he was executed. Although he had several followers, the influence of his Greek confession appears to have been limited.[88]

Another Greek translation of the Belgic Confession was published in 1648 by the well-known publisher Elzevier in Leiden.[89] It was part of an edition of the Dutch church book that also contained the catechism, the liturgical forms and the church order, the same documents Revius had already published in Greek. The main difference between these editions is that Revius' translation was written in classical Greek, whereas the 1648 edition was translated in "the common language of the Greek," as the title page indicates. This formulation indicates that the purpose of this publication was not teaching Dutch students Greek, but rather to make the Reformed doctrine known among the Greeks themselves.

---

87. See the extensive discussion of the confession in Schlier, *Der Patriarch Kyrill Lukaris*, 50-92.

88. Hadjiantoniou, *Protestant Patriarch*, 112-13, 127-31, 136-37.

89. The main title of this publication is *Toon Ekklesioon tes Belgikes Christianike kai Orthodoxos Didaskalia kai Taxis* (Leiden: B. and A. Elzevier, n.d.), and the content consists of four sections: Confession, Catechism, Liturgy and Church Order. Posthumus Meyjes remarks that Revius was not involved in this Greek edition; see *Jacobus Revius*, 141.

The translator wrote an extensive foreword in which he explained the different parts of the book, but neither on the title page nor in the foreword of the publication did he reveal his identity. The translation has been attributed to the abbot Hierotheus,[90] who stayed three years in Leiden at the expense of the States General of the Netherlands in order to make this publication available to the Greek people.[91] Nothing is known about him,[92] but it is possible that he used a pseudonym while in the Netherlands.

However, it may be possible to find the translator among the followers of Cyril. There was a priest by the name of Nathaniel Conopius, who wrote an account of Cyril's martyrdom. After the death of Cyril, he traveled to Western Europe to study in Oxford. Following this, he went to the Netherlands in order to continue his study at Leiden University.[93] He registered as a student in theology on June 16, 1645. However, there is no record that he confirmed his registration, and he did not register again in 1646.[94] Background, time and place make it likely that it was Cyril's follower Conopius who translated into contemporary Greek the confessional and liturgical documents of the Reformed church in the Netherlands, including the Belgic Confession.

The translator added a lengthy foreword to this edition, explaining all the sections of his publication. Among other things, he states that the following confession is in agreement with the Reformed confessions of England and Scotland, of France and Germany.[95] Preceding the confession itself, the terms used for minister, elder and deacon are explained, as are the names used for the ecclesiastical meetings. The articles of the confession are accompanied by explanatory marginal notes, and each article is followed by the references to Scripture, which have been written out. These features confirm the statement on the title page that the purpose of this edition was to make known to the Greek church the teaching and structure of the Reformed churches in the Netherlands. However, it is not known whether this Greek version of the confession ever reached the people for whom it was translated and published.

---

90. Alphonse Willems, *Les Elzevier: Histoire et annals typographiques* (1880; reprint, Nieuwkoop: B. De Graaf, 1962), 155-56; Nauta, "Die Verbreitung des Katechismus," 45 (sub #57). This goes back to a study by Christiaan Sepp, *Bibliographische mededeelingen* (Leiden: Brill, 1883), 230-35.

91. Jan N. Bakhuizen van den Brink, "Cyrillus Lukaris," in *Winkler Prins*, 6:600.

92. Willems, *Les Elzevier*, 156.

93. Hadjiantoniou, *Protestant Patriarch*, 135.

94. I wish to thank Ms. Marjolein Kranse of the Library of Leiden University for providing these data.

95. See *Toon Ekklesioon tes Belgikes Christianike kai Orthodoxos Didaskalia kai Taxis*, *2.

English Translations

Already during the sixteenth century, English Protestants had moved to the Netherlands, where they established their own churches. At the beginning of the seventeenth century, voices were raised advocating that these churches should come together in a federative unity. This was realized in 1621, when they united as an English synod under the umbrella of the Reformed churches in the Netherlands, just as the Walloon churches had done. These English churches were required to follow the church order of the Dutch churches, to use the Dutch liturgical forms and to implement several rules for the worship services.[96] No regulations were made concerning the confession, and the English synod did not pursue an English translation of the Belgic Confession.

The result was that the first English translation of the Belgic Confession had its origin in England. In 1645, the ministers and elders of the Dutch congregation at London published a book containing their important documents in English. Included in this book was an English translation of the Belgic Confession.[97] The purpose of this book appears not to have been liturgical. Since it was published during the time of the Puritan revolution, the Reformed church probably wanted to make known its own basic documents in the context of the struggle between the High Church ideal propagated by Laud and his followers and the Low Church ideal of the Puritans. However that may be, this edition of their church book was never used during the service of the Dutch congregation in London, for they were not allowed to organize an English worship service.[98]

In the meantime, the situation of the English churches in the Netherlands had changed. The English synod had changed from being an ecclesiastical organization into a fellowship of like-minded Congregationalists, who practiced freedom in worship.[99] In response, the Dutch Reformed churches disbanded the English synod as a separate organization within the Dutch churches, requiring these churches to join the Reformed classis in their area.[100] This incorporation meant that these churches needed English translations of the Dutch confessional statements adopted within these churches.

---

96. On the development in general, see Keith L. Sprunger, *Dutch Puritanism: A History of English and Scottish Churches of the Netherlands in the Sixteenth and Seventeenth Centuries* (Leiden: Brill, 1982), 289-306. The specific rules can be found on page 306.

97. Daniel J. Meeter, "Puritan and Presbyterian Versions of the Netherlands Liturgy," *Nederlands archief voor kerkgeschiedenis* 70 (1990): 68-74; see also his *"Bless the Lord, o My Soul": The New York Liturgy of the Dutch Reformed Churches 1767* (Lanham: Scarecrow, 1998), 24. Meeter adds that the translator of these documents was probably Gribius, pastor of the English congregation in the Dutch city of Middelburg.

98. Meeter, *"Bless the Lord, o My Soul"*, 24.

99. Sprunger, *Dutch Puritanism*, 305; Meeter, "The Puritan and Presbyterian Versions," 59-60.

100. Sprunger, *Dutch Puritanism*, 375-77.

It took a while before the required English translations were ready. This appears to have begun in 1651 when the consistory of the church in Amsterdam ordered an English translation of the Heidelberg Catechism to be made, which was published in the next year.[101] The decision to begin with the catechism was probably caused by the requirement in the Reformed Churches in the Netherlands that it should be used for the instruction of the youth of the church and for expounding the doctrine in the afternoon service. An English translation of the Belgic Confession was obviously seen as less urgent, for it was published much later, in 1689. This is an unusual edition, for the confession and the liturgical forms were published together in one book, but the catechism was not included,[102] presumably because this had already been published separately. A translation of the liturgical forms was necessary as these were used in the worship services, but usually the Belgic Confession did not have a liturgical function.[103] Its inclusion in this edition of official documents confirms that for the English churches in the Netherlands this confession was authoritative as a rule of faith.

This English version of the Belgic Confession was reprinted several times together with the Heidelberg Catechism and the liturgical forms. The 1721 edition was printed in Middelburg. The contents are still the same as in the previous editions, but according to the title page it had been newly revised and mistakes had been corrected. This edition was followed by two other editions. In 1744, the same content was printed for the use of the church in Amsterdam, in a smaller and in a larger format. The 1772 edition was a new printing, using the text of 1744.[104] The fact that these editions were all made for use in the churches is an indication that the English churches in the Netherlands actually used the same confessional and liturgical documents as their Dutch counterparts.

North American Editions

The first mention of an American edition of the Belgic Confession can be found in 1747. In an advertisement in the *New York Evening Post*, subscriptions were solicited for the publication of the Dutch church book in the English language. For several months afterward the same paper continued to run the notice stating that this new edition had been published.[105] The content was specified and it included the

---

101. Meeter, "The Puritan and Presbyterian Versions," 66 n. 59.
102. Meeter, "The Puritan and Presbyterian Versions," 67 n. 61.
103. An exception was Balthasar Bekker, see footnote 31 above.
104. Meeter, "The Puritan and Presbyterian Versions," 67 n. 61.
105. Meeter, "The Puritan and Presbyterian Versions," 72: "Just published and to be Sold by the printer hereof. The whole Book of Forms, and the Lithurgy [sic] of the Dutch Reformed Church." Around the same time, the elderly minister Gualtherus Du Bois complained that the Dutch language

Belgic Confession. However, as no copy of this edition has surfaced, the question must be considered whether it was ever printed.

The initiative for this publication had not come from a consistory, but from a publisher. According to the advertisement, the publisher of the newspaper, Hendrik De Foreest, was both publisher and seller of this edition. It may therefore be assumed that this advertisement was intended to gauge the interest of the public in a projected English edition, but that the book itself was never actually printed for lack of interest.[106] However that may be, the advertisement is clear on the issue of which translation was going to be used. It was not the printer's intention to come with a newly translated version, for it is stated: "Carefully translated from the Original, and formerly Printed at Amsterdam."[107] This is the English edition mentioned above.

It took another twenty years before an American edition of the Belgic Confession was published.[108] The background of this publication can be found in a letter sent in 1763 to Reverend Archibald Laidlie, a Scot who, after having ministered at the English church in Vlissingen in the Netherlands, had received a call to serve as a minister of the Reformed Dutch church in New York.[109] He was advised by his future consistory not to take along copies of an English language church book printed in the Netherlands. The main reason appears to have been that the Americans did not like the version of the Psalms in the church book, but an additional reason was that "the Catechism and other Forms in said book are not as Elegantly or accurately translated as we could wish, and therefore will be by us Rectified in ours."[110] This remark implies that the consistory knew the English version used in the Netherlands, but did not want to adopt it. Rather, the consistory had decided to make its own translations, consulting existing translations. It also implies that the impetus for an English edition did not come from the minister, but from the consistory itself. At the request of the consistory, a committee made the translation, using the 1744 version but revising it thoroughly. This edition of the Belgic Confession was published in 1767.[111]

---

was more and more neglected; see Meeter, *The "North American Liturgy": A Critical Edition of the Liturgy of the Reformed Churches in the Netherlands, 1793* (Ann Arbor: UMI, 1994), 114-15.

106. Meeter considers it possible that the edition was not well received since at the time the English language would be seen as a threat rather than an opportunity ("The Puritan and Presbyterian Versions," 72). This would explain why the edition would not be mentioned, but it fails to explain why copies have not been found.

107. Meeter, "The Puritan and Presbyterian Versions," 72, adds that the survey of the content matches that of the recent Amsterdam edition of 1744.

108. Los, *Tekst en toelichting*, 91, called John H. Livingston the father of the constitution of the Reformed Church in America, but this must be corrected on the basis of newer information.

109. On Laidlie, see the article by W. J. R. Taylor, "Laidlie," in *Cyclopaedia of Biblical, Theological and Ecclesiastical Literature*, 12 vols., ed. John McClintock and James Strong (n.p.: Harper and Brothers, 1867-1887; reprint, Grand Rapids: Baker Book House, 1981), 5:195.

110. The whole letter is printed in Meeter, *The "North American Liturgy,"* 127-28.

111. Meeter, "The Puritan and Presbyterian Versions," 73.

About twenty-five years later, this English version was officially adopted.[112] In 1792, the Reformed Dutch Church in the United States of America adopted a constitution which contained English translations of the Belgic Confession, the Heidelberg Catechism and the Canons of Dort (without the Rejection of Errors).[113] The text of the Belgic Confession was left intact, but in the preface of this publication certain qualifications were made concerning expressions in articles 18 and 36, in which the Anabaptists were condemned in harsh terms. It was maintained that at the time of the Reformation there were people "who held to the erroneous and seditious sentiments which in those articles are rejected, and who by their fanaticism and extravagance rendered themselves abhorred by all sober and religious men." The preface continues by stating openly that these statements are not "intended to refer to any denominations of Christians at present known."[114] The issue of article 36 came up again in the twentieth century, when in an overture the general synod was requested to remove this article from the text and to place it in a footnote since the Reformed Church in America holds to a separation of church and state. In 1972, it was decided not to accede to this request for the reason that the confession is a historical document and not subject to revision.[115]

The Christian Reformed Church was confronted with the need for a new English translation at the turn of the twentieth century. The decision to actively pursue an English translation was relatively late. The committee for a German translation had already been appointed in 1902, but a committee for the English text was appointed two synods later, in 1906.[116] The committee was not ready to deal with the confession at the next synod of 1908, but it could report at Synod 1910 that the existing translation of the Belgic Confession had been scrutinized. They concluded that it was a very good translation, but some improvements could be made. Suggestions for minor improvements were presented in connection with articles 2, 7, 9, 12 and 21. They also pointed out that in the proposed translation of article 36, the section dealing with the task of the government was different in content than the original Dutch text. As the churches had not yet discussed this issue, the committee for translation alerted synod to this difference without proposing a formulation for

---

112. For this period during which the transition from Dutch to English took place, see Gerald F. De Jong, *The Dutch Reformed Church in the American Colonies* (Grand Rapids: Eerdmans, 1978), 211-27.

113. This book was entitled *The Constitution of the Reformed Dutch Church in the United States of America* (New York: W. Durell, 1793).

114. *The Constitution of the Reformed Dutch Church*, vi-vii.

115. Mildred W. Schuppert, *A Digest and Index of the Minutes of the General Synod of the Reformed Church in America* (Grand Rapids: Eerdmans, 1979), 8, referring to the *Acts and Proceedings of the 166th Regular Session of the General Synod* (Somerset: Somerset Press, 1972), 99-100.

116. *Acta der Synode 1906*, 18, article 35. 9. c.

the task of the government.[117] Synod's advisory committee stated that this translation had not been scrutinized for lack of time. Synod approved the proposal to appoint a committee to evaluate this translation and make a decision at the next synod.[118]

The next synod, which was held in 1912, adopted the English text of the Belgic Confession. Concerning the task of the government in article 36, it was decided to leave the statement intact but to add an explanatory note emphasizing religious freedom.[119] In 1938, the synod decided to remove the discrepancy concerning religious freedom that was noted between text and footnote by changing the text of the article.[120]

During the 1970s, several synods of the Christian Reformed Church dealt with the English translation. At the recommendation of the Liturgical Committee, Synod 1977 decided to appoint a committee to prepare a new translation of the Belgic Confession, including a review of the textual references.[121] This committee presented to Synod 1979 a translation based on the original 1561 text of the confession.[122] At synod, this choice for the 1561 text caused considerable discussion, resulting in an extensive mandate for this committee. In addition to the submitted translation of the 1561 edition, it had to provide a translation of the 1619 text, and to summarize the development of the Belgic Confession from 1561 till 1619.[123] In 1982, the committee reported it had not been able to complete the work, but during the next year, two reports were presented to synod, resulting from a different evaluation of the historical development.[124] The majority of the committee advocated using the Dort 1619 text as the basis for a translation, but a minority, evaluating the changes in the later editions as accommodation to the government, was in favor of using the original 1561 text.[125] Synod 1983 decided to replace the statement "we detest the Anabaptists . . ." with "we denounce the Anabaptists . . ." and to submit the new translation of the 1619 text to the churches for study.[126] Synod 1984 only dealt with

---

117. *Acta der Synode 1910 van de Christelijke Gereformeerde Kerk* (Grand Rapids: Christelijke Gereformeerde Kerk, n.d.), 126-27.

118. *Acta der Synode 1910*, 69.

119. *Acta der Synode 1912 van de Christelijke Gereformeerde Kerk* (Grand Rapids: Christelijke Gereformeerde Kerk, n.d.), 47.

120. *Acts of Synod 1938 of the Christian Reformed Church* (Grand Rapids: Office of the Stated Clerk, n.d.), 16-20.

121. *Acts of Synod 1977* (Grand Rapids: Christian Reformed Church Publications, 1977), 88.

122. "Report 33," in *Acts of Synod 1979*, 534-604, see especially 540. See also chapter 6 above.

123. *Acts of Synod 1979*, 126-27.

124. *Acts of Synod 1983* (Grand Rapids: Christian Reformed Church Publications, 1983), 272-78, 396-405.

125. On this issue, see chapter 6.

126. *Acts of Synod 1983*, 647-48.

the formulation of article 36.[127] This issue was decided at Synod 1985 by placing in a footnote the whole section concerning the rejection of the Anabaptists in article 36, thereby indicating that what is stated in this paragraph is no longer the confession of the Christian Reformed Church. Following this, the new translation of the 1619 text of the Belgic Confession was adopted as the committee had proposed.[128]

A third North American translation of the Belgic Confession was made within the Canadian Reformed Churches, which have their origin in the Dutch immigration after the Second World War. The transition to English took place in the 1960s, as can be seen from the fact that in 1968 the language of the *Acts of General Synod* was changed from Dutch to English. At the same synod it was decided to bring together English versions of the rhymed psalms and hymns, confessions, liturgical forms and the church order in a *Book of Praise*.[129] After some initial work had been done, Synod 1977 decided that an English text of the Belgic Confession was to be made that was a faithful rendering of the original. The biblical quotations were to be taken from a newer Bible translation.[130] At the next synod, in 1980, the committee presented its translation of 23 articles on the basis of the Dort 1619 text. Synod agreed with the committee that the Dort 1619 text should be taken as the basis for their translation.[131] The discussion in the Christian Reformed Church is reflected in the report for the following synod. The committee not only presented a complete English text, but it also provided several reasons why the 1561 text should not be used as a basis for its translation. It was argued that the church should not follow the first, personal version of Guido de Brès, but rather the text authenticated by the church. Moreover, going back to the 1561 text would mean that important changes and improvements would be lost.[132] Synod adopted the proposed translation in 1983.

As a result, two updated English versions of the Belgic Confession exist side by side. Although the Christian Reformed Church had started working on the revision earlier than the Canadian Reformed Churches, due to their initial preference for the first edition their version was finalized later.

---

127. *Acts of Synod 1984* (Grand Rapids: Board of Publications of the Christian Reformed Church, 1984), 441, 609.

128. *Acts of Synod 1985* (Grand Rapids: CRC Publications, 1985), 789.

129. *Acts: General Synod Orangeville, 1968, of the Canadian Reformed Churches* (Fergus, ON: R & R Printing, n.d.), 29-30.

130. *Acts: General Synod Coaldale, 1977, of the Canadian Reformed Churches* (Winnipeg: Premier Printing, 1977), 28.

131. *Acts: General Synod Smithville, 1980, of the Canadian Reformed Churches* (Winnipeg: Premier Printing, 1980), 91-93.

132. *Acts: General Synod Cloverdale, 1983, of the Canadian Reformed Churches* (Winnipeg: Premier Printing, 1983), 149-50. In its report, the committee also rejected the reconstruction of the historical situation, as presented in the report for the synod of the Christian Reformed Church to defend its choice in favor of the 1561 text as the basis for its translation.

South African Translations

During the seventeenth century, the Dutch extended their influence to Africa. In 1650, the Dutch trading company decided to establish a settlement at the Cape, which later grew to become Capetown.[133] This also led to the establishing of a Reformed church in South Africa. When the first two elders were ordained in Capetown, they declared with their signature that the Confession of the Reformed Churches was good and in agreement with the Word of God.[134] They would have used a Dutch text of the Confession.

An English text of the Belgic Confession was published in South Africa during the nineteenth century, but there is no record of a text in the South African language.[135] It was not until well into the twentieth century that a South African text of the confession was published. This edition was made by representatives of three churches from a Dutch background in South Africa, and it contained not only the Belgic Confession, but also the Heidelberg Catechism, the Canons of Dort and the liturgical forms. The translation was made by the same persons who had translated the Bible into Afrikaans. This translation was also published in a book containing the documents of the federated Dutch Reformed Church in South Africa, which was obviously intended for ecclesiastical purposes.[136] The same version of the Belgic Confession was also published separately.[137]

Translations for Indonesia

The Dutch have long been involved in Indonesia. Translations of the Heidelberg Catechism were published several times,[138] but no early translation of the Belgic Confession is known. In the nineteenth century, J. Wilhelm translated not only the Heidelberg Catechism but also the Belgic Confession into the Javanese language, but

---

133. Pieter Coertzen, "Die koms van de Franse vluchtelinge na Suid Africa," in *Studia historiae ecclesiasticae I: Referate gelewer by vergaderinge van die kerkhistoriese werkgemeenschap van Suid-Afrika 1971, 1973* (Stellenbosch: Kerkhistoriese Werkgemeenschap van Suid Afrika, n.d.), 47.

134. This statement can be found in the decisions book of the consistory of Kaapstad (Capetown); see J. P. Claasen, "Aspekte van die afrikanisatie van die kerk gedurende die Europese lidmaatsverplanting: Die oriëntering van die Afrikaanse kerke," in *(Suid-) Afrika en die kerkgeschiedenis: Referate gelewer by die jaarvergadering 1975* (Stellenbosch: Kerkhistoriese Werkgemeenschap van Suid Afrika, 1976), 65.

135. The title is *The Doctrinal Standards and Liturgy of the Reformed Dutch Church. Published by Authority and for Account of the Reformed Dutch Church of South Africa.* A revised edition was published in Capetown in 1876. See Nauta, "Die Verbreitung des Katechismus," 57.

136. Nauta mentions in his survey of translations of the catechism that there were two editions, one published in 1636 and another in 1950 ("Die Verbreitung des Katechismus," in Coenen, *Handbuch zum Heidelberger Katechismus*, 57).

137. I have seen an undated copy of the third edition and an obviously later copy dated 1962.

138. Nauta, "Die Verbreitung des Katechismus," 55.

there is no indication that this translation was ever published.[139] Another translation was made for the Toraja churches on the island of Celebes, because its church order mentioned the Belgic Confession in addition to the Heidelberg Catechism and the Canons of Dort. However, this translation was never completed, and the regulation in the church order has been deleted.[140]

A minister on the island of Sumba, Boleh N. Radjah, made a translation of the Belgic Confession in cooperation with the missionary J. Klamer. This text serves the Reformed churches of Sumba, Savu and Timur, which adopted the Belgic Confession, the Heidelberg Catechism and the Canons of Dort. The translation was made during the 1980s, and published together with the liturgical forms in 1990.[141]

A new translation was made to be included in a collection of Reformed documents. It contains a number of Reformed confessions, including the Belgic Confession, several catechisms, church orders and liturgies. The Indonesian translation of the Belgic Confession, the Heidelberg Catechism and the Canons of Dort was made by Thomas Van den End. This edition was not intended for use in the churches but for study purposes.[142]

Spanish Translation

Around 1950, a Spanish translation of the confession was published. The original impetus came from Dr. Borkent in the Netherlands, who received the support of the well-known Dutch preacher Gerard Wisse.[143] This translation, entitled *Confesíon Belga*, includes the section on the civil government in article 36, which was deleted by the Reformed Churches in the Netherlands in 1905. This version was adopted by the Reformed Churches in Venezuela, and it is being used by several Spanish-speaking Reformed Churches in Spain, Latin America and the United States of America.

---

139. Thomas Van den End, "Transfer of Reformed Identity on the Missionfield in Indonesia," in *Changing Partnership of Missionary and Ecumenical Movements*, ed. Leny Lagerwerf, Karel Steenbrink and Frans Verstraelen (Leiden: Interuniversity Institute for Missiological and Ecumenical Research, 1995), 120; referring to D. Pol, *Midden Java ten Zuiden*, 147.

140. Van den End, "Transfer of Reformed Identity," 121. I wish to thank former missionaries in Indonesia, and in particular Dr. Van den End for providing information on the translation of the Belgic Confession into Indonesian.

141. This version can be found in the publication *Buku Geraja* (n.p.: BPK Gunung Mulia, 1990).

142. Van den End, ed., *Enam Belas Dokumen Dasar Calvinisme* (Jakarta, 2000).

143. Gerard Wisse, *Memoires: Onvergetelijke bladzijden uit mijn levensboek* (Utrecht: W. M. Den Hertog, 1953), 208-10. See also the article by W. M. Stougie, "Gerard Wisse," *BLGNP*, 4:453-55. I wish to thank Rev. W. J. Keesenberg, missionary in Venezuela for the information he provided.

Portuguese Translations

During the 1980s, the Belgic Confession and the Heidelberg Catechism were translated into Portuguese. The initiative for this translation came from the yearly conferences of Reformed missionaries in Brazil. A translation for internal use, made by missionaries, was published in 1988. Later, it was published in a more official version,[144] although it has not yet been officially adopted by any church in Brazil.

However, there is another, earlier translation in Portuguese. During the 1970s, many Portuguese who lived in African countries such as Mozambique and Angola moved to South Africa. The result was that a Portuguese classis was established. For these churches, a Portuguese translation was made of the three confessional standards of the Reformed Church in South Africa, including the Belgic Confession. This translation was published in 1990.[145]

Conclusion

This survey shows that the Belgic Confession, originating in Belgium and initially approved by a limited number of Reformed churches, has been translated into many languages. It is remarkable that this confession, published during persecution and pursued and mostly destroyed in its first year of existence, has been made available in so many languages. To this day it is being used by churches in all continents.

---

144. *Confissão de Fe e Catecismo de Heidelberg*, Cambuci (São Paulo: Casa Presbyteriana "Cultura Christâ," 1999).

145. The text of the Belgic Confession was published in *Três Confissôes da Igreja Reformada*, trans. L. Leal and Rev. M. Taute (Pretoria: M. Taute, 1990). I wish to thank former missionary Dr. Peter W. Van de Kamp and Rev. Abraham De Graaf, who presently works as a missionary in Brazil, for providing me with this information.

Appendix

Document 1 - Commissioners' Letter (Nov. 2, 1561)

The following document contains a description of the circumstances leading to the first discovery of the Belgic Confession.[1] It is part of a letter written by the committee for investigating the disturbances in Doornik. The letter is dated November 2, 1561; the described events must have taken place during the previous night.

"Madame ce jourd' huy à l'ouverture de la porte de ce chasteau à esté trouvé, jecté endedens la premiere fermeture un certain pacquet cloz et caceté; ou il y avoit ung long escript adreschant à nous ou en n[ost]re absence à Ceulx de ceste ville, faict au noms des bourgeois manans et habitans d'icelle, contenant leurs plainctes allencontre des persecutio[n]s qui se font p[rese]ntement pour la foy de Jesu-Christ (qu'ilz di[s]ent) chose toujours predicte par luy et ses apostres, et que cela ne sert que a soustenir la tyrannie du Pape et de ses ministres, ayant faict plusieurs constitutions pour esteindre l'honneur de Dieu, fonder son ambition avarice et idolatrie, disant qu'ilz ne sont turbateurs du repos publicque ny rebelles au princes, bien est vray qu'ilz ne pouvoient louer les chanteries icy faictes, qui disoient estre advenuz par avollez et gens subornez par les p[res]b[yt]res de ceste ville, pour esmouvoir ceste persecution contre eulx, et affin que schaichons la pureté de leur doctrine, nour p[rese]ntoient le livret icy encloz, conten[ant] leur confession qu'ilz disoient plus de la moictié de ceste ville, nous p[rese]nter d'un com[m]un accord, a quoy plus de cent mil ho[mm]es des pays si consente[n]t pareillement et que pour perdition de biens, tourmens, calamitez, mortz ou feuz ne la changeront, ni se leisseront divertir de la pureté de la doctrine de Dieu. Enfin allegue[n]t aucunes sentences en latin, grec et hebrieu prinses de l'escripture. Nous envoiont a V[otre] A[lteze] led[i]t petit livre, duquel en avions trouvé un semblable en la maison de Jan du Mortier, voires ung long escript faict sur mesme matiere de persecution des vrays chrestiens escript d'une mesme main que celuy p[rese]nt, qui est ca[us]e que retenons ledict escript, pour povoir averer l'auteur et interroguer sur ce noz prisonniers, par lequel nous admonestons

---

1. In this and many of the following documents, abbreviations were used. To facilitate understanding, the omitted letters will be inserted between brackets. Misspellings have not been corrected.

aussy de prendre exemple au magistrat de France, lequel pour avoir persecuté ainsy les bons fidelles a la poursuyte des p[re]b[st]res leurs ennemys en sont en perplexité de conscience. Voions assez le stil estre d'un francois, et pour la prolixité dud[i]t escript le temps ne souffre d'en faire la copie, mais luy envoyons un petit extraict, dont le demeura[n]t de l'escript se poeult estimer."

Source: Van Langeraad, *Guido de Bray*, 32-33. The original can be found in the *Papiers d'Etat*, Correspondence de Tournay, 1561-1563, fols. 50v - 51r.

Document 2 - Commissioners' Letter (Nov. 15, 1561)

The following report is part of the final confession made by Gilles Espringalles during an interrogation on November 15, 1561. The "escript" that is mentioned refers to a letter to Guido de Brès, which had been discovered by the committee for investigation and was shown to Espringalles during the interrogation.

"Interrogué, qui luy a baille *la confession des fideles, quil dict estr[e] d'Anvers*, dont il faict me[n]tion par sond[i]t escript aud[i]t Guy. Dict que p[er]sonne, ne luy a baillé, et que jamais ne la veu, et ce quil en parle p[ar] sond[i]t escript est pour aultant quil en avoit oy parler aud[i]t personnaige. Et sur ce que luy a este dict, q[ue] par plussieurs lieux de son escript, il monstre assez de scavoir, que c'est de lad[i]te Confession, d'aultant quil le juge bonne, mesmes quil dict que led[i]t Jerome l'attacha et publya aux portaulx. A persisté quil ne le scavoit q[ue] par led[i]t Jerome. Dict quil ne scet qui est l'auteur de lad[i]te Confession.

Dict aussy quil ne scet, quy l'a imprimé. Requis de dire quelle correspondance ceulx de ceste ville ont avec ceulx de France. Dict quil n'en scauroit a parler, parce quil ne les a hanté. Co[mm]e aussy ne scauroit a parler quelle intelligen[ce], ceulx de ceste ville ont avec ceulx Danvers, Valenciennes et Lille etc."

Source: Van Langeraad, *Guido de Bray*, 39. The original can be found in the *Papiers d'Etat*, Correspondence de Tournay, 1561-1563, fol. 99r.

Document 3 - Commissioners' Letter (Dec. 19, 1561)

The following is the first part of the summary report, dated December 19, 1561, which was sent to the king of Spain. It deals first with the "chanteries," which caused the investigation in Doornik, and later with the Belgic Confession.

"L'affaire de Tournay (dont p[ar] mes p[re]cedentes j'ay adverty v[ot]re ma[jes]té) a este une multitude de poeuple temerairem[ent] levée p[ar] aucuns jeusnes gens quy se sont mis a chanter, les pseaulmes de Dauid en rithme françois, traduictz p[ar] Marot, et en cest estat discourir p[ar] les rues, et com[m]encha d'un boult de la ville a l'ault[re], continua deux jours suyvantz scavoir est le jour Sainct Michiel dernier, et le lendemain. Le premier jour estoient trois ou quat[re] cens p[er]sonnes, ta[n]t hom[m]es, femmes que enffantz, et le lendemain le double à dire depuis les VII heures du soir, jusques ap[re]z IX essuyuans.

Le chant finy se meit un harengue p[ar] un sayetteur de Tournay, qui les renvoya en leurs maisons, disant quilz remerchiassent Dieu, de ce quil leur avoit donné la grace de ainsy chanté ses louanges. Et ne fut esté, que ceulx de la ville le IIIe jour drescharent ung ghibet, et firent deffendre sur la hart de chanter, et que pour execu[ti]on ondonnarent un bon ghuet sur le marchié, estoient en volunté de continuer led[it] IIIe jour.

Est trouvé que ces jeusnes gens estoie[n]t seduictz et mal sentans de la foy, qui ne desiroient que conciter la poeuple a les suyvre, et a tenter quelque chose de nouvelle sy leur fust este passe p[ar] dissimula[ti]on et quelque dilligence que l'on ayt faict denuoyer les com[m]issaires pour informer devant leur vienne la pluspart de ces autheurs estoient fugitifz, hormis les deux que ceulx de la ville avoient apprehendé et tost relaxez, sonbz caution de leurs peres, lesquelz entendans la venue desd[its] com[m]issaires se sont reunduz fugitifz pour lequel faict ont depuis este perpetuellem[ent] bannis des pays de pardeça de v[ot]re ma[jes]té avec pris a ceulx qui les pourroient rendre vifz, en quelque justice, que ce fut desd[its] pays. Et au regard de leurs peres, ils sont este tenus p[ri]sonniers et mulctez damends, selon quil a este trouvé co[n]venir, et ceulx qui ont esté trouvez avoir esté en la trouppe des chanteurs ont esté diversem[ent] pugnis et chastiez, selon leurs demerites, et qualitez de leurs delictz.

En prenant laquelle informa[ti]on, sur les affaires que dessus, ont esté oultre descouverts plussieurs lieux ou se tenoient co[n]venticulles, et faisoient p[ar] les hereticqs preschementz secrets, ce que l'on n'auvoit sceu p[ar] avant descouvrir, tellement q[ue] a esté executé p[ar] le feu, ung dogmatisant hereticq pertinax. Et sont encoires detenus aucuns opiniastres hereticqs, et au regard des aultres qui avoient esté seduictz et sont repentans ont esté pugnis extraordinairem[ent] p[ar] repara[ti]on honorable et abdica[ti]on canonicq[ue], ch[acu]n diversem[ent], selon la qualité de soy mesmes.

Ont esté aussy trouvées trois maisons quy estoient receptacles des heresiarqs esquelles com[m]unem[ent] se faisoient les assamblees de sorte que lesdites mais[ons] en detesta[ti]on du faict sont ordonnees est[re] demolies, et ruees p[ar] terre, sans pouvoir estre reëdiffiees.

Lesdictz com[m]issaires tienne[n]t encoires en prison aultres hereticques, de tous lesquelz se fera la justice exemplaire, selon leurs demerites, et que a esté advisé icy sur ch[ac]un diceulx, ausy que l'estat des affaires p[erso]n[elle]s, et le bien de la religion requiert.

Et quant a aucuns dogmatiseurs, receptateurs, diacres, som[m]eurs surveillans, daultres ministres et hereticques principaulx (dont lesd[its] com[m]issaires en ont descouvert assez bon nombre) si ava[n]t q[ue] l'on ne les a sceu apprehender, a esté procedé allencont[re] d'eulx p[ar] telle dilligence et rigueur quilz sont ban[n]is perpetuellem[ent] des pays de pardeça, avec confisca[ti]on de leurs biens, donnant non seullem[ent] pardon ... a ceulx q[ui] les pourront livrer vifz, ou mortz (pourveu que ce ne soit crime de leze ma[jes]té ou ault[re] detestable) mais aussy pris et mercede d'argent.

Que plus est leurs noms sont proscriptz en tableaux publiquem[ent] aud[it] Tournay, et s'envoyeront en certaines villes de pardeça, affin quilz ne prinssent nulle part demeure en ces pays, chose quy doibt donner grand terreur a tous semblables hereticques, affin de les povoir entheirem[ent] enterminer [read: exterminer].

Com[m]e aussy cont[re] les fugitifz a esté fort rigoreusement procedé, ainsy q[ue] dit-est, au contraire usé de quelque considera[ti]on cont[re] les vrays penitens, retournez a grace et misericorde de v[ot]re ma[jes]té. Ce que a esté trouvé co[n]venir pour la grande multitude de ceulx q[ui] sont trouvez aud[it] Tournay entachez de ce mal, affin de ne desasperer tout le peuple mais monstré au constrictz et repentans quelque chemin de grace, moiennant abjura[ti]on et penitence co[n]venable.

Lesdictz com[m]issaires ont aussy trouvez quelques escriptz fort scandaleux q[ue] aucuns mauvois espritz ont faict, sur la forme des livres que les Calvinistes de France ont exhibé parcidevant a leur roy, affin de leur permectre vivre a leurs phantasies et discre[ti]on et de deleisser toute persecu[ti]on contre eulx.

Encoires ont este trouvez petitz livrets, imprimez en nom des fidelles subjectz de pardeça adreschantz a v[ot]re ma[jes]té, contenans leur confession, plain de tous erreurs et perverse doctrine de Calvin, et sur la fin une remonstran[ce] aux magistratz ad ce quilz les voeulle[n]t endurer. Parquoy incontine[n]t l'on a mandé p[ar] tout ad ce que tels livres ne fussent p[er]mis es pays de pardeça, et sy on en trouvoit aucuns que l'on les levast pour scavoir dont ils venoient, quy en estoit autheur, et ou ilz estoient imprimez, neantmoings n'en a encoires riens peu scavoir certainem[ent]. Sinon que l'on dit, quil est composé en France et imprimé a Rouen, et que ces malingz esprits de Geneve ou France font cecy, pour seduire et conciter les subiectz de p[ar]deça."

Source: Van Langeraad, *Guido de Bray*, xv-xvii. The original can be found in the *Papiers d'Etat*, Correspondence de Tournay, 1561-1563, fols. 114r - 117r.

Document 4 - Commissioners' Letter (Jan. 10, 1562)

This is the first part of a letter the commissioners sent to the Governess, in which they report that the hiding place and the library of Guido de Brès had been discovered. The report is dated January 10, 1562.

"Est (madame) que nous avons faict telle dilligen[ce] qu'avons descouvert la maison, ou ce Guy de Bresse, aultrement Hierome, ministre et predicant solloit resider en ceste ville, en la paroisse St. Brixe. Et desirans empoigner un nom[m]é Jan de Gand et sa femme, desquelz ledict Guy tenoit sa dicte maison en arrière louaige, et luy faisoit ses provisions, avons failly de mectre la main sur eulx, mais seullement ont esté saisiz leurs biens.

Si avons pareillement ordonne de constituer prissonnier un nom[m]é Piat Moyeulx, cousturier et sa femme, lesquels estoient des familiers dudict-ministre, et des plus advanchez en la congrega[ti]on des hereticques, mais n'ont peu estre trouvez, pourquoi le procur[eur] du bailliaige de ceste ville par nostre charge a procedé par saisissement de leurs biens.

Et entendant que led[i]t Piat avoit encoires un aultre louaige d'un jardin et quelque petite maisonnete en lad[i]te paroisse de St. Brixe tenant les remparts assez pres la maison dudit Guy, y est alle avec quelques sergeans et lui arrivé illec a trouve tout le voisinage assemblé pour estaindre le feu que un quidam jusques ad present incognu, le mesmes jour a l'aprèz disner, ayant descendu audit jardin par une eschelle estoit venu mectre dedens une grande multitude de livres et de papiers amassez ensemble en lad[i]te maison, tellement que tous se meirent a estaindre ledit feu et saulver lesdictz papiers et livres, si avant quilz poeurent.

Entre lesquelz ont este saulvez environ deux-cens exemplaires d'un petit livret intitulé: Confession de foy des fidelles des Pais-Bas dont par ci-devant en avions envoie un semblable a V[otre] A[lteze] et pour ce que led[i]t peuple en prendoit a discre[ti]on nous les avons faict rapporter par un edict fort rigoreux contre ceulx qui les retiendroient.

Ont aussy este trouvez plussieurs livres tres pernicieux de Calvin, Luther, Melanchton, Ocolampadius, Zwinglius, Bucerus, Bullingerus, Brentius et tous aultres heresiarcques tant en francois que en latin, avec aucuns livres en grec, et aultres divers livres rammassez la plus part hereticques et deffenduz.

Comme pareillement ont este trouvez grande multitude de pappiers et livretz et entre iceulx plussieurs memoriaulx, recoeulx de s[e]rmons, minutes, l[iv]res, extraictz, annota[ti]ons et choses samblables tant en francois qu'en latin, ou sont inserees plussieures sentences de l'escripture saincte et aucuns auteurs, la plus part en grec et quelques unes en hebrieux, le tout escript de mesme l[ett]re et caractere (co[mm]e avons veu par conference) que la missive qui nous fut envoyee et jectee dedens la premiere porte de ce ch[ate]au qui nous donne asseurance que lesd[ite]s missives ont esté escriptes et composées enthierement par led[i]t Guy, et parta[n]t nous oste le scrupule, qu'avons eu jusques ad p[rese]nt pour scavoir quy les avoit escript et composé.

Que plus est entre lesd[i]ts pappiers l'on a recouvert plussieures l[ett]res de plussieurs costez escriptes aud[i]t Guy, et entre icelles une l[ett]re de Jan Calvin de l'an 1556 par lesquelles il respond à certaines questions que luy avoit propose led[it] Guy, dont envoions extraict a v[ot]re Alteze co[mm]e aussy y avoit l[ettr]es d'un nom[m]é Pierre Dathey qui se dit ministre des Flamengs a Francfort lequel intitule led[it] Guy ministre de la parole de Dieu es pays-bas, et trouvons que led[it] Guy a faict le com[m]encheme[n]t de ses erreurs a Lozane et a Geneve, aussy une aultre l[ett]re de Jan Crespin de l'an 1559, qui luy demande le catalogue des martirs qui ont estez pardeca les quelz il scavoit digne de ce tiltre et reng, veu quil en faisoit l'estat tant en francois que en latin.

Comme pareilleme[n]t trouvons divers escriptz a luy adreschantz, sur les choses qui passent p[rese]nteme[n]t en France, avec divers escriptz venans de diverz lieux de ces pays, la plus part sans nom, ny lieu dont ilz sont escriptz, le tout parlant des matieres et affaires hereticques.

Par ou voions estre satisfaict a plusieures choses que nous desirions entendre, ascavoir que led[it] ho[mm]e s'appelle Guy de Bresse, natif de Mons co[mm]e avons trouvé escript de sa prop[r]e main en aucuns de ses livres tant en latin, grecque et francois ayans les aucuns d'iceulx ce mot Guy efface, et au lieu d'icelluy mis Hieromme, pour se rendre tant plus incognu, est marye, ayant eu un filz le dernier daoust 1560 q[ue] le lendemain il feit baptiser et appeler Israel, selon que voyons par sesd[it]s memoriaulx escriptz de sad[it]e main.

Ledict ho[mm]e est le surveilla[n]t et ministre general de ces sectaires Calvinistes, principallement en ceste ville, Lille, Valencien[n]es ou il a ses congrega[ti]ons qu['] il appelle egl[is]e des fidelles avec ses som[m]eurs et aultres ses suppostz et aydes."

Source: Van Langeraad, *Guido de Bray*, 45-47. The original can be found in the *Papiers d'Etat*, Correspondence de Tournay, 1561-1563, fols. 136-38.

Document 5 - Calvin's Letter (March 3, [?])

The following advice was written by Calvin on behalf of the ministers in Geneva. The year of the response is not given, but it deals with a question some unidentified ministers submitted to Calvin. However, the content proves that this advice deals mainly with confessions in general and with the Belgic Confession specifically.

"Hac ubique astutia molitur Satan Christi ecclesiam pessumdare, quando puram doctrinam, quae est veluti anima, prorsus exstinguere non potest, ut fracta et soluta disciplina nervos corporis incidat, unde luxatis membris paulo post sequatur tristis dissipatio. Atque utinam probe expenderent, quicunque iugo reiecto permitti volunt cuique effraenem [read: effraenam] licentiam, hoc modo se quaerere ruinam ecclesiae et vastitatem. Certe non tantum moderationi studerent, sed placido mansuetoque spiritu se ipsi quoque subiicerent communi disciplinae. Sed quoniam hac de re prolixius disserere non est nobis propositum, breviter literis vestris respondebimus, optimi et integerrimi fratres. Ubi nos primum consulitis: An adigendi sint ad fidem suam publice testandam, qui se in ecclesiam admitti postulant: deinde sententiam nostram rogatis de ipsa confessionis apud vos receptae forma, tandem quaeritis, annon excommunicandi sint e coetu fidelium, qui vel sua contumacia vel turpitudine vitae ordinem pervertunt? Nos autem non videmus cur grave sit homini, qui inter ecclesiae domesticos censeri vult, Christo capiti in solidum nomen dare. Quod fieri non potest, nisi diserte subscribat sincerae pietati, et ingenue errores damnet, quibus sinceritas religionis corrumpitur. Iam errorum detestatio saepe ex circumstantia temporum pendet. Quia prout novas turbandi rationes excogitat Satan, prudenter occurrere necesse est. Scimus quantopere nobis commendet Paulus unitatem spriritus, in vinculo pacis (Ephes. 4, 3). Porro ad fovendum et retinendum inter pios consensum, plusquam necessaria est illa solennis fidei professio. Denique quicunque optabunt ecclesiam Dei stare incolumem, non aegre ferent, hoc adminiculo eam fulciri. Non putamus esse, qui litem moveant de generali illa professione: sed frigeret illa nisi distincte quisque tam haereticis, quam perversis dogmatibus renunciet. Iam in forma vestrae confessionis nihil animadvertimus, quod non sit sacris Dei oraculis et fidei orthodoxae consentaneum. Itaque summam doctrinae quae illic habetur libenter probamus. Tantum vellemus epistolam ad Hebraeos non adscribi Paulo, quum firmis argumentis persuasi simus alium esse autorem. Neque tamen volumus nostro suffragio obstringi conscientias, vel quasi praeiudicio ligari ecclesiam, quominus liberum sit singulis in medium proferre, si quid eos a subscriptione impediat. Etsi autem nobis displicet eorum morositas, qui ob leves scrupulos a publico consensu discedunt: si quis tamen verbum aliquod durius, vel loquutionem amplecti nequeat, modo conveniat de re ipsa, tolerari forte poterit eius infirmitas, ne ob res quasque minimas scindatur ecclesia. Hortamur interea pios omnes ad hanc modestiam et sobrietatem, ut potius quisque ad reliquos omnes accedat, quam sua pervicacia speciem praebeat tentandae religionis. Caeterum, non aliter consistet ecclesiae incolumitas, quam si ad eam purgandam, fraenandas libidines, tollenda flagitia, corrigendos perversos mores vigeat excommunicatio: cuius moderatum usum quisquis recusat, praesertim admonitus, se ex Christi ovibus non esse prodit. Valete eximii viri, et nobis ex animo colendi fratres. Dominus semper vobis adsit, vos gubernet suo spiritu, et virtute sua confirmet ad implendum sanctae suae vocationis cursum.

Genevae, 3. Nonas Martii.

Ioannes Calvinus fratrum nomine."

Source: *Calvini Opera*, 10/1: 224-26.

Document 6 - Saravia's Letter (April 13, 1612)

Adrianus Saravia wrote an extensive letter to Johannes Uytenbogaert, in response to a letter he had received from him. The second part is reproduced here. Earlier in this letter, he discussed the authority of the government in ecclesiastical affairs. In that context, he mentions the Belgic Confession, referring to the fact that the original edition of the Belgic Confession began with an appeal to the government. He goes on to recount how he was involved in an attempt to bring the confession to the attention of noblemen. This leads to another section providing information concerning the author of the Belgic Confession.

"Huius rei testis est epistola ad Hispaniarum Regem et Ordines Belgicarum Provinciarum, quae olim praefixa fuit fidei Confessioni Ecclesiarum et tecum reputa cuius Religionis illi fuerint, quantum tamen illis tribuerimus in fidei negotio. Ego tunc temporis Minister eram Ecclesiae Gallicanae Antverpiae, et exemplaria illius Confessionis Principi Auriaco et Comiti Egmondano offerenda curavi. Frater uxoris meae erat Comiti Ludovico à cubiculis, qui me ad dominum suum adduxit, ut illi innotescerem et exemplaria recens editae Confessionis darem ulterius principibus distribuenda. Congregavi primum tunc temporis Ecclesiam Bruxellis auxilio Domini de Tolossa, fratris Domini sanctae Aldegundae, ex aulicis et paucis quibusdam civibus Gallici sermonis. In altercationibus Leidanis illam fidei Confessionem et Catechismum allegari et urgeri video, ac si ipsum esset Dei verbum. Homines improbi Confessionem Augustanam audacter despiciunt; et qui modestiores haberi volunt, in illa esse aliquid, quod mutatum vellent, desiderant; in sua vero Confessione, ac si fidei Canon esset, nihil mutari patiuntur. Ego me illius Confessionis ex primis unum fuisse authoribus profiteor, sicut atque Hermanus Modetus; nescio an plures sint superstites. Illa primo fuit conscripta Gallico sermone à Christi servo et martyre Guidone de Bres. Sed antequam ederetur, Ministris verbi Dei quos potuit nancisci, illam communicavit et emendandum, si quid displiceret, addendum, detrahendum proposuit: ut unius opus censeri non debeat. Sed nemo eorum qui manum apposuerunt, unquam cogitavit fidei canonem edere, verum ex Canonicis scriptis fidem suam probare. Nihil tamen meo iudicio in illa est quod reprehendam aut mutare velim. Quod si sint aliqui quibus non omnia probentur, audiendos censeo et ex verbo Dei docendos si quod reprehendunt secundum Dei verbum. Nemo temere inter impios censendus est qui doceri paratus est. Articulorum non idem omnium est pondus; esse possunt nonnulli à quibus si dissentiant sunt ferendi, non ab Ecclesia idcirco alienandi. Idem censeo de Catechismis vestris, quos ipse aliquando tam in Gallicis quam Teutonicis Ecclesiis docui. Ab illis tamen dissentio ex expositione descensus Christi ad inferos; postquam à vestris eiectus huc sum reversus, mutavi sententiam, melius hic in Anglia edoctus concionibus et scriptis tum doctissimi viri Reverendi Episcopi

Vintoniensis tum aliorum doctorum hominum, qui nulla in parte aut Calvino aut Bezae cedunt. De qua re ad Ecclesias quae Reformatae dicuntur duos conscripsi libros, qui nondum viderunt lucem. Sunt hic plures de hoc argumento hinc inde scripti libri sermone Anglico. Tibi per vestrum tabellarium brevi mittam descriptum exemplar; interea iubeo te salvare et pro veritate fortiter stare.

Cantuariae die 13 Aprilis stilo Angliae 1612."

Source: Vinke, *Libri Symbolici*, xii-xiii; cf. Van Langeraad, *Guido de Bray*, 140-41; Nijenhuis, *Adrianus Saravia*, 356-57. This letter was first published in 1662 as a Dutch translation, in the Remonstrant publication *Brieven van geleerde mannen*, 52-57.

Document 7 - Thysius' *Leere ende orde* (1615).

During the debates between the Remonstrants and the Counter-Remonstrants, the Reformed theologian Thysius published a book on the doctrine and church order of the Reformed churches in the Netherlands in 1615. In the preface of this book he discussed, among other issues, the historical background of the confession. His summary of the early history of the Belgic Confession is followed by some remarks on the second edition.

"Ende eerstelyck soo veel de Confessie ende Bekentenisse aengaet, die, in twee *Copyen* (1563 en 1582) teghen den anderen overghestelt, voor aen staet, Is eerst int Walsch int Jaer 1562. geschreven, ende des Jaers daerna in druck wtghegheven: niet datse van de Walsche Kercken alleen gestelt sy, maer om dat dese sprake, beyde in ende buyten Nederlandt, ghemeyner ende kennelijcker is als de Nederduytsche, voornemelijck den Koninck van Spangien ende de[n] Nederlantsche[n] Overheden, wien sy toe-gheschreve[n] is: oock is stracx in 't Jaer daernae, in Nederduytsch ende ook in Hoochduytsch te Heydelberch overgheset, ghedruct gheworden. Ende al-hoe-wel het niet ghenoechsaem aen den dach en is, wie den Schryver oft Schryvers der selver zijn geweest (waer aen oock weynich gelegen is) so isse nochtans van Gheleerde, Godtsalighe mannen gheschreven, die gheen onsekere ende alleen in de hersenen vlietende, maer een ghewisse ende dadighe kennisse van Godt ende Goddelijcke saken onser salicheyt betreffende, hebben ghehadt, haer bloet niet kostelyck achtende tot bevestinghe der Waerheyt in deselvighe begrepen: ende, soo wy van de oude bericht worden, van dien in Godts Woort ende alle Godtsalicheyt wel gheoeffenden trouwen Dienaer ende Martelaer Iesu Christi, WIDO DE BRES, ende syne Mede-helpers in de Ghemeynten van Ryssel, Casselereye, Doornick, Valencyn etc. ende GODEFRIDUS WINGHIUS, wiens sonderlycke gheleertheyt in de Theologie ende gheschiktheyt in de Griecksche en andere Spraken, ghenoechsaem aen den dach is, als die ons het niew Testament van nieus overgeset heeft, wtgesonde[n] zijnde van de Emdische Kerck tot opbouwinghe der eerst-ghestichte Vlaemsche Ghereformeerde Ghemeynten, neffens syne mede-arbeyders in Vlaenderen, Brabant, Hollandt ende elders. Dan het sy daer mede als het wil, is evenwel niet ghemaect noch wtgegaen dan met voorgaende *Communicatie* ende *Approbatie* (als sulck een wichtich werck vereyschte, gheschreven zijnde in ghemeynen naem der Kercken aen den Koninck van Spangien ende Overheden deser Nederlanden) ghenomen met, ende gegeven van de ghetrouwe Dienaers, die toen ter tijdt in den Nederlandtschen Kercken over-al waren: soo in-landische, als GEORGIUS WIBOTIUS, anders SYLVANUS, CHRISTOPHORUS FABRITIUS, ende andere gheleerde mannen binnens landts meer, te langh om te verhalen: als wt-landische, namelijck met CORNELIO COLTHUNIO, eertijts Pastoor tot Alckmaer, NICOLAO CARENAEO, 't Emden, PETRO DATHENO, ende GASPARO HEYDANO, te Franckendael; VALERANDO POLLANO, te Francfort; IOHANNE TAFFINO, ende PETRO COLONIO te Mets; NICOLAO GALASIO, PETRO COGNATO, PETRO ALEXANDRO, eertyts Bicht-Vader ende Hof-prediker van Vrouw Marie Coninghinne van Hungarien ende Regente deser Nederlanden, ende PETRO DELENO, te Londen; ende waerschijnelijck oock met dien Hoochgeleerden ende God-salighen Theologo ANDREA GERARDI van Iperen, Professoor der wyt-beroomde Universiteyt van Marborch. Iae selfs is van dien seer geleerden; Godtsaligen ende yverighen JOHANNE CRISPINO, vertoont ende ghecommuniceert met de Kercken-dienaren, ende vooral met dien wtnemenden ende dieren man Gods JOHANNE CALVINO, te Geneven, alwaer se oock eerst ghedruct is. Waer wt genoechsaem blyckt dat se niet van eenige gheringhe ende ongheoeffende persoonen, elders wt eenen duysteren hoeck is voortsgecomen, als sommighe hooch-dunckende lieden stoutelijck haer derven laten verluyden.

Wyders, so is deselvige int Iaer 1565, by goetduncken ende last der *Synode* oft Kerckelycke By-een-comste, 't Antwerpen onder het Cruys gehouden, (alwaer oock tegenwoordich geweest is PHILIPS VAN MARNIX, HEER VAN SINT ALDEGONDE) van nieus overzien geworden, namelyk door FRANCISCUM JUNIUM, Dienaer Godts in de Nederlanden, (als tselvige van hem in syn leven verhaelt wort) wel een Iongher-man, maer als eenen rechten TIMOTHEUS, neffens syne sonderlinge geleertheyt, stemmich ende ernstig boven syne iare, ende naderhandt een voornemen en treffelyck *Professoor* ende Leeraer in de H. Schrift, in de wyt beroemde Universiteyten van *Nieustadt, Heidelberg* ende *Leyden*. Ende is die, alsoo verbetert zijnde, niet in de sake selfs, maer eyghentlyck in den aert ende wyse van schryven, corter ende duydelycker stellinghe, by order der voor-ghemelder Vergaderinghe na Geneven gesonden, om by advijs van dien voortreffelijkcken Leeraer THEODORI BEZAE ende syne Mede-dienaers des Euangeliums, alsoo te Geneven gedruct te werden, dwelck door den voorseyden CRISPINO int Iaer 1566, (gelyck de voorgaende *Copye*) ghesciet is: al ist dat de Nederduytsche-Kercken haer aen deselve eerste Copye eenighe Iaren na den anderen ghehouden hebben: waerop FRANCISCUS SONNIUS, dien bloedighen Kettermeester, ende een van de nieuwe Bisschoppen, Bisschop van Antwerpen, int Iaer daer na, onderstaen heeft te antwoorden."

Source: Van Langeraad, *Guido de Bray*, 103-4, 130. The original can be found in the preface of Thysius, *Leere ende order der Nederlandsche, soo Duytsche als Walsche, Ghereformeerde kercken* (1615).

Document 8 - The Synod of Dort (1618-19) on the Confession

The Synod of Dort 1618-19 dealt with the Belgic Confession on several occasions. The following reports are taken from the Dutch language version of the Acts; they will be presented in chronological order.

In the 144th session, held in the afternoon of April 29, 1619, the representatives of the States General at the Synod of Dort reported that the States General had been informed that Canons had been drafted and that all members had subscribed to this. They conveyed the approval of the States for what had been done. They added that the States particularly wanted the custom of a national synod to review the Belgic Confession, in this case to be carried out in the presence of the foreign delegates.

"Dat dit oock voor al den wille der Hoogh: Mogh[ende] Heeren Staten was / dat de Confessie des gheloofs der Gereformeerde Nederlantsche kercken / nae ghewoonte der Nationale Synoden / inde tegenwoordicheyt der uytheemsche Theologen over-lesen en[de] ondersocht soude worden. Ende dat yeder lidt des Synodi so wel uytheemsche als inlantsche / vrijelick soude verclaren / so sy yet in dese Confessie mochten aenghemerckt hebben / 'twelcke de Leer-puncte[n] ende substantie der Leere betrefte / en[de] 'twelcke met de waerheyt va[n] Godes geopenbaerde woort / ofte met de Confessie[n] van andere Gereformeerde Kercken / niet al te wel en soude schijnen te accorderen. Doch wat de methode ofte manieren van spreken / ende de regieringe ofte ordere der Kercke aenginck, dat dat selvighe nader hant van de inlantsche alleen naerder ondersocht soude worden. Is derhalven vermaent ter selve tijdt / dat volghens dien den 31. en[de] 32. Artijckel / niet en behoefde geexamineert te worden: dewijle in beyde ghehandelt wiert vande Kerckelicke ordere / die sommighe uytheemsche vande onse verscheyden hebben.

Naer ghedaene provisie van exemplaren der Nederlantsche Confessie / zyn ordentlick voorgelesen alle de Artijckelen deser Confessie. Ende is yeder een versocht / dat naer behoorlicke ende neerstighe ende ernstige examinatie der selvighe / voorts vrymoedelijck ende oprechtelijck souden willen verclaren / of sy in de Leer-stucken in de Confessie begrepen / yet hadden waer ghenomen / 'twelck met Godes Woordt niet en soude accorderen / ende derhalven oordeelden nootsaeckelick verandert te moeten worden."

Source: *Acta ofte Handelinghen des Nationalen Synodi . . . tot Dordrecht*, 1:345.

The delegates from Great Britain gave their opinion during the 145th session, held on the morning of April 30, 1619:

"De E[erweerdighe] Theologe[n] van Groot Britannien / hebben verclaert dat sy de Nederlantsche Confessie neerstelick hadden gexamineert / ende niets daer in ghevonden / aengaende de Leer-stucke[n] des geloofs / of ten quam over een met Godes woort / niet teghenstaende de bedenckinghen der Remonstranten: de welcke sy betuyghen met de selve moeyte ondersocht te hebben / ende dat de selve meestendeel sodanighe waren / die op alle Confessien der Gereformeerde Kercken conden aengeteyckent worden."

Source: *Acta ofte Handelinghen der Nationalen Synodi . . . tot Dordrecht*, 1:346.

During the 146th session, which was held in the afternoon of the same day, the other delegations were given the opportunity to evaluate the Belgic Confession:

"Syn af-ghevraeght de oordeelen van de andere / soo uytheemsche als inlantsche Theologen vande Leere inde Nederlantsche Confessie begrepen: ende is by allen ende een yeder verclaert met eenstemmige advijsen / dat sy oordeelden / dat in dese Confessie gheen Leer-stuck begrepen en was / 'twelck met de waerheyt in de heylige Schriftuere uytgedruckt / was strijdende: maer ter contrarien dat alles met de selvige waerheyt / en[de] met de Confessien van andere Ghereformeerde Kercken wel accordeerde.

Daer-en-boven zijn de inlantsche vermaent van de uytheemsche Theologen / in dese rechtsinnighe / Godsalighe ende eenvoudighe Confessie des gheloofs / stantvastelick te willen volherden / de selve den nacomelinghen onvervalscht te willen naer laten / ende tot de comste toe onses Heeren Jesu Christi / onvervalscht te willen bewaren. Hebben oock de inlantsche eendrachtelic verclaert / dat haer voornemen was / inde professie deser rechtsinnighe Leere / stantvastelick te willen volherde[n] / ende de selve in dese Nederlantsche Provincien suyverlick te leeren / neerstelick voor te staen / ende voorts onvervalscht door de ghenade Gods te bewaren. Den welcken sy oock voor dat minnelicke accoort / soo wel der uytheemsche als inlantsche gedanckt hebben / ende de E[erweerdighe] Heeren Ghecommitteerde uyt name der Kercken gebeden / dat sy by de Hoog: Mogende Heeren Staten souden willen intercederen / dat den selvighen Hoogh: Mogende Heeren believe dese rechtsinnige Leere inde Nederlantsche Kercken voortaen door hare authoriteyt ongheschent te hanthaven ende te bevestighen.

De Ghedeputeerde[n] der Walsche Kercken hebben aanghedient / dat de selvighe Nederlantsche Confessie in de Nationale Synode der kercken van Vrancrijck / in de Stadt van Vitrii / anno 1583. ghehouden / solemnelicken gheapprobeert hadde gheweest. Twelcke sy uyt de Acten des selvighen Synodi bevestighden."

This is followed by an excerpt from the Acts of the Synod of Vitrij, and by the full text of the Belgic Confession.

Source: *Acta ofte Handelinghen des Nationalen Synodi . . . tot Dordrecht*, 1:346-7.

After the foreign delegates had left, Synod of Dordrecht continued meeting in order to deal with national issues. Although these events, too, were officially recorded, their records were not included in the Latin *Acta* published in 1620, nor in the Dutch *Handelinghen*, published the year after. They were published many years afterwards, in Latin in 1668 and in Dutch in 1669. During this later, national part of the synod, the Belgic Confession was again discussed. In session 171, held in the morning of May 23, synod dealt with improvements in the text:

"De verbeterde Fransche ende Nederlantsche editien vande belydenisse der Nederlantsche kercken zyn voorgelesen, de Nederlantsche van *Godefrido Udemanno* ende de Fransche van *Daniele Colonio*: ende is doorgaens rede vande verbeteringe aangewezen."

During session 172, held in the afternoon of May 23, synod continued scrutinizing the text, until it was confronted with an issue in connection with article 22 of the Belgic Confession:

"Men is noch voortgegaen int voorlesen vande voorgemelte verbeteringe, ende deselve affgelesen zynde, is een yder affghevraecht, zoo zy meynden, datter in dese recognitie yets nagelaten ware, waer op te letten stont, dat hij t' selve zoude willen aanwijsen.

De Praeses heeft te kennen gegeven, dat de Theologi van Geneven bij hem gelaten hadden eenighe notulen op onze Confessie; waerop gelet is. Dat oock bij hem gelaten waren twee vermaen stuckxkens; het eene vande Theologis vande Paltz, ende het andere vande Theologis van Hessen, die oock voorgelesen zijn. Ende ter occasie van dien is ghevraecht oft niet geraden ware datmen in den 22e Art. onser Confessie in plaetse vande woorden, *Ende zoo veel zijne alderheylichste wercken, die hij voor ons ghedaen heeft*, stelde het generale woort *ghehoorsaemheyt Christi*. Maer also dese vraghe werde tegengesproocken, ende de tyt nu verloopen was, is de saecke uijtgestelt tot s' anderdaechs: ende de Broeders zyn vermaent, dat zy collegialiter wilden antwoorden."

A decision was made during session 173, held in the morning of May 24:

"Is besloten met eendrachtighe stemmen aller Collegien, datmen bij de sententie, die inde Nederlandsche ende Fransche Confessie uytgedruckt is, ganschlijck zal blyven, ende dat het geensints geraden zij, datter eenighe veranderinghe inde woorden vande selve Confessie gheschiede, waer toe van velen treffelycke redenen zyn bijgebracht. Nochtans is ten versoecke van sommige goetghevonden, dat inden selven Art. bij de woordekens *voor ons* tot nader verclaringhe zouden bijgevoecht worden de woordekens *ende in onse plaetse*.

Ende na dat de andere Broeders oock hare observatien byghebracht hadden, ende deselve al te samen geexamineert zyn gheweest, zoo zyn noch enighe dinghen met gemeyn advys verandert: Ende zyn also beyde de exemplaria in beyde de talen Nederlantsche en Fransche, zoo ghebetert, gheapprobeert. Ende is verclaert, datmen voortaen alleen dese exemplaria voor authentike houden zal, ende deselve tot zulck een eynde metten aldereersten zal affschryven, ende doen drukken."

Source: H. H. Kuyper, *De post-acta*, 222-25.

Document 9 - Trigland's *Kerckelycke geschiedenissen* (1650)

The Reformed Dutch historian Trigland published his *Kerckelycke geschiedenissen* ("Ecclesiastical Histories," 1650) as a response to a book entitled *Kerckelycke historie* ("Ecclesiastical History," 1646) written by the Remonstrant Uytenbogaert. In his book, Trigland calls Uytenbogaert "de Histori-schrijver," in the sense of "the author of the History." Throughout the work, Trigland includes extensive quotations from Uytenbogaert's book, which were printed using Latin type. These are followed by his own views on the development of the Dutch church, which are printed in Gothic type. Below, Uytenbogaert's statements are distinguished from Trigland's by being set in *italics*. In addition, a comparison between Trigland's *Kerckelycke geschiedenissen* and Thysius' *Leere ende order* shows that Trigland derived much of his argument from Thysius. In what follows, it will be indicated which sections are dependent on Thysius, and which are Trigland's own.

Two lengthy quotations are reproduced here, both focusing on the authority of the confession. The first quotation shows this in connection with the church. Trigland presents his argument in five sections, which is here clarified by beginning each of these section with a new paragraph. The second quotation deals with the submission of the confession at the Diet at Augsburg in 1566.

[In the following, Trigland is dependent on information from Thysius.]
"Van die Confessie zijn in voorige tijden twee Copyen geweest / d'eene wat breeder / d'andere in sommige poincten wat korter ingetogen. De eerste is eerst inde walsche of Fransche tale gheschreven / inden Jare 1562. ende des volghenden jaers in druck uytgegeven. Dit is gheschiet / niet om datse van of voor de Walsche kercken alleen ghestelt zy gheweest / maer om dat de Fransche tale / die byde walsche in 't schrijven ghebruyckt wordt / binnen ende buyten de Nederlanden ghemeyner ende kennelijcker is als de Nederduytsche / voornamelijck den Coninck van Spaenjen / ende den Nederlantschen Overheden / den welcken zy is toegheschreven. Ende is terstont des jaers daer aen / namelijck inden jare vijftienhondert drie ende 't sestich / uytgegeven in Nederduytsch / alsmede in 't Hoochduytsch overgeset / en[de] te Heydelbergh gedruckt /
[Trigland continues on his own and quotes Uytenbogaert at length.]
gelijck ick die dit schrijve / een exemplaer heb ghesien / als oock noch eenige voorhanden zijn / van dien genoemde[n] druck inden jare vijftien-hondert drie-en t'sestich. Waer uyt blijckt / met hoe weynich waerheyts den Histori-schrijver gheseyt heeft ter voor geallegeerde plaetse/ pag. 150, col. 2. *dat de Ghereformeerde noch gheene bysondere Confessie hebbende, haer behielpen met dien tijtel vande Ausbursche Confessie, tot dat zy eene andere souden ghesmeet hebben.* Want den tijt vanden welcken hij daer spreeckt / op den welcken hy seyt *datse noch gene Confessie en hadden,* was het jaer 1566 / ende hare bysondere Confessie was

alghemaeckt inden jare 1562. ende inde Nederduytsche tale ghedruckt inden jare 1563. soodanige exemplaren men noch soude konnen thoonen / des noot zijnde. Den Histori-schrijver seyt pag. 151. col. 2. *Wat persoon of personen, leeraren of andere, dese geseyde Nederlantsche Confessie oorspronckelijck ghestelt, en[de] op den naem van alle de Nederlantsche Ghereformeerde kercken, over ende uytgegeven hebben, en kan ick niet seeckerlijck seggen. Ick vinde niet dat eenighe Synodale, oft andere Generale vergaderinge der Nederlantscher kercken, daer over te voren zy ghehouden, of dat daer toe eenige ghenerale last van allen zy ghegeven, weyniger dat die oorspronckelijck van allen ghetoetst, ende wel ondersocht soude zijn, aen ende nae Godts woort, om met voorgaende kennisse van saecken, by allen, als het selve woordt in allen deelen gelijkformich, aenghenomen, oock nae de selve gheleert ende ghelooft te moeten worden, soomen daer nae inghevoert ende ghewilt heeft te moeten gheschieden. Ick heb ghesien ende ghelesen een brief, gheschreven met de eyghene hant van D. Adrianus Saravia, wylen Professor inde Theologie tot Leyden, daer in hy seyt, dat de selve Confessie is gestelt geweest, alleen van drie of vier Predikanten, waer van hy selve een was, daer in zy meest hadden ghevolght de Fransche Confessie, Oock dat hy Saravia selve te dier tijt ghebruyckt wierdt, om die aende Heeren, den Prince van Oraenjen, ende Grave van Egmont, (in welcker Hoven hy kennisse hadde) te leveren, om voort-ghecommuniceert te worden. Ende D. Franciscus Iunius zal[iger] heeft my geseyt, dat Guy de Bres, walsch Predikant, (nae om de Religie ghedoodt) met Hermannus Moded, Saravia, ende hy Iunius, doe* [read: *die*] *noch jonck zijnde, meest tot het schrijven in 't Fransch ofte Walsch ghebruyckt wierdt, ende noch een of twee andere my nu vergeten, daer mede zijn besich gheweest.* Dus verre d' Historischrijver.

Hier op staet aen te mercken / Ten eersten / Dat onse Voorsaten / vande oude / die onder de kruys-kercken verkeert hadden / bericht zijn geweest /
[Here Trigland again borrows heavily from Thysius.]
dat de vroome / ende in Goddelijcke saecken wel gheoeffend martelaer Christi / *Guido de Bres*, met goetvinden van syne medehulpers inde Gemeynten van Rijsel / Cassellrye / Doornick / Valencijn etc[etera] ende de seer gheleerde ende Godvruchtighe Godefridus Winghius, die vande Embdische kercke / tot op bouwinghe vande eerstgestichte vlaemsche Ghereformeerde Ghemeynten / ghesonden is gheweest / met kennisse van syne medearbeyders in Vlaenderen / Brabant / Hollant / etc[etera] de eerste stellers van die Confessie zijn gheweest;
[Trigland himself adds the following.]
die / ghelijck van gheleertheyt / Godtvruchticheyt / ende ghetrouwicheyt beroemt / wel hebben gheweten / ende ghetrouwelijck uytghedruckt / 't ghene dat hare medehulpers alomme inde Ghemeynten / neffens haer / leerden / ende de vroome martelaers met haer bloet besegelden.

Ten tweeden / Datmen niet en leest van eenighe Synodale / of Generale vergaderinghe / die daer overgehouden zy / is gheen wonder. Want een yeder kan wel bevroeden hoe kommerlijck het zy / in sulcke sware tijden / onder soo wreede vervolgingen / vergaderinghen te houden / insonderheyt die groot zijn: doch even wel dattet niet en is gheschiet sonder soodanige communicatie alsmen in sulcke tijden hebben kan.

[Trigland again follows Thysius.]

Ten derden / datse ghemaeckt zijnde / niet en is uytghegaen / dan nae voorgaende communicatie met veel Godsalighe ende treffelijcke mannen / die te dier tijt inde Gereformeerde kercken waren / niet alleen binnen / maer oock buyten slants / als met *Georgio Wibotio*, ende *Christophoro Fabritio* binnen slants; ende buyten slants met *Cornelio Coolthunio*, eertijts gheweest Pastoor tot Alckmaer / ende *Nicolao Carenaeo*, beyde tot Embden / *Petro Datheno* ende *Casparo Heydano* tot Franckendael / *Valerando Pollano* tot Franckfoort, *Joanne Taffino* ende *Petro Colonio* te Mets / *Nicolao Galasio, Petro Cognato, Petro Alexandro* (gewesen Biechtvader ende Hofprediker van vrouw *Maria*, Coninginne van Hongarien / ende Regente der Nederlanden) ende *Petro Deleno* tot London etc[etera].

Ten vierden / Datse inden jare 1565. met goetduncken ende last van een kerckelijcke byeenkomste / by de welcke oock teghenwoordich is gheweest d' Edele ende seer gheleerde *Philips van marnix* Heere van St Aldegonde / ghehouden t' Antwerpen onder 't Cruys / van nieus oversien is geworden. Waer van de vermaerde Theologant *D. Franciscus Junius*, inde beschryvinghe van zijn eyghen leven / eenich gewagh maeckt in deeser manieren.[2]

[What follows is again Trigland's own contribution.]

Daer hebben wy immers klaer eene Synodale vergaderinge / door welckes last die Confessie is oversien / waer uyt blijckt dat op die selve sonderlinghe is gelet gheweest. Evenwel is in dat jaer de selve noch gedruckt gheworden in het Nederduytsch na de oude forme / daer eenighe Artijckelen wat langer zijn ghestelt. Maer naderhandt zijn eenighe Artijckelen wat inghetrocken ofte bekort inden jare 1566. in het Walsch / ende inden jare 1581. in het nederduytsch/ ende des jaers daar aen alsoo inden druck uytgegeven; in welcke forme de selve is overgheset in 't latijn / ende ghestelt inde Harmonie der Confessien. Ende dit is de korter Copie / die nu meest in handen vande kercken is. Daer uyt schijnt afgenomen te worden / dat / indien *D. Adrianus Saravia* in dat stuck yet ghedaen heeft / dattet gheschiet is in het laetste hernemen ende oversien vande voorsz[eide] Confessie.

Ten vijfden / Den Histori-schrijver / hebbende hier voor aenghetoghen de forme vande kerckelijcke regieringhe / ghestelt binnen London byden Heere *Joannes à Lasco*, om quansuys te bewijsen / dat de eerste Gereformeerde Christenen van Nederlant met de Remonstranten souden hebben ghevoelt /

---

2. This lengthy quotation from Junius has been omitted. Part of his statement can be found in chapter 2, footnote 29. For further discussion, see chapter 6.

heeft dat boexken daer mede authoriteyt willen gheven / dattet vande kercken deurgaens was aengenoomen ende gherecommandeer[t] / goet ghekent ende ghepresen. Op dat fundament voorwaer mach veel meer de voorsz[eide] Confessie / by alle Predikanten ende Litmaten vande Gereformeerde kercke haer aensien hebben / nae dien datse / op soodanige wyse gestelt ende gherevideert zijnde / als nu ghehoort is / voorts byde Ghereformeerde kercken alomme is erkent ende aenghenomen / ende / neffens andere Confessien / inde ghemeene Harmonie aller Confessien is in-verlijft. Dat de voornoemde Synode onder 't Cruys die Confessie heeft aengenomen / als den woorde Godts ghelijckformich / blijckt uyt de gantsche saecke. Darenboven inden jare 1571. eer de Nederlantsche Ghereformeerde kercken eenighen voet in haer Vaderlant hadden / is inden Synodo nationali ghehouden tot Embden / goet gevonden dat alle kercken-dienare[n] die confessie / als schriftmatich / ofte den woorde Godts gelijckformich / souden onderschrijven / om te betuyghen datse alle met malkanderen stonden in een recht / gesont / ende schriftmatich ghevoelen / ende sulcx hare Gemeynten eendrachtelijck voordroegen ende in planteden; 't welck nergens anders toe konde strecken / als tot behoudenisse der H[eilige] waerheyt / ende goede broederlijcke eenicheyt onder malkanderen."

Later, Trigland reported about the presentation of the Belgic Confession to the emperor by a number of noblemen.

" . . . die oock Anno 1566. onder den naem der gener die begeeren van gantscher herten te ghelooven ende te leven nae 't Evangelium des Soons Godts / op den Rijcxdach tot Augsburg / aenden Keyser Maximiliaen / door eenige afgesondene / overghegeven hebben een Supplicatie / ofte ootmoedige bede / die oock in volle Staten des Rijcx gelesen is / met een bygaende oratie aende hoogh-gedachte Keyserlijcke Majesteyt / aengaende de Reformatie der kercke; inde welcke sy haer niet alleen beroepen hebben op de gedachte hare / ende der Gereformeerder Nederlandtscher kercken / Confessie / maer de selve oock byde voornoemde Supplicatie ende Oratie ghevoecht. 't Is wel sulcks dat daer mede niet veel en is uytgheright / so door de nootwendige krijchs-rustinghe des Keysers tegen den Turck / als oock door de instantie van des Paus legaet / die last hadde tegen alle handelingen vande Religie te protesteren: doch evenwel blijckt daer uyt den goeden yver van die kloeckmoedighe Heeren tot de ware Religie / mitsgaders in hoedanighe achtinghe de voorsz[eide] Confessie by haer is gheweest."

Source: Trigland, *Kerckelycke geschiedenissen*, 144-46.

Document 10 - Schoock's *Liber de bonis vulgo ecclesiasticis dictis* (1651)

In 1651, Schoock published a book on church properties, in which he included a section on the history of the churches in the Netherlands. In the following section he deals with the Belgic Confession, which he calls a "general consensus formula in Belgium," and provides further information appealing to unpublished sources.

"A quibus primitus haec universalis consensus in Orthodoxia formula per Belgium, concepta fuerit, diversimode a variis refertur. Ego ex certis documentis, pleniori opere cum bono Deo suo tempore exhibendis, ita hanc rem se habere didici. Iam anno 1559, Guido de Bres vir pientissimus, (quippe, uti antea patuit, veritatem Evangelicam sanguine suo obsignavit) maxime quod furibundi Anabaptistae ab Inquisitoribus eodem loco cum Orthodoxis haberentur, instituit quosdam articulos consensus Orthodoxi colligere, quos cum Hadriano Zaraviae accincto ad iter Genevense primitus exhibuisset, per eum Calvino et aliis Theologis Genevatibus sub finem illius anni ostensi fuerunt; sed cum ab Authore lingua Gallica (quod Belgis plerisque ea ex parte aut vernacula esset, aut saltem familiaris) concepti essent, Zaraviae authores fuerunt, moneret tum Authorem, tum reliquos per Belgicam ministros, potius cum fratribus Gallis consentirent in Confessionem, quae in prima Synodo Parissina recenter eodem anno condita erat, die videlicet 19. May, redux paulo post in Belgium Zaravia, Authori tum viva voce, tum per literas, quas a Genevatibus deferebat, consilium Calvini, aliorumque illius Collegarum exposuit, pressitque hos articulos Bresius usque ad annum 1561. quo ex consilio Godefridi Wingii, cuius jam antea fuit facta mentio (renuente licet Zaravia, qui contendebat iterato Genevates consulendos esse) eosdem misit ad Ecclesiam Emdanam, in qua cum viveret Cornelius Cooltuyn Wingio familiaris, ipse eosdem cum paucis ex Collegis (quod non putaret, omnes privati ministri positiones, tanquam definitam formulam consensus plurium nationum, probaturos esse) expendit, probavitque; postea missi fuerunt ad varios in Belgio ministros, item ad ministros Metenses, quorum iam antea facta fuit mentio, nec non Frankendalium ad Petrum Dathenum et Casparum Heidanum, ut et Francfurtum ad Vallerandum Pollanum, nec non ministros Ecclesiae Belgicae Londini, itemque eos, qui ibidem Ecclesiae Gallicae praeerant, Nicolaum scil. Galasium, Petrum Cognatum, et Petrum Alexandrum quondam Confessionarium Mariae Ungariae reginae; neque enim consultum fuit visum, iterum adire Genevates, quod mallent Belgas Gallicae Confessioni, hoc ipso anno 1561. vulgatae subscribere. A plerisque in Belgio Ministris visa cum esset haec Confessio, taciteque probata, Walonico idiomate, primitus concepta erat ab Authore, vulgata est anno 1562, ac mox anno sequenti, sive anno 1563 in Belgicam traducta linguam per omnes Ecclesias non solum fuit disseminata; verum etiam ab hoc tempore coepit esse formula consensus. At cum complures ex Zaravia didicissent Genevatibus displicuisse hoc consilium Belgarum de edenda nova Confessione, mense Maio anno 1565 inter sexcentas difficultates et pericula, ex praecipuis Belgii ministris, qui tum noti erant, Antverpiae occulto Synodus, cur [read: cui] et ipse Philippus Marnixius interfuit, et ad quam vocatus quoque erat Zaravia, collecta fuit; relectaq[ue] Confessione ab omnibus probata fuit, sic tamen ut expostularetur super ea consilium Genevensium; quod cum jussus esset Franciscus Iunius, Theologis illis familiarior, explorare, mense Novembri (ut aliis documentis allatis probabitur) ab iis responsum est, se articulos (in quibus pauca mutata erant) ab initio, cum exhiberentur, admisisse quidem ut orthodoxos, caeterum existimasse pro eo tempore, Ecclesias Belgicas non indiguisse Confessione, quae cum iam vulgata sit, revocari non posse, probareque se eam tanquam verbo Dei consentaneam. Huic Confessioni ab hoc subscripserunt non solum ministri, verum ultro quoque Ludovicus Nassovius Guilielmi Aurangiae Principis frater, Comes Columburgicus, Comes Bergensis, et Dominus de Brederode, aliique ex proceribus, quibus aeternum devotam se esse agnoscere debet patria atq[ue]; sic scriptum initio privatum, factum est formula universalis consensus."

Source: Vinke, *Libri symbolici*, xiii-xv, quoting Schoock, *Liber de bonis vulgo ecclesiasticis dictis* (1651), 519-22. The text can also be found in Van Langeraad, *Guido de Bray*, 97-98 n. 4, 129-30, n. 1.

Bibliography

Acta der Generale Synode van de Gereformeerde Kerken in Nederland, gehouden te Utrecht 1905. Amsterdam: Höveker en Wormser, n.d.

Acta der Synode 1906 van de Christelijke Gereformeerde Kerk. Grand Rapids: Christelijke Gereformeerde Kerk, n.d.

Acta der Synode 1908 van de Christelijke Gereformeerde Kerk. Grand Rapids: Christelijke Gereformeerde Kerk, n.d.

Acta der Synode 1910 van de Christelijke Gereformeerde Kerk. Grand Rapids: Christelijke Gereformeerde Kerk, n.d.

Acta der Synode 1912 van de Christelijke Gereformeerde Kerk. Grand Rapids: Christelijke Gereformeerde Kerk, n.d.

Acta et scripta synodalia Dordracena ministrorum Remonstrantium in foederato Belgio. Herder-Wiici: Ex officina typographi Synodalis, 1620.

Acta ofte handelingen der nationalen Synodi . . . tot Dordrecht, Anno 1618 ende 1619. Dordrecht: Isaack Iansz. Canin, 1621.

Acta van de Generale Synode van de Gereformeerde Kerken in Nederland, Kampen 1975. Enschede: J. Boersma, n.d.

Acta van de Generale Synode van de Gereformeerde Kerken in Nederland, Groningen-Zuid 1978. Haarlem: Vijlbrief, n.d.

Acta van de Generale Synode van de Gereformeerde Kerken in Nederland, Arnhem 1981. Haarlem: Vijlbrief, 1981.

Acts and Proceedings of the 166th Regular Session of the General Synod / Reformed Church in America. Somerville: Somerset Press, 1972.

Acts: General Synod Cloverdale, 1983, of the Canadian Reformed Churches. Winnipeg: Premier Printing, [1983].

Acts: General Synod Coaldale, 1977, of the Canadian Reformed Churches. Winnipeg: Premier Printing, 1977.

Acts: General Synod Orangeville, 1968, of the Canadian Reformed Churches. Fergus, ON: R & R Printing, n.d.

Acts: General Synod Smithville, 1980, of the Canadian Reformed Churches. Winnipeg: Premier Printing, [1980].

Acts of Synod 1938 of the Christian Reformed Church. Grand Rapids: Office of the Stated Clerk, n.d.

Acts of Synod 1977. Grand Rapids: Christian Reformed Church Publications, 1977.

Acts of Synod 1979. Grand Rapids: Christian Reformed Church Publications, 1979.

Acts of Synod 1983. Grand Rapids: Christian Reformed Church Publications, 1983.

Acts of Synod 1984. Grand Rapids: Board of Publications of the Christian Reformed Church, 1984.

Acts of Synod 1985. Grand Rapids: CRC Publications, 1985.

Arminius, Jacobus. *The Writings of Arminius.* 3 vols. Translated by James Nichols and W. R. Bagnall. Grand Rapids: Baker, 1956.

Baird, Henry M. *Theodore Beza: the Counsellor of the French Reformation*. 2nd ed. New York: B. Franklin, 1970.

Bakhuizen van den Brink, Jan N. "Het convent te Frankfort 27-28 September 1577 en de Harmonia Confessionum." *Nederlands archief voor kerkgeschiedenis* 32 (1941): 235-80.

———. *De Nederlandse belijdenisgeschriften*. 2nd ed. Amsterdam: Bolland, 1976.

———. "Quelques notes sur l'histoire de la Confession des Pays-Bas en 1561 et en 1566." In *Ecclesia II: Een bundel opstellen door Dr. J. N. Bakhuizen van den Brink*, 296-335. Den Haag: Martinus Nijhoff, 1966.

———. "De tekst van de Belijdenisgeschriften en van de Liturgische Formulieren der N. H. Kerk." *Nederlands archief voor kerkgeschiedenis* 40 (1954): 207-50.

Bangs, Carl. *Arminius: A Study in the Dutch Reformation*. Nashville: Abingdon, [1971].

Beets, Henry. *De Christelijk Gereformeerde Kerk in Noord America: Zestig jaren van strijd en zegen*. Grand Rapids: Grand Rapids Printing Company, 1918.

Bekker, Balthasar. *De leere der gereformeerde kerken van de vrije Nederlanden, begrepen in derselver geloofsbelydenisse*. Amsterdam: Daniel van den Dalen, 1696.

Belijdenisse oft verklaringhe van 't ghevoelen der leeraren die in de gheunieerde Nederlanden Remonstranten worden genaemt over de voornaemste Articulen der Christelijcke Religie. N.p., 1621.

Beuker, Gerrit J. "German Oldreformed Emigration: Catastrophe or Blessing?" In *Breaches and Bridges: Reformed Subcultures in the Netherlands, Germany and the United States*, edited by G. Harinck and H. Krabbendam, 101-13. Amsterdam: VU Uitgeverij, 2002.

———. *Umkehr und Erneuerung: Aus der Geschichte der Evangelisch-altreformierten Kirche in Niedersachsen 1838 - 1988*. Bad Bentheim: A. Hellendoorn KG, 1988.

Beza, Théodore. *The Christian Faith*. Translated by J. Clark. East Sussex: Focus Christian Ministries Trust, 1991.

———. *La confession de foi du chrétien*. Translated and edited by Michel Réveillaud. *La Revue réformée* 6 no. 23-24 (1955): 1-158.

———. *Confession de la foy chrestienne . . . Reveue et augmentee de nouveau par luy, avec un abregé d'icelle*. N. p.: Conrad Badius, 1559.

———. *Correspondence de Théodore de Bèze*. Vol. 3. Collected by H. Aubert. Edited by A. Dufour, F. Aubert, and H. Meylan. Geneva: Droz, 1963.

Biesterveld, Petrus, and Herman H. Kuyper. *Kerkelijk handboekje, bevattende de bepalingen der Nederlandsche synoden . . .* Kampen: Bos, 1905.

Bijlagen bij de Acta van de Generale Synode, 1955-56. Kampen: Kok, n.d.

Blaise, Albert. *Dictionnaire Latin-Français des auteurs chrétiens*. Turnhout: Brepols S.A., 1954.

Bode, W. "Onze Duitse gemeenten." In *Gedenkboek van het vijftigjarig jubileum der Christelijke Gereformeerde Kerk 1857-1907*, edited by Jakob Noordewier et al., 71-84. Grand Rapids: Semi-Centennial Committee, [1907].

Bouvy, D. P. R. A. *Kerkelijke kunst*. Bussum, 1965.

Braekman, Émile M. "Anvers - 1562: Le premier Synode des Églises Wallonnes." *Bulletin de la société royale d'histoire du protestantisme Belge* 102 (1989): 25-40.

———. *Guy de Brès: Sa vie*. Bruxelles: Éditions de la Librairie des éclaireurs unionistes, 1960.

———. *Le protestantisme Belge au 16e siècle*. Carrières-sous-Poissy: La Cause, 1998.

————. "Les sources de la Confessio Belgica." *Bulletin commission de l'histoire des églises Wallonnes* 7 (1961): 2-24.

Brandt, Caspar. *The Life of James Arminius*. Translated by John Guthrie. Nashville: E. Stevenson and F. A. Owen, 1857.

[Brandt, Geeraert]. *Brieven van verscheyde vermaerde en geleerde mannen deser eeuwe*. Amsterdam: Jan Riewertsz, 1662.

————. *Historie der reformatie*. 4 vols. Amsterdam: Jan Riemertsz and Hendrik & Dirk Boon, 1671-1704.

Brinks, Herbert J. "Ostfrisians in Two Worlds." In *Perspectives on the Christian Reformed Church: Studies in its History, Theology and Ecumenicity*, edited by Peter De Klerk and Richard R. De Ridder, 21-34. Grand Rapids: Baker, 1983.

Brouwer, Wayne. "The German Element in the CRC: European Background." *The Banner* 115 (April 11, 1980): 10-12.

Calvin, John. *Institutes of the Christian Religion*. 2 vols. Edited by John T. McNeill. Translated by Ford Lewis Battles. Philadelphia: Westminster, 1960.

————. *Ioannis Calvini opera quae supersunt omnia*. 59 vols. Edited by Guilielmus Baum, Eduardus Cunitz, and Eduardus Reuss. Brunswick: Schwetschke, 1863-1900.

————. *Johannes Calvins Lebenswerk in seinen Briefen*. 3 vols. Translated by R. Schwarz. Neukirchen: Neukirchener Verlag, 1962-63

Claasen, J. P. "Aspecte van die Afrikanisatie van die kerk gedurende die Europese lidmaatsverplanting: Die oriëntering van die Afrikaanse Kerke." In *(Suid-) Afrika en die kerkgeschiedenis: Referate gelewer by die jaarvergadering 1975*, 63-87. Stellenbosch: Kerkhistoriese werkgemeenskap van Suid-Afrika 1976.

Coertzen, Pieter. "Die koms van die Franse vlugtelinge na Suid-Afrika." In *Studia historiae ecclesiasticae I: Referate gelewer by vergaderinge van die kerkhistoriese werkgemeenskap van Suid-Afrika 1971, 1973*, 40-65. Stellenbosch: Kerkhistoriese werkgemeenskap van Suid Afrika, n.d.

Confissâo de Fee e Catecismo de Heidelberg. Cambuci, Sâo Paulo: Casa Presbyteriana "Cultura Christâ," 1999.

[Conopius, Nathanael]. *Toon eklesioon tes Belgikes Christianike kai Orthodoxos Didaskalia kai Taxis*. Leiden: B. and A. Elzevier, n.d.

The Constitution of the Reformed Dutch Church in the United Stated of America. New York, Willem Durell, 1793.

Crespin, Jean. *Histoire des martyrs*. 3 vols. Toulouse: Société des Livres Religieux, 1889.

Dankbaar, Willem F. *Hoogtepunten uit het Nederlandsche Calvinisme in de zestiende eeuw*. Haarlem: H. D. Tjeenk Willink & Zoon, 1946.

De Brès, Guido. *Le baston de la foy chrestienne* . . . N.p.: Nicolas Barbier et Thomas Courteau, 1558.

————. *Bekanntnusz Christliches Glaubens der Niderlendischen Kirchen* . . . Heidelberg: Johannes Meyer, 1566.

————. *Confession de foy, faicte d'un commun accord par les fideles qui conversent és pays bas* . . . [Rouen: Abel Clémence], 1561.

————. *Confession de foy, faicte d'un commun accord par les fideles qui conversent ès pays Bas* . . . N.p., 1562. [Major]

————. *Confession de foy. Faicte d'un commun accord par les fideles qui conversent és Pays Bas* . . . N.p., 1562. [Minor]

————. *Confession de foy, faite d'un commun accord par les fideles qui conversent és pays bas* . . . [Lyon: Jean Frellon], 1561.

————. *La Racine, source et fondement des Anabaptistes* . . . [Lyon]: Abel Clémence, 1565.

Deddens, Detmer. "De eerste synode der Franse gereformeerde kerken te Parijs 1559." *Lucerna* 1 no. 3 (1959): 99-120.

————. "De Nederlandse Geloofsbelijdenis: Een en ander over haar geschiedenis." *De Reformatie* 37 no. 6 (1961): 46-47.

————. "Rondom het eerste geschrift van G. de Brès, 'Le Baston de la Foy.'" *Lucerna* 3 no. 6 (1962): 817-31.

De Greef, Wulfert. *The Writings of John Calvin: An Introductory Guide.* Translated by Lyle D. Bierma. Grand Rapids: Baker, 1993.

De Jong, Gerald F. *The Dutch Reformed Church in the American Colonies.* Grand Rapids: Eerdmans, 1978.

Dekker, Eef. "Was Arminius a Molinist?" *Sixteenth Century Journal* 27 no. 2 (1996): 337-52.

————. *Rijker dan Midas: Vrijheid, genade en predestinatie in de theologie van Jacobus Arminius.* Zoetermeer: Boekencentrum, 1993.

De Lind van Wijngaarden, Jan D. *De Dordtsche Leerregels.* 2nd ed. Utrecht: G. J. A. Ruys, 1905.

De Moor, Bernardus. *Commentarius perpetuus in Johannis Marckii compendium.* Vol. 5. Leiden: Johannes Hasebroek, 1768.

Denzinger, Henricus, and Adolf Schönmetzer. *Enchiridion symbolorum definitionum et declarationum de rebus fidei et morum.* 33rd ed. Barcinone: Herder, 1965.

Dirkse, Paulus W. M. "De katholieke kerk en haar genadeleer." In *Geloof en satire anno 1600*, 20-24. N.p.: RMCC, 1981.

Doekes, Lourens. *Credo: Handboek voor de gereformeerde symboliek.* Amsterdam: Ton Bolland, 1975.

[Dwinglo, Bernardus]. *Historisch Verhael van 't ghene sich toegedraeghen heeft binnen Dordrecht in den jaeren 1618. ende 1619.* Published together with *Oorspronck ende Voortganck der Nederlantsche Kerckelijcke verschillen tot op het Nationale Synodus.* N.p., 1623.

Ens, Johannes. *Kort historisch berigt van de publieke schriften rakende de leer en dienst der Nederduitsche kerken.* Completed and published by Regnerus Ens. N.p., 1733. Reprint, Kampen: S. Van Velzen, 1864.

Faber, Jelle. "Textus Receptus of the Belgic Confession." In *H.E.R.O.S. lustrumbundel 1925-1989*, 93-116. Kampen: Van den Berg, 1980. An earlier version in four articles was published in *Clarion* 28 (1979): 310-11, 354-55, 458-60, 510-12.

Gardy, Frédéric. *Bibliography des oeuvres théologiques, littéraires, historiques et juridiques de Théodore de Bèze.* Genève: Librairie E. Droz, 1960.

Gilmont, Jean-François. "Premières éditions de la Confessio Belgica (1561-1562)." *Quaerendo* 4 no. 2 (July 1972): 173-81.

————. "La seconde édition française de la Confessio Belgica [Lyon, Jean Frellon] 1561." *Quaerendo* 6 no. 3 (July 1974): 259-60.

Godfrey, William R. "Calvin and Calvinism in the Netherlands." In *John Calvin: His Influence in the Western World*, edited by J. Stanford Reid, 95-120. Grand Rapids: Zondervan, 1982.

Goeters, J. F. Gerhard. *Die Akten der Synode der Niederländischen Kirchen zu Emden vom 4.- 13. Oktober 1571*. Neukirchen: Neukirchener Verlag, 1971.

Gootjes, Nicolaas H. "The Earliest Report on the Author of the Belgic Confession (1561)." *Nederlands archief voor kerkgeschiedenis* 82 no. 1 (2002): 86-94.

———. *De geestelijkheid van God*. Franeker: Wever, 1984.

———. "Problems with Proof Texts: The Proof Texts of Article 11 of the Belgic Confession and Their Implications for the Confession." *Calvin Theological Journal* 36 (2001), 372-78.

Hadjantoniou, George A. *Protestant Patriarch: The Life of Cyril Lucaris (1572-1638) Patriarch of Constantinople*. Richmond: John Knox, 1961.

Hall, Peter, ed. *The Harmony of Protestant Confessions*. 1842. Reprint, Edmonton: Still Waters Revival Books, 1992.

Hollweg, Walter. *Neue Untersuchungen zur Geschichte und Lehre des Heidelberger Katechismus*. Neukirchen: Neukirchener Verlag, 1961.

Hommius, Festus. *Specimen controversiarum belgicarum*. Leiden: Elzevier, 1618.

Hooyer, Cornelis. *Oude kerkordeningen der Nederlandsche hervormde gemeenten (1563-1638) . . . Verzameld en met inleidingen voorzien*. Zaltbommel: Noman, 1865.

Houtman, Cornelis. *Nederlandse vertalingen van het Oude Testament*. 's Graven-hage: Boekencentrum, 1980.

Jahr, Hannelore. *Studien zur Überlieferungsgeschichte der Confession de foi von 1559*. Neukirchen-Vluyn: Neukirchener Verlag, 1964.

Jansen, Gerhard. "De muurschilderingen in de Galileërkerk te Leeuwarden." *Gildeboek* (May 1942): 3-9.

Janssen, Hendrik Q. and J. J. Van Toorenenbergen. *Brieven uit onderscheidenen kerkelijke archieven*. Werken der Marnix-vereeniging. Series 3. Vol. 2. Utrecht: Kemink & Zoon, 1878.

Junius, Franciscus. *Opuscula theologica selecta Francisci Junii*. Edited by A. Kuyper. Amsterdam: Fredericus Muller, 1882.

Kaajan, Hendrik. *De groote synode van Dordrecht in 1618-1619*. Amsterdam: De Standaard, 1918.

Kamphuis, Jacob. *Kerkelijke besluitvaardigheid*. Groningen: De Vuurbaak, 1970.

Kimmel, Ernst J. *Libri symbolici ecclesiae orientalis*. Jena: Carolus Hochhausenius, 1843.

Kist, Nicolaas C. "Synoden der Nederlandsch Hervormde kerken." *Archief voor kerkelijke geschiedenis, inzonderheid van Nederland* 9 (1837): 152-54.

Knipscheer, Frederik S. *De invoering en de waardering der gereformeerde belijdenisgeschriften in Nederland voor 1618*. Leiden: A. H. Adriani, 1907.

Kuyper, Abraham. *Revisie der revisie-legende*. Amsterdam: J. H. Kruyt, 1879.

Kuyper, Herman H. "Guido de Brès." *De Heraut*, 1943-44, #3426-51. [A series of 26 articles.]

———. *De opleiding tot den dienst des woords bij de gereformeerden*. Den Haag: M. Nijhoff, 1891.

————. *De post-acta of nahandelingen van de nationale synode van Dordrecht in 1618 en 1619 gehouden*. Amsterdam: Höveker & Wormser, 1899.

Leal, L., and M. Taute, eds. *As Três Confissões da Igreja Reformada*. Pretoria: M. Taute, 1990.

Le Long, Isaac. *Kort historisch verhaal van den eersten oorsprong der Nederlandschen gereformeerden onder 't kruis*. Amsterdam: S. Schouten en zoon, 1751.

Lilje, Hans. *Portret van Luther in de lijst van zijn tijd*. Edited by Willem J. Kooiman. Amsterdam: W. Ten Hoor, 1967.

Los, Frans J. *Tekst en toelichting van de geloofsbelijdenis der Nederlandsche Hervormde Kerk*. Utrecht: Kemink & Zoon, 1929.

Marnef, Guido. *Antwerp in the Age of the Reformation: Underground Protestantism in a Commercial Metropolis, 1550-1577*. Translated by J. C. Grayson. Baltimore and London: John Hopkins University Press, 1996.

Meeter, Daniel J. *"Bless the Lord, o My Soul": the New York Liturgy of the Dutch Reformed Church 1767*. Lanham: Scarecrow Press, 1998.

————. *The "North American Liturgy": A Critical Edition of the Liturgy of the Reformed Dutch Church in North America, 1793*. Ann Arbor: UMI, 1994.

————. "The Puritan and Presbyterian Versions of the Netherlands Liturgy." *Nederlands archief voor kerkgeschiedenis* 70 (1990), 52-74.

Meijer, Johannes A. "De oosterse confessie van Cyrillus Lukaris." In *Bezield verband*, edited by J. Douma, J.P. Lettinga and C. Trimp, 134-51. Kampen: Van den Berg, 1984.

Mooi, Remko J. *Het kerk- en dogmahistorisch element in de werken van Johannes Calvijn*. Wageningen: H. Veenman & Zonen, 1965.

Moreau, Gérard. *Histoire du Protestantisme à Tournai jusqu' à la veille de la révolution des Pays-Bas*. Paris: Les Belles Lettres, 1962.

————. "Les synodes des églises Wallonnes des Pays-Bas en 1563." *Nederlands archief voor kerkgeschiedenis* 46 (1965-1966): 1-11.

Müller, E. F. Karl. *Die Bekenntnisschriften der reformierten Kirche*. Leipzig: A. Deichert, 1903. Reprint, Zürich: Theologische Buchhandlung, 1987.

Muller, Richard A. "Calvin and the 'Calvinists': Assessing Continuities and Discontinuities Between the Reformation and Orthodoxy." Part I, *Calvin Theological Journal* 30 no. 2 (November 1995): 345-75; Part II, *Calvin Theological Journal* 31 no. 1 (April 1996): 125-60.

————. *God, Creation and Providence in the Thought of Jacob Arminius*. Grand Rapids: Baker, 1991.

————. "The Myth of 'Decretal Theology'." *Calvin Theological Journal* 30 no. 1 (1995): 159-67.

Nauta, Doede. *Hoogtepunten uit het Nederlandsche Calvinisme*. Franeker: Wever, 1949.

————. "Die Verbreitung des Katechismus, Übersetzung in andere Sprachen, moderne Bearbeitungen." In *Handbuch zum Heidelberg Katechismus*, edited by L. Coenen, 39-62. Neukirchen: Neukirchener Verlag 1963.

————. "Wezel (1568) en Emden (1571)." In *Opera minora: kerkhistorische verhandelingen over Calvijn en de geschiedenis van de kerk in Nederland*, edited by D. Nauta, 30-56. Kampen: J. H. Kok, 1961. This article can also be found in *Nederlands archief voor kerkgeschiedenis* 36 (1949): 220-46.

De Nederlandse belijdenisgeschriften. Den Haag: Boekencentrum, 1983.

Nijenhuis, Willem. Adrianus Saravia: Dutch Calvinist. Leiden: Brill, 1980.

————. "The Controversy Between Presbyterianism and Episcopalianism Surrounding and During the Synod of Dordrecht 1618-1619." In Ecclesia Reformata: Studies on the Reformation, 207-20. Leiden: Brill, [1972].

Outhovius, Gerardus. Ter waerschouwinge aan alle Kristenen. Emden: H. Van Senden, 1723.

Panchaud, Eduard. Souvenir du jubilé tricentenaire de la publication de la confession de foi. Brussels: Librairie chrétienne évangélique, 1861.

Pannier, Jacques. Les origines de la Confession de Foi et la Discipline des églises Réformées de France. Paris: Librairie Félix Alcan, 1936.

Pearson, John, ed. "Mr. Hales Letters from the Synod of Dort." In Golden Remains of the Ever Memorable Mr. John Hales. 2nd ed. London: Th. Newcomb, 1659.

Pettegree, Andrew. Emden and the Dutch Revolt: Exile and the Development of Reformed Protestantism. Oxford: Clarendon, 1992.

Plomp, Jan. "De kerkorde van Emden." In De Synode van Emden oktober 1571, edited by D. Nauta, 88-121. Kampen: Kok, 1971.

Polman, Andries D. R. Onze Nederlandsche geloofsbelijdenis. 4 vols. Franeker: T. Wever, 1948-53.

Postumus Meyjes, Egbert J. W. Jacobus Revius. Amsterdam: Ten Brink & De Vries, 1895.

Raitt, Jill. The Eucharistic Theology of Theodore Beza: Development of the Reformed Doctrine. Chambersburg: American Academy of Religion, 1972.

Reitsma, Johannes, and Sietse D. Van Veen. Acta der provinciale en particuliere synoden: gehouden in de noordelijke Nederlanden gedurende de jaren 1572-1620. Vol. 1. Groningen: J. B. Wolters, 1892.

"Report 33." In Agenda for Synod 1979, 360-430. Grand Rapids: Christian Reformed Church Publications, 1979.

Rozemond, Keetje. "De eerste uitgave van de belijdenis van Cyrillus Lucaris." Nederlands archief voor kerkgeschiedenis 51 no. 2 (1970-71): 199-208.

Rullmann, J. C. Kuyper-bibliografie. Vol 2. Kampen: Kok, 1929.

Rutgers, Frederik L., ed. Acta van de Nederlandsche synoden der zestiende eeuw. 1899. Reprint, Dordrecht: J. P. Van den Tol, 1980.

————. Calvijns invloed op de Reformatie in de Nederlanden. Leiden: Donner, 1899.

Schaff, Philip. The Creeds of Christendom: With a History and Critical Notes. 3 vols. 6th ed. New York: Harper and Row, 1931. Reprint, Grand Rapids: Baker, 1990.

Schlier, Richard. Der Patriarch Kyrill Lukaris von Konstatinopel: Sein Leben und sein Glaubensbekenntnis. Marburg: Druckerei Bauer, 1927.

Schoock, Martinus. Liber de bonis vulgo ecclesiasticis dictis. Groningen: Johannes Nicolai, 1651.

Schriftelicke conferentie, gehouden in 's Gravenhaghe inden jare 1611 tusschen sommighe kerken-dienaren, aengaende de Godlicke praedestinatie metten aencleven van dien. 's Gravenhaghe: Hillebrant Jacobsz, 1617.

Schuppert, Mildred W. A Digest and Index of the Minutes of the General Synod of the Reformed Church in America. Grand Rapids: Eerdmans, 1979.

Sepp, Christiaan. Bibliographische mededeelingen. Leiden: Brill, 1883.

Sinnema, Donald N. *The Issue of Reprobation at the Synod of Dort (1618-1619) in Light of the History of This Doctrine.* Ph.D. diss., Toronto School of Theology, 1985.

Sprunger, Keith L. *Dutch Puritanism: A History of English and Scottish Churches of the Netherlands in the Sixteenth and Seventeenth Centuries.* Leiden: Brill, 1982.

Strauss, Siebrand A. "John Calvin and the Belgic Confession." *In die Skriflig* 27 no. 4 (1993): 501-17.

Taylor, W. J. R. "Laidlie." In *Cyclopaedia of Biblical, Theological and Ecclesiastical Literature,* 12 vols., edited by John McClintock and James Strong, 5:195. N.p.: Harper and Brothers, 1867-1887. Reprint, Grand Rapids: Baker Book House, 1981.

Te Water, Willem. *Tweede eeuw-getyde van de geloofs-belydenisse der gereformeerde kerken van Nederlant.* Middelburg: Pieter Gillissen, 1762.

Thysius, Anthonius. *Leere ende order der Nederlandsche, soo Duytsche als Walsche, ghereformeerde kercken.* Amsterdam: Pieter Pietersz, 1615.

Trigland, Jacobus. *Kerckelycke geschiedenissen.* Leiden: A. Wijngaerden, 1650.

Van den End, Thomas, ed. *Enam Belas Dokumen Dasar Calvinisme.* Jakarta, 2000.

———. "Transfer of Reformed Identity on the Missionfield in Indonesia." In *Changing Partnership of Missionary and Ecumenical Movements,* edited by Leny Lagerwerf, Karel Steenbrink and Frans Verstraelen, 113-30. Leiden: Interuniversity Institute for Missiological and Ecumenical Research, 1995.

Van der Zwaag, Klaas. *Onverkort of gekortwiekt? Artikel 36 van de Nederlandse Geloofsbelijdenis en de spanning tussen overheid en religie.* Heerenveen: Groen, 1999.

Van Itterzon, Gerrit P. *Johannes Bogerman.* Amsterdam: Ton Bolland, 1980.

Van Langeraad, Lambregt A. *Guido de Bray, zijn leven en werken: bijdrage tot de geschiedenis van het Zuid-Nederlandsche protestantisme.* Zierikzee: S. Ochtman & Zoon, 1884.

———. "De liturgie bij de Hervormden in Nederland I." *Theologisch tijdschrift,* 35 (1901): 123-59.

Van Toorenenbergen, Johan J. *Eene bladzijde uit de geschiedenis der Nederlandsche Geloofsbelijdenis ter gedachtenisviering bij haar derde eeuwgetijde . . . met de oorspronkelijke bescheiden.* Den Haag: M. Nijhoff, [1862].

Van 't Spijker, Willem, ed. *De Synode van Dordrecht in 1618 en 1619.* Houten: Den Hertog, 1987.

Veltenaar, C. *Théodore de Bèze et ses relations avec les théologiens des Pays-Bas.* Kampen: J. H. Kok, 1904.

Vinke, Henricus E. *Libri symbolici ecclesiae reformatae nederlandicae.* Utrecht: J. G. Van Terveen et fil., 1846.

Voetius, Gisbertus. *Politicae Ecclesiasticae.* Vol. 4. Amsterdam: Johannes Jansonius à Waesberge, 1676.

Vonk, Cornelis. *De voorzeide leer, III: De Nederlandse geloofsbelijdenis.* 2 vols. Barendrecht: Drukkerij Barendrecht, 1955-56.

Voorvelt, Gebhard. "De fresco-fragmenten van Leeuwarden en het Haarlemse paneel." *De Vrije Fries* 38 (1946): 69-85.

Weerda, Jan. *Holbein und Calvin: Ein Bildfund.* Neukirchen, Kreis Moers: Verlag der Buchhandlung des Erziehungsvereins, [1955].

Willems, Alphonse. *Les Elzevier: Histoire et annals typographiques*. 1880. Reprint, Nieuwkoop: B. De Graaf, 1962.

Wisse, Gerard. *Memoires: Onvergetelijke bladzijden uit mijn levensboek*. Utrecht: W. M. Den Hertog, 1953.

Subject Index